Katherine Anne Porter's Women

❖ THE EYE OF HER FICTION

by Jane Krause DeMouy

UNIVERSITY OF TEXAS PRESS, AUSTIN

First edition, 1983

Requests for permission to reproduce material
from this work should be sent to:
    Permissions
    University of Texas Press
    Box 7819
    Austin, Texas 78712

Publication of this work has been made possible in part
by a grant from the Andrew W. Mellon Foundation.

LIBRARY OF CONGRESS CATALOGING IN PUBLICATION DATA
DeMouy, Jane Krause, 1942–
    Katherine Anne Porter's women.
    Bibliography: p.
    Includes index.
    1. Porter, Katherine Anne, 1890–1980—Characters—
Women.   2. Women in literature.   I. Title.
PS3531.O752Z55   1983   813'.52   82-17489
ISBN 0-292-79018-X

Grateful acknowledgment is made for permission to reprint the following
poems by Emily Dickinson: No. 338, No. 1129, No. 1732. Reprinted by permission of the publishers and the Trustees of Amherst College from THE
POEMS OF EMILY DICKINSON, edited by Thomas H. Johnson, Cambridge,
Mass.: The Belknap Press of Harvard University Press, Copyright 1951,
© 1955, 1979 by the President and Fellows of Harvard College.

For Lou, Maura, Amy, and Bridget

KATHERINE ANNE PORTER'S WOMEN
The Eye of Her Fiction

Contents

Acknowledgments

I have been blessed with intelligent and generous friends who supported me in this effort: Nancy Traubitz, Starr Solomon, Sr. Maura, S.S.N.D., and Carl Bode. Jackson Bryer has given me invaluable advice and encouragement, and Beth Alvarez generously guided my work on the index. Leo Weigant, who read the manuscript and offered insightful criticism on more than one occasion, was of immeasurable help. Lewis Lawson, my longtime mentor and friend, brought sensitivity, good humor, and uncommon intellect to our discussion of the issues in this study, and he did so with tireless enthusiasm. His good sense and his insight are in these pages. I am especially grateful to him and to my husband, Lou, whose warmth, generosity, and unflagging support of my work helped me produce this book.

KATHERINE ANNE PORTER'S WOMEN
The Eye of Her Fiction

Tell all the Truth but tell it slant—
Success in Circuit lies
Too bright for our infirm Delight
The Truth's superb surprise
As Lightning to the Children eased
With explanation kind
The Truth must dazzle gradually
Or every man be blind—

                    Emily Dickinson (no. 1129)

❖ *Introduction*

Katherine Anne Porter contributed gem-like fiction to American literature for over fifty years. Yet she is hard to place. Literary history would make her the contemporary of Hemingway and Fitzgerald; born in 1890 in Indian Creek, Texas, she experienced all the "millennial change"[1] that thrust America into the twentieth century (and she experienced more of this change than her male counterparts could, since the first quarter of the century gave to women particularly a greater freedom and mobility and, most important, a political voice). She accomplished her best work during the twenties and thirties, lived the bohemian life in Mexico and Europe, as much expatriated as any of that generation could claim to be, although she did not flaunt that position. She is justly called a Southern writer, believing as she does that all literature comes from "myth and memory" and setting many of her stories in the Southwest, her native country. Her ironic voice and her compressed, economic style label her a contemporary. She is part of yet not contained by these classifications.

Always a loner, determined to write in her own voice, she taught herself style by imitating Laurence Sterne and by holding herself aloof from the literary society that might influence her to write in the manner of someone else. When "María Concepción," the first of her collected stories, was published in 1922 in *Century* magazine, it was she who decided it was ready for publication, and the story was not edited. Because she has revealed little about her apprenticeship, saying only that she has burned trunkfuls of her stories, readers have assumed that these carefully wrought stories sprang full-blown from the head of their creator.

Since the publication in 1930 of her first volume of stories, *Flowering Judas*, Porter has enjoyed the regard of critics and fellow writers, who have consistently noted two things about her work: the brevity of her canon (three volumes of short stories, *Flowering Judas, Pale Horse, Pale Rider*, and *The Leaning Tower*, and one novel, *Ship of Fools*) and the high quality of her work. Her place in American letters has never been disputed, but it has been hard for commentators to name that place, for a third characteristic of her oeuvre, identifiable over the years, is its apparent diversity. She has written of the South, but she has also recreated Mexico and its culture in her fiction; her stories breathe life into images of nineteenth-century Texas, but she also characterizes the anxiety-ridden era of plague-infested World War I America as well as Berlin on the eve of World War II. Her protagonists are often artists—both female, like herself, and male—but they also include dirt farmers, poor Irish and Mexican peasants. She is a realist who nevertheless deals in dreams and myths. It has been hard to find an informing principle for such plenitude.

Nevertheless, Porter has not wanted for commentators. She was fortunate enough to be taken up at the outset of her career by intelligent, insightful readers like Ivor Winters and Allen Tate. The prominence of such critics, along with the clarity of their comments on her as a twentieth-century master of the short story, undoubtedly helped establish her reputation in spite of the small quantity of her work. On the other hand, because she uses many different settings and characters as well as intricate imagery and symbolism, her critics have been unable to suggest a comprehensive interpretation of her canon. No one has established a thematic unity in her work; with little agreement as to the content of her stories, the real nature of their artistic form has remained elusive.

In actuality, Porter does have a subject, although she approaches it from so many different angles that it is obscured. Her stories do not mirror each other pattern for pattern, but are rather like the spokes of a wheel, originating from a common source or single perception, made of similar characters and techniques, and yet separate and distinct from each other. Her territory is not Mexico, or New York, or Texas, or even childless marriages; it is not geographical, but psychological and mythic. A failure to recognize this has led to frustrated critical comments like John W. Aldridge's:

> Her stories are considered to be distinguished examples of
> their type and have undoubtedly had enormous influence on
> the contemporary development of the form. Yet the precise na-
> ture of her artistic qualities continues to be one of the great
> unsolved mysteries of modern literature. She remains the sym-
> bol and custodian of an excellence that is almost everywhere
> appreciated but almost nowhere clearly understood.[2]

Surely there is no easy formula to explain how or why Porter wrote as she wrote. We must begin, however, by identifying what she is writing about, and stress that her imagination is not so analytical as the presence of wit and irony in her work may suggest. The reader who wishes to understand Katherine Anne Porter's best works must recognize the mythic mind at work in them as well. Patterns are often circular, not linear; alogical realities may be the norm; images project more than one meaning, and those meanings may be paradoxical and simultaneous, like the elements of a dream. Her power is evocative, which accounts for an intensity in her stories that moves far beyond actual setting, character, and plot. But, most important, Porter's stories do constitute a canon, based on a specific experience and perspective.

The first thing one notes in looking at the stories together is that practically all of Porter's protagonists are women. As early as 1944, Edmund Wilson noted the significance of her stories about women,[3] and Cleanth Brooks, writing in 1971, asserts that Porter's stories and essays reveal "a wide streak of the feminist."[4] Robert Penn Warren,[5] among others, notes that her heroines search for identity and independence. M. M. Liberman finds Porter's portrayal of feminine sexuality more compelling than D. H. Lawrence's.[6] In more recent substantive comments, Jane Flanders[7] and Judith Fetterley[8] both focus on the problems of growing up female under the Old Order.

While Katherine Anne Porter has played the citizen of the world, she has been first and foremost a woman, who from childhood had a fierce curiosity about who she was and what her feminine identity meant. Her fiction chronicles what she discovered in various times and places, particularly how women were affected psychologically by attitudes in their society and by the other women they encountered.

Miranda—Porter's primary character—and her point of view have been much discussed, but no one has attempted to describe the feminine psychology represented by the whole of Porter's work; nor has anyone examined its significance or its relationship to Porter's "negative" tone. Porter's stories are one response to John Stuart Mill's insistence that women themselves must tell what they know about being women. In them we find a woman writer, most often writing out of her own experience and her own history—certainly out of her own psychology—who details time after time both the interior and exterior experience of femininity, a double experience about which Porter's women have ambivalent feelings.

Thus, although scholars have seen little unity in the diversity of Katherine Anne Porter's fiction, a close reading of the short stories which made her reputation[9] reveals a thematic unity that suggests what motivated them in the first place. Virtually every one of the stories illustrates a basic psychological conflict in the protagonist: a desire, on the one hand, for the independence and freedom to pursue art or principle regardless of social convention, and, on the other, a desire for the love and security inherent in the traditional roles of wife and mother.

Sometimes the conflict is personified by two specific characters; sometimes it is contained in two different personas that a character assumes; and sometimes, in the most complex stories, the conflict is internalized in the deepest psyche of the protagonist, resulting in emotional and sexual frigidity. The protagonists in the stories from "María Concepción" through "Hacienda" express this conflict through Jungian archetypes and Freudian symbolism, particularly Earth Mother and Venus figures, and through image clusters which suggest that sexuality, birth, and either psychic or physical death are always contiguous.

In the stories contained in "The Old Order" and *Pale Horse, Pale Rider*, Porter's principal persona, Miranda, takes shape. The sources of feminine conflict emerge from the careful characterization of the role models who influenced Miranda's childhood: the beautiful cousins who were the romantic belles of family myth; her matriarchal grandmother, a Southern lady who really survives because of her aggressiveness and grit; and other female relatives who are bluestockings and crusaders for female suffrage. These stories are also an exposition of Miranda's decision to separate herself from the double life led by other Porter protagonists. Ultimately, she rejects love and death, choosing instead independence and art. "Old Mortality," "Pale Horse, Pale Rider," and "Holiday" illustrate how painfully she learns that being free means being alone. Two principal women in *Ship of Fools*, Mrs. Treadwell and Jenny Brown, characterize that choice and the settled conflict.

Of her major stories, only "Noon Wine" and "The Leaning Tower" fall outside this framework and are not analyzed here. But even they utilize elements of Porter's familiar pattern. "Noon Wine," although it is by no stretch of the imagination Mrs. Thompson's story, does demonstrate, in the principal male characters, Porter's preoccupation with duality. Her use of psychological doubling constitutes part of the powerful impact of the story, as Thomas F. Walsh has illustrated.[10] Consequently, even this exception appears to prove the rule.

"The Leaning Tower" also has a male protagonist, but he does not illustrate any psychic dilemma. Although he shares the sensitivity of Miranda, he is more like the women of *Ship of Fools*. His psyche is settled, and he suffers no personal dichotomy, unlike the male artist who is the protagonist of "That Tree." Published in 1944, and prefiguring both the political backdrop and the skeptical tone of *Ship of Fools*, "The Leaning Tower" represents a point in Porter's career when her thinking had shifted from its original perspective— the individual woman's own psychological conflict—to broader concerns for humanity's capacity to survive without love.

The same is true of two other stories published in the same period. Lacey Mahaffy, the wife in "A Day's Work," is bitter, but not divided. And Stephen, the sensitive little boy in "The Downward Path to Wisdom," shares the clear-eyed perception Miranda has as a child in the Old Order stories, but the only thing he learns is the sad truth that he must survive alone. Thus, although these stories are linked in both content and technique to her other work, they do not represent the crux of Porter's fiction: the peculiar dilemmas inherent in being woman.

Significantly, Katherine Anne Porter declined to be called a feminist; unlike Miranda's cousin Eva, she is no strident polemicist, but a woman born into the tradition of white Southern Victorian society, writing about what she knows. There are many illustrations of the well-documented givens of feminine experience: women are valued more for their beauty than their wit; female activity outside the home and family is shameful and unfeminine; female children are naturally drawn to the roles of the adult women around them; active "masculinized" women who reject their preordained role bring upon themselves either physical or psychic death.

But what seems most prominent in the stories up to 1935 is a perception of duality in womanhood. There is the remnant of the Old Order—the traditional femininity imaged in a bit of handmade lace, a gold purse, or a delicate comb—that speaks to her protagonists from their blood, and refuses to be denied even while it is restrained. In opposition is the emerging persona who rejects subjugation and accepts independence for the sake of her art.

This duality is both an ancient and a contemporary truth about the nature of women which Porter was well equipped to perceive. Her own grandmother, like Miranda's, projected a contradictory image, being a genteel lady of uncommon toughness. Porter herself had to confront the historical conflict inherent in having been bred to the manners of the South at a time when that culture was already receding before a new, faster, and cruder century. These experiences perhaps gave her insight into other paradoxes and possible conflicts in woman's experience. In any case, her stories reveal an intuitive and profound understanding of the human concept of the feminine in all its paradox.

Certainly Porter is aware that, on the archetypal level, femininity is primally associated with both maternity and sexuality, and with both birth and death. On the psychological level, she understands that contemporary woman needs independence as much as she needs love: she needs an androgyny that society will deny her. Porter sees that, on the physical/emotional level, woman's sexuality thus becomes an area of conflict: what does she do with her sexual nature if she chooses not to marry and mother? If she chooses to deny her sexuality, what happens to her capacity to love? These issues, in all their possible combinations, are the stuff of Porter's stories, many of them contemporary statements of archetypal truths.

Anthropologists hypothesize that primitive humans who valued life and the continuance of their kind above all else first worshiped motherhood, projecting their experience in the womb with its security and life-sustaining comfort in the form of rotund and bulbous rocks which eventually evolved into explicitly sexual representations of grossly pregnant female deities. But security was not the whole experience. Human beings expressed their awareness of the complexity and even the doubleness of their experience of maternity by characterizing aggressive and even terrible aspects of their matriarchal goddess.

The functions of femininity and maternity were bloody, and birth was precarious; it might result in life or death. Consequently, the eternal feminine was at one and the same time a double figure who was Great Mother and Terrible Mother—she who nurtures and she who devours. The womb was simultaneously the sea of life and the dark abyss, both cradle and grave. Duality was the first attribute of femininity (and probably will be the last, as the prevalence of dark and fair women in our own literature attests).[11]

As human rationality developed, human beings no longer perceived this doubleness as integrated. Ancient peoples who worshiped the maternal now not only depicted her in terms of feminine symbols of fertility but gave her masculine symbols as well. Thus, statues of the Cretan mother goddess represent a beautiful young woman with heavy breasts and round belly whose arms are entwined with phallic snakes and whose sacrificial tool is a double-bladed ax.

By the time patriarchal religions overtook the primitive worship of the Great Mother, this archetypal knowledge of the complex character of the feminine was being expressed in explicit images of anthropomorphized goddesses who often conflicted with each other. The Greek pantheon is typical: Hera, the mother goddess and wife of the father god Zeus; Hestia, the guardian of hearth and home; Diana and Athena, virgins and warriors, patronesses of battle and the hunt; and Aphrodite, seductress, goddess of beauty and love.

Thus was the androgynous nature of womanhood split into several different—and mutually exclusive—personalities. It was only a small further step for modern society to strip away the religious image and reduce woman to the types we recognize so easily in our literature: mother, virgin, temptress, faithful wife, castrating bitch. It is this separation of the parts of the feminine character—this insistence that if a woman is body (sexual), she may not be soul (nurturing)—that creates conflict in female identity. Significantly, primitive societies, to whom an awareness of duality suggested that humankind was composed of two essences, body and soul, saw the importance of integration. Separation of these essentials was seen as a dangerous fragmentation that left one vulnerable. Restoration, then as now, was accomplished by a "soul doctor."[12]

It is this fragmentation and vulnerability that Porter writes about. In "María Concepción," the first work in her *Collected Stories,* integration is possible, and she deftly uses psychological doubles in two principal characters not only to suggest a fragmented personality but also, as Otto Rank has indicated, to dramatize her protagonist's search for identity, which hinges on her incorporation of the alter ego.[13] In her later stories, she demonstrates that integration is not possible within existing societal structures, and her women must therefore make hard choices, denying one part of themselves in order to be another, for woman is not whole in the human imagination. Meanwhile, in the first half of her career, Porter declined to take the simple view. In the second half of her short stories, produced in 1935–1936 in a burst of intense creativity which suggests how important these visions were to her, she dramatized situations which illuminate how such ambivalence occurs and the choices a woman may make in the face of it.

Certainly the most prominent fact of Porter's—and Miranda's—experience is its duality. Born only ten years before the beginning of the twentieth century, into a Southern tradition hearkening back to the antebellum period, Porter grew up in a society peopled with legends and ghosts, but she grew into a world of hard realities, where legends had to be verified and ghosts laid. It is this doubleness of experience that informs Porter's concept of womanhood and forms the basis of irony and tension in her work. Her ambivalent desire to hold onto her roots while moving beyond them is projected, as Freud said it would be,[14] into conflicting images of womanhood in her stories.

There is, first of all, the overpowering image of her childhood, the beautiful belle. The "early training" with which her heroines are always obsessed is training in the appearance, behavior, grace, and decorum which will enhance their marriageability. In white Southern society, woman was not so much a person as she was an ideal, created not out of man's rib but out of his imagination. Pure, innocent, submissive, and physically weak, she was made to love, honor, and obey her husband and to bear his children.[15] Her beauty and grace charmed all about her and assured her of the male protection that was apparently her only natural right.[16] Any other traits or tendencies were aberrations to be vigorously uprooted or, failing that, restrained and buried. Man, not humanity, must be served, for man was woman's lord and master.[17] Her virginity was her principal virtue; if she had beauty as well, she was doubly blessed. After all, her job was to charm her potential protectors, for only as a wife and mother could she hope for any kind of individuation at all. Of course, Victorian society as a whole believed that being a wife and mother was woman's "natural" role, but this dogma was held with particular fervor in the South.[18]

Even in 1944, Helene Deutsch, a disciple of Freud and the author of the classic *Psychology of Women*,[19] whose definitions of certain types of female personality are still valuable, described the "normal" feminine woman in terms that suggest the Southern Victorian ideal. The "erotically feminine" woman, Deutsch felt, was one who existed to love and be loved:

> . . . they are ideal collaborators who often inspire their men
> and are themselves happiest in this role. They seem to be
> easily influenceable and adapt themselves to their companions
> and understand them. They are the loveliest and most unag-
> gressive of helpmates and they want to remain in that role;
> they do not insist on their own rights—quite the contrary.
> They are easy to handle in every way—if one only loves
> them.[20]

In the "Old Order" stories, Porter provides valuable insight into how women responded to their society's image of them. The small glimpse we get of Miranda's mother, Mariana, in "Old Mortality" suggests that she comes close to the ideal and fits the description of Deutsch's passive, erotically feminine woman. However, she dies too young to influence Miranda, who grows up surrounded by more active, aggressive models, like her matriarchal grandmother and her legendary, coquettish Aunt Amy. Deutsch defines the matriarch as an active type of woman who is not necessarily ambitious or competitive with men, but who will direct her extraordinary willpower and certainty of purpose toward nurturing many children or some substitute for them. She is conservative but decisive in supporting her values, and rules over both home and family members.[21] Her identity is separate from man, and her strength may outshine any forcefulness in her husband; her sons will tend to be passive. Juanita Williams points out that this type is like a "mythological matriarch" and that Deutsch sees her as a type of Earth Mother.[22] Interestingly, this is the way Porter portrays Miranda's paternal grandmother in "The Source." One would have to be blind not to recognize her here: a benevolent despot who has single-handedly raised a large family of children and overseen a number of servants and grandchildren, a provident woman who has established homes and planted trees that still bear fruit in three states.

Furthermore, this same type of woman has a sense of duty, which leads her to serve social values and to defend the underdog (with whose plight she identifies psychically) in society. As is characteristic of women in puritanical societies, she may be ascetic and obsessionally neurotic.[23] While one would not ordinarily associate Laura in "Flowering Judas" or Miriam in "That Tree" with Miranda's grandmother, Deutsch's description clearly illustrates a relationship.

Furthermore, Deutsch states, should a girl mistakenly identify with her father—that is, desire active power that she is not prepared to integrate with motherhood—she may react against fear of her own passivity by becoming sexually aggressive, like the coquette, who is embodied so well in Miranda's Aunt Amy and also in Rosaleen O'Toole, whose "active coquetry is . . . an aggression."[24] Femininity, according to Deutsch, is only a mask for these women, who use their narcissistic charm to snare men whom they then sadistically reject.[25] This is apparently what the young woman in "Theft" is accused of by the lover who writes to break off their relationship.

Finally, there is yet another type of woman in whom active and aggressive tendencies predominate and who displays what Deutsch calls a "masculinity complex," here summarized by Juanita Williams: "The classic example of such a woman is the intellectual, who sacrifices her feminine affectivity for the arid pursuit of goals which are defined as masculine: achievement in the arts, business, or the professions."[26] These "masculinized" women, Deutsch explains, having turned from their natural femininity in identifying with their fathers, experience conflict in their personalities, with half of their psyches identifying with feminine tendencies and half with masculine tendencies. To Deutsch, such androgyny is abnormal. To Porter, even without psychological terminology, it is an identifiable conflict that she writes about again and again.

Unfortunately, Deutsch does not explain what happens when

the model herself, like Miranda's grandmother, has been ambiguous, but Porter's stories suggest the result, since Amy the coquette is the matriarch's daughter and Miranda, the professional woman and loner, is her granddaughter. Obviously, Porter's literature, written out of her own experience and before Deutsch's *Psychology,* is corroborated by the psychoanalyst's descriptions, suggesting how universally astute Porter's characterizations of feminine tension are. But her insight doesn't stop there. More than one conflict is inherent in the experience Porter perceives.

In addition to creating women of universal significance, Porter's stories demonstrate what happens to a woman's sexuality in a historical period that denies her physical nature. Southern Victorian society assured itself that white women were not so crass as to have sexual needs. Any libidinal energy they had was meant to be sublimated in childbearing and mothering. But Porter's work dramatizes woman's curiosity about sex itself and her anxiety over her femaleness and the blood rites associated with it: menstruation, defloration, and childbirth. It is hard for women living on a pedestal to come to terms with their bodies. They cannot control menstruation—although Eva Parrington tells Miranda that Amy took lemon juice and salt to suppress her periods—but they can exercise some control over their virginity and maternity by keeping a distance from men.

For nineteenth-century belles like Amy, that simply means avoiding marriage; but for twentieth-century women who live outside the strictures—and protection—of a moralistic society, that means restraining themselves as well. Avoiding sexual temptation of any kind creates a constriction portrayed in Laura, Miriam, and the protagonists in "Theft" and "Hacienda." These women are celibate, repressed, and retentive almost to the point of catatonia. They have good reason for their avoidance. Fear of menstruation, defloration, and birth, which are painful, bloody experiences, becomes, in psychic terms, a primal fear—fear of death. It is easier to let sexual experience go, from Laura's point of view, and the young woman in "Theft" feels that letting it go is ultimately a protection of her more essential self.

As castration is to a man, so initial intercourse may seem to a woman: it injures her physical integrity. Furthermore, orgasm causes an "eclipse of consciousness," and a woman may fear that she will be unable to regain that consciousness.[27] Beyond intercourse itself, she may become pregnant, carrying in her body a new life over which she has no real control. She

must obey its power; its rule is expected, yet invisible, impla-
cable. It is inside her and yet unknown and irresistible. Because of these very qualities it necessarily produces fear. This
knowledge of an event that will happen on a certain date, upon
which one depends, and which, nevertheless, one cannot influence, this mixture of power and submission, has something
fatal and inevitable about it, like death.[28]

And, certainly, impregnation *is* death—death to the virginal belle
that Southern society adores, even while it is also the birth of a new
life for a child and of a new role for its mother. A woman may automatically associate coitus with impregnation and birth with death if
her childhood knowledge of birth has been unhappy. This is true of
Miranda, whose own mother dies in childbirth; furthermore, Miranda is born at a time when many women died in childbirth; those
who survived could expect their marriages to become a "grim and
terrible race of procreation."[29] Anne Scott notes that the idealization
of the role of mother in Southern society failed to emphasize "the
darker side of maternity": " . . . only in private could women give
voice to the misery of endless pregnancies, with attendant illness,
and the dreadful fear of childbirth, a fear based on fact. The number
of women who died in childbirth was high. When the mother survived the family tended to be large."[30] The plaintive comment written by one Southern wife in 1862 readily characterizes how Miranda
must have felt upon recognizing her sexuality in "The Grave": "I'm
not fit for anything but to have children, and that is nothing but
trouble and sorrow."[31] Even after modern medicine significantly reduced the threat of death in childbirth, Helene Deutsch would write
that "fear of death has not been eliminated with the real dangers.
[Woman] has merely transferred her motivation from reality to psychic life."[32]

Thus, although a young woman might long for an Edenic happiness with a perfect man, as Granny Weatherall does and as Miranda
does in "Pale Horse, Pale Rider," that way is fraught with perdition
and death, if not for the body then certainly for the soul. Love in
blessed weddedness is never really a choice for Porter women, as illustrated by "Rope," and "The Cracked Looking-Glass," and her
other portraits of childless, unhappy marriages. There is only one
choice beyond remaining virgin and alone, as we have already noted.
Beyond the first year of marriage, a woman like Granny Weatherall
or the grandmother in "The Source" and "The Journey" need never
wonder who she is. She is Mother and will eventually be translated

by the passage of years into a matriarch, thus integrating her "masculine" desire for power with her "feminine" desire to nurture. This woman

> became, as the myth assured her she must, a wife and mother as soon as the opportunity offered. Thereafter she was likely to work hard for the rest of her life, having a baby every year or so, developing in the process of her experience a steely self-control, and the knowledge that the work she did was essential gave meaning to her life.[33]

Miranda's legacy from the Old Order is the knowledge that she may be a belle, then a matriarch, and establish an identity which has little to do with her personality and which depends particularly on her ability to restrain and control herself. In other words, by containing her real self, she may project an image that others expect. But Miranda chooses to please herself rather than others. At the end of "Old Mortality," she resolves to find her own truth and to make her own mistakes. With the death of Gabriel, Amy's legend may be laid to rest, and Miranda takes a last leave of her father and Eva and the Old Order they represent when she makes her *non serviam*. The real courage of her action is that she doesn't know whether there are any other choices. She simply sees that those before her will not suit. The individualist who evolves is inherent in that choice of the unknown, but at the time she makes it, she cannot know what she will become. It is a progressive discovery that Miranda gradually apprehends over years of remembering personalities and possibilities. Thus, only the totality of Porter's work can illustrate who Miranda is and whence she has come. The same is true of Porter. Each story contributes to her evolving portrait of the artist as a young woman, and only her canon can reveal who Porter is as an artist. What seems certain is that, for Porter, woman is the linchpin, and feminine psychology is the perspective from which Porter's fiction must be examined.

The Porter protagonist is, after all, really only one woman: not Miranda, but a universal, an Everywoman, an archetypal female who feels her vulnerability but acts as an Earth Mother and tower of strength. She sometimes appears in the guise of Mother (Granny Weatherall, the Grandmother), Virgin (Violeta, Amy), or Artist-Creator (the protagonists in "Theft" and "Hacienda"). What fascinates about "Flowering Judas," among other things, is that Laura carefully balances herself among all three roles by playing teacher, immovable object, and revolutionist at one and the same time.

In addition, Porter's essays, collected in 1970, make a fascinating if adjunct gloss to her fiction because they provide a rational rather than creative or intuitive statement of the central issues of her world view. While this study does not attempt to examine the essays in detail, it is worth noting that they contain uncompromising statements about the subjects Porter treated mythically, symbolically, or in dream figures when she produced a story. In essays on Rilke ("Orpheus in Purgatory") and Edith Sitwell ("The Laughing Heat of the Sun"), to name only two, she writes about the significance of love both as a civilizing force and as a personal, human relationship. And in "Letters to a Nephew" and "A Wreath for the Gamekeeper," she explores the relationship of human sexuality to love. In the classic "St. Augustine and the Bullfight," one finds her understanding of basic human psychological issues like the excitement—and sexual overtones—of flirtation with danger and death. And in essay after essay, she speaks of the necessity of bringing order out of chaos: "Chaos *is*—we are in it. My business is to give a little shape and meaning to my share of it . . ."[34] Many of her characters seek that shape and meaning through love relationships, but Porter's own response to that ideal is a single-minded pursuit of excellence in art, best expressed in her introduction to the 1940 edition of *Flowering Judas*: the arts "are what we find again when the ruins are cleared away."[35] As one might expect, the informing attitudes behind the essays and the stories are the same.

In the whole of Porter's work, then, we discover that being a contemporary woman means being torn by a need for love and a conflicting desire for individual identity and assertion of personal ideals (revolution) or talents (art). This conflict surfaces again and again, sometimes with the two tendencies personified and warring directly with each other, as is the case in "María Concepción," at other times with the conflict internalized in the deepest psyche of the protagonist, as it is in Granny Weatherall, Laura, the young woman in "Theft," and Miranda herself.

Finally, the value of reading Katherine Anne Porter's work from the viewpoint of feminine psychology extends in two different directions. First of all, this viewpoint provides a unity to her work not usually found in the diversity of her stories. Second, the stories themselves, when read in conjunction with each other, provide a sensitive prophecy for contemporary femininity: no longer limited to the simple reproduction of life, women can reject the cocoon, but then they must assume the burden of freedom.

Furthermore, the motivating force behind Porter's most significant stories is the conflict between, on the one hand, the feminine desire for love and for the traditional female role sanctioned by the

Old Order, and on the other, by the assertion of self and of one's ideals and talents, made possible by the social upheaval of the twentieth century. She seems to suggest that in order to define their identities, women must choose between love and work. Refusing to make the womanly role one's work can only result in fragmentation; on the other hand, doing so often requires self-delusion and brings about dissatisfaction and even despair. This pattern is illustrated in a chronological overview of Porter's stories. (A chronology of Porter's fiction is found in the Appendix.)

The early stories, written and published in the twenties, are portraits of women in conflict with themselves or with societally imposed roles. All are trying desperately to control what is essentially beyond their control. By focusing on women separated from her by class, heritage, and culture, Porter deals with their conflict in fairly objective terms, as if gradually defining what will be the informing concept of her work. But it is a mistake to try to classify Porter's work on the basis of objective details like setting or situation. In these diverse stories, she uses mythic structures, images, symbols, and irony to create a broad but not deep view of feminine conflict. Only in "Virgin Violeta" does she begin the kind of psychological penetration that she will embrace and finely hone in her most complex stories. Her canon is a movement backward from objectivity, a descent into the psyche which provides an intense view of female duality.

In the next group of stories, published in 1929–1930, this feminine conflict emerges in all its psychological depth, reiterated in Porter's first complex projection of subconscious states like dream and memory and combined with psychological penetration and present-tense realism that is typical of Porter's best writing. Published within one year and linked in theme and technique, "The Jilting of Granny Weatherall," "Theft," and "Flowering Judas" collectively represent an intense effort to come to terms with feminine division by examining it in its utter depths.

Interestingly, Violeta and the anonymous protagonist in "Theft" seem to be early versions of a Miranda-like character, and it is another anonymous woman—but an implicit Miranda—who will finally confront her dichotomy decisively by examining all the ramifications of her choices and then making the only real choice open to her in terms of her values. This occurs in "Hacienda," a pivotal story which marks, along with "That Tree," the end of her fiction about Mexico. Significantly, in "Hacienda" artistic pursuits are defined as essentially masculine; in "That Tree" the artist is male and his double a domesticated woman who tries to subvert his real nature.[36]

After this decisive juncture, Porter produced the "Old Order" stories and *Pale Horse, Pale Rider*, two movements backward into even more personal depths, which utilize the double vision and hindsight she learned in writing "Hacienda." In the intensely re-membered vignettes of "The Old Order," which climax in the psy-chological complexity of "The Grave," Porter returns through mem-ory to the sources and models which give the adult Miranda her perspective. Miranda's experiences in "Pale Horse, Pale Rider" and in "Holiday" indicate that in the contemporary world love is not really possible, but that it is possible, even without love, to survive. With these stories, Porter's canon essentially ends.

Apparently the intensive writing of these stories functioned as a kind of exorcism, or the problem "settled itself," for after 1936 Por-ter did not significantly address the issue again. In *Ship of Fools* both Jenny and Mrs. Treadwell think about their choices and the effects these choices have had on their lives, but both are opposed to mar-riage and traditional domestic roles. For them, integration has been impossible; they have made the only choice they could make and be true to themselves.

Perhaps, too, life had conspired to settle the issue for Katherine Anne Porter. By early 1938, when "Old Mortality" and "Pale Horse, Pale Rider" had been published, she was forty-eight years old. Her professional reputation was irrefutable; her earlier marriages had been unsuccessful, and she was in the midst of her last marriage, which was fated to end in divorce. She had no children. Undoubtedly she felt that she had made her choice, even if by instinct, by virtue of the innumerable decisions she made through the early years to place herself in living situations—in Mexico, Paris, New York—where do-mesticity was the aberration rather than the choice of a single, pro-fessional life. She told Barbara Thompson of the *Paris Review*:

> I was living almost as instinctively as a little animal, but I real-
> ize now that all that time a part of me was getting ready to be
> an artist. That my mind was working even when I didn't know
> it, and didn't care if it was working or not. It is my firm belief
> that all our lives we are preparing to be somebody or some-
> thing, even if we don't do it consciously. And the time comes
> one morning when you wake up and find that you have be-
> come irrevocably what you were preparing all this time to be.[37]

In the majority of her stories, Porter suggests that her women fear the dependence and loss of freedom that love seems to imply. Having ascertained her own personal freedom in the face of the threats possible from her experience, and having come to understand the sacrifices that freedom necessitates, she focused in *Ship of Fools* on the physical and psychological separation of men and women, seeing in that primal disunity the potential destruction of the civilized world.

PART I

The Mirror Image: Virgin and Mother

1922–1934

The first six stories in The Collected Stories of Katherine Anne Porter *were published between 1922 and 1928. They are marked by an objectivity characteristic of 50 percent of Porter's work. This objectivity is created by a detached, omniscient narrator, an ironic tone that can reduce the subject to comedy, and an absence of obvious autobiographical parallels to the author, unlike those which will be examined in Chapter 5.*

These are stories about people removed from Porter's class and culture; they are objective and realistic in setting and plot, even where psychological insight into character is offered. In them, Porter experiments with characterization, technique, form, and length.

Yet they share one not always apparent consistency with her other work: they are all stories of women caught in constricting circumstances who must recognize and confront two burdens in their lives: their sexuality and their social position. (Even "He," despite its title, is the mother's story.) In these stories, Porter pursues her predominant theme of divided women in search of their souls, but she also examines feminine stereotypes and conventional feminine roles as viable identities for women.

She writes out of a consciousness that intuitively understands the complexity of womanhood. In her early stories she examines the archetypal duality of womanhood and concludes that integration can exist only in the most primitive cultural circumstances. The more structured the society, say these stories, the more difficult integration becomes and the more trapped woman is. What that circumstance means to her women psychically is the subject of her next two groups of stories, in which her protagonists are characterized even to the roots of their minds. The stories written in the second half of her career are penetrating psychological studies of a persona who must repeatedly refuse her society's attempt to type her and who must find her way out of the labyrinth of her own divided self.

The relatively new sciences of anthropology and psychology have taught us most about the way human beings conceptualize. Human beings concretize what is significant, even critical, in their experience in symbols which are in turn reproduced in their objects of worship, their visual arts, and their stories and songs. This is as true of the contemporary artist as it is of the primitive. Katherine Anne Porter has said repeatedly that she writes out of experience, which does not clarify why she writes about certain experiences and not others, nor why she writes about a paradigmatic situation over and over again. Presumably she seizes on a certain donnée *because it illuminates her sense of what is psychically significant, and even essential.*

1 ❖ *Reflections*

"María Concepción"

"María Concepción," published in 1922, is a story based on the same images, symbols, and feminine archetypes contained in the last story Porter would publish, forty years later.[1] Superficially, it sounds like a Hollywood script: it is the story of three Mexican Indians caught in a triangular relationship nursed by love, jealousy, and revenge. María Concepción, the independent protagonist, who is married to Juan Villegas, is pregnant. She discovers that her husband is making love to María Rosa just before Juan and his mistress run off to war together. María Concepción becomes stolid, refusing even to cry when her child is born and dies. When Juan and María Rosa return, María Rosa delivers a healthy child, but before the day is out, she has been fatally knifed by María Concepción. Everybody knows the wife's motives for vengeance, but when the police investigate, both Juan and the other villagers protect her. She takes María Rosa's baby for her own and goes home with husband, child, and sanity restored.

A plot summary cannot approximate the psychological characterization Porter achieves in this story, one of her most complete and compelling portraits of womanhood. A paradigm for many later stories, it is a kind of morality play in which two strongly defined feminine principles fight to the death, not over the love of a man, but for ascendancy.[2] The triangular relationship of María Concepción, Juan, and María Rosa, in conjunction with the bloody sacrifice and the presence of the infant son, is enough to suggest the author's conscious or unconscious use of the most ancient archetype in human experience: the eternal feminine or the Great Mother, whose office is the continuation of life. In "María Concepción," it is manifest in the Aztec mythology which is part of the cultural heritage of these Indians, despite their Christianization.

It is evident from the beginning of the story, even from the title, that María Concepción manifests the character and attributes of the archetypal mother goddess. She is, first of all, Mary of the Conception, designated a mother from birth by her name. She is also pregnant, serenely and pridefully so: "The shape of her body was easy, the swelling life was not a distortion, but the right inevitable proportions of a woman. She was entirely contented" (p. 3).

Furthermore, she is superior to her fellows, even her husband, whose work in the "damp trenches" of the ancient buried city marks him as a servant of the womb. He exists primarily to impregnate her. She needs him for nothing else. She has skill and money. She is an independent, energetic, proud woman who initiates her marriage to Juan Villegas by paying for the license and who then sets herself above her more common neighbors by paying the priest to marry them in church. The announcement of their banns of marriage is an "adventure" to the community, and the proclamation lends a regal air to their union. Even Givens, Juan's employer, who "liked his Indians best when he could feel a fatherly indulgence for their primitive childish ways" does not condescend to María Concepción; he admires her nerve and her "grand manner," which makes him think of "royalty in exile" (p. 7).

Even her small, enclosed house sits shrine-like "halfway up a shallow hill" (p. 3), while her rival, María Rosa, lives in the valley, attended by Lupe, the medicine woman, whose pagan charms and cures María Concepción eschews. This queen-like woman, with her hens, symbols of fertility, slung over her shoulder, her body swollen with pregnancy, and her long-bladed knife at her waist suggests a primal goddess like the Cretan mother figure, full-breasted and armed with her double-bladed ax. Finally, the bloody business which is her livelihood, the slaughtering of her chickens, is a task she carries out by beheading, the favored form of sacrifice to the goddess because it allowed blood from the severed neck to flow freely.

By contrast, María Rosa is clearly the feminine love principle whose passionate, seductive nature is suggested by her association with the flower of love.[3] The sheltered nature of her femininity is underscored by the fact that she lives with her godmother, Lupe, a priestess figure who looks after the "pretty, shy child only fifteen years old" (p. 4). Nothing could be more appropriate to a goddess of love than that she keep bees and dispense honey to the village. Her presence there among the hives is a statement of both the sweetness and the sting of love that Juan will come to know through her. Everything about her milieu is sensual; a drowsy, warm, and fragrant air hangs over her hive-like house and the mounded hives themselves are surrounded by "a dusty golden shimmer of bees" (p. 5).

Whereas María Concepción is described by objects, her manner, and her pregnancy, María Rosa is defined by references to the movement of knees and thighs and by her physical beauty: ". . . her halfraveled braids showered around her shoulders. . . . Her dark red mouth moved . . .; her long black lashes flickered with the quick-moving lights in her hidden eyes" (p. 5). Everything about her is sultry, soft, and consenting as she disappears under the cornstalks with Juan. Truly, she is like honey to him, as he later tells Givens.

Although he runs away to war with María Rosa, he returns with her a year later. Significantly, he is not able to gainsay either one of "his" women. A vain little peacock of a man, he merits all of the irony in the story. His "primitive childish ways" allow Givens the "fatherly indulgence" of saving him from one scrape after another. When Juan returns from the revolution, María Concepción has lost her child and María Rosa is pregnant. Givens warns him against María Concepción's vengeance: "You be careful. Some day María Concepción will just take your head off with that carving knife of hers." Juan, who swaggers and poses with the best of them, favors Givens with an expression that is "the proper blend of masculine triumph and sentimental melancholy. It was pleasant to see himself in the role of hero to two such desirable women." He responds to Givens "handsomely, as one man of the world to another: 'My chief, women are good things, but not at this moment. Let us forget María Concepción and María Rosa. Each one in her place. I will manage them when the time comes.'" (p. 12).

The time comes without his planning and sooner than he thinks. He returns to María Rosa and their newborn son, but after a morning of celebratory drinking, he finds himself "unaccountably in his own house, attempting to beat María Concepción by way of reestablishing himself in his legal household" (p. 13). She responds with amazing assertion for a woman of her class, refusing to yield to her husband's right to beat her, and even hitting back at him. However, her anger is not directed at him. María Rosa is her enemy, the temptress who has taken her man and caused through this trauma the death of María Concepción's child. It is Lupe who recognizes that the loss of her child has transformed María Concepción into the Terrible Mother. "She is mere stone," Lupe says of her, reminding us that Terrible Mothers like Medusa killed by turning their victims to stone; to be stone, of course, is to be immobile and therefore to lack life. Death will be the mother's office so that new life may be generated. It is no surprise, then, that after Juan falls asleep, his wife suffers an agony of soul before she realizes what she must do to reestablish her fecundity.

On the literal level, if she wants motherhood again, she must recapture Juan's sexual attention by obliterating her rival, María Rosa. On the mythic level, the necessity for María Rosa's bloody sacrifice is even more complicated and is illuminated by its parallel-ism to ancient Aztec mythology.

The mythology of many cultures contains a triangular relation-ship between the goddess of the corn (a mother of fertility), a young maiden, and a youth, often the goddess's daughter and son. In Mex-ican tradition, the Aztec mother goddess was originally "the goddess of the obsidian knife with which bodies are dismembered,"[4] who in time evolved into the fertility goddess of the corn. She nevertheless still demanded blood, sacrifice, and death, for fecundity requires death, as the life cycle in nature demonstrates. In some ceremonies a male god becomes identified with the corn mother after the behead-ing of a woman goddess, whose blood fructifies their union and as-sures the birth of the son, who represents the corn.

More specifically, the Aztec triangle is seen in the relationship of Xochipilli, Xochiquetzal, and the Great Mother goddess. Xochi-pilli is "the beautiful prince of flowers" and "the young god of life, of the morning, of procreation and of foodstuffs, a typical god of the sun, of love, and of vegetation . . . he is also the butterfly and the 'flower prince.'"[5] It is hard not to think of Juan as he appears on his return from war, dressed in bright finery that María Rosa has scav-enged for him: "He was walking in the early sunshine, smelling the good smells of ripening cactus-figs, peaches, and melons, of pungent berries dangling from the pepper trees, and the smoke of his ciga-rette under his nose. . . . His situation was ineffably perfect . . ." (p. 12).

Xochiquetzal, a virgin, is "the goddess of love's pleasures and of sins; of amusements, dances, songs, and art; of spinning and weav-ing. She is goddess of the marriage bond, and the patroness of har-lots."[6] She is identified with the third member of the trio, the Great Mother, and in effect is subsumed by her.

> The archetypal marriage of the Great Mother with the son
> who appears as god of the light, of the maize and the flowers,
> is celebrated also in Mexico, and here again a rejuvenated
> daughter goddess appears beside the terrible mother goddess,
> with whom she is identical.[7]

Thus, in marrying her lover, the son of the Terrible Mother, the daughter goddess reinforces her identification with the mother god-dess; her own identity is subsumed in the matriarch, just as María Rosa's position as common-law wife to Juan necessitates her re-moval and the assumption of her role by María Concepción. In Az-tec ritual, likewise, Xochipilli must be identified as a successful adulterer and warrior, as is Juan, thus ensuring his sacrifice to the Great Mother also.

Other parallel aspects of the triangular relationship are found in the tales associated with Quetzalcoatl, the hero god of the Aztecs. He is a phallic god whose name means "plumed serpent" (again, we think of Juan's silver tassels, his bright yellow shirt, his tooled red belt); he overindulges in drink and/or sexual pleasure with a harlot named Xochiquetzal, who is brought to him by demons. He thus destroys paradise and himself. Of course, we already know that Xochiquetzal is identical with the Great Mother, thus, Quetzalcoatl, seduced by her, becomes synonymous with Xochipilli.[8]

The parallels to our three principals are fairly obvious, and an understanding of this ancient mythic pattern helps explain several confusing elements in Porter's plot and characterization. First, it demonstrates why Juan feels he needs both women, even though he has earlier abandoned María Concepción. It explains, at a level beyond simple vengeance, why María Concepción, after knifing María Rosa, says, "For me everything is settled now" (p. 15). Juan wishes suddenly to repent "as a very small child" and just as suddenly values the wife he has rejected, for "she had become invaluable, a woman without equal among a million women, and he could not tell why" (p. 16).

It also explains why Lupe, who is, after all, María Rosa's godmother, and Soledad, the wise woman of the village, not only do not accuse María Concepción, but defend her with cunning. They attribute the murder to "an evil spirit," an accurate description of the Terrible Mother as killer. They claim that she is "a woman of good reputation" among them and support her with "a secret and mighty sympathy." In fact, the bonding of these women in the candle-lit hut over the body of a sacrificial victim has a ritualistic character which reminds us that, for all its Christian trappings, this culture remains essentially pre-Christian. María Concepción may be named for Mary, the virgin mother of a patriarchal god, but Porter's use of the name is ironic rather than literal. Although she has been married in church, María Concepción's blood is Aztec, not Catholic. Listening to the defenses raised for her, María Concepción feels "the forces of life . . . ranged invincibly with her against the beaten dead" (pp. 19–20), and she is restored to life-giving power. When María Concepción claims the newborn child, who "spat blood the moment it was born" (p. 17), the women who had defended her recognize her claim to this new life and, with it, her resumption of her office as Great Mother and goddess of fertility.

At the end of the story, we are reminded that it is not only María Rosa, but Juan, too, who has been sacrificed for the sake of continuing life. Exhausted from his ordeal, he understands no reason for what he has done to save his wife. He strips off his peacock's clothing, his plumage, and falls backward into sleep, "his arms flung up and outward" in a position of crucifixion.

In recognizing that his days of excitement as a soldier and adventurer are over, he broods over his return to the womb-like trenches of the buried city, reminding the reader that life is a continuum; that human beings bring history to the present and that they, in the present, themselves create what will become history. Juan associates the buried city with María Rosa's death and interment. In so doing, he reiterates a cluster of images that reverberate in this and other Porter stories. The trench, the grave, the womb, life and death and burial in life are images so closely related here as to be literally inseparable, moving eternally into each other, as do Juan and María Rosa into the eternal serenity of being that is María Concepción, who is ultimately in harmony with all the rhythms of the earth, new life "cradled in the hollow of her . . . legs" (p. 21).

On the psychological level, María Concepción and María Rosa may be viewed as doubles; the story then becomes a struggle between alter egos or conflicting aspects of one personality. Classic literary examples of the split personality, like Oscar Wilde's Dorian Gray, deal with men, but these two women illustrate the archetypal fight to the death over a love object, in this case, Juan and his son.

One sign of the struggle between the two is the gauntness that characterizes María Concepción ("as if something were gnawing her life away inside") and María Rosa's leanness, despite her advanced pregnancy. Juan spends a year with each woman before the final struggle ensues, and on his return to the village he declares to his chief that he cannot harm María Concepción because he married her in church, while María Rosa pleases him more than any woman. He must have both of them, for he needs the stability and security of one and the love of the other.

From María Concepción's point of view, she cannot bear children or solve her psychic agony until she has found a way to absorb the erotic into her personality. This she achieves by overcoming María Rosa. Significantly, when she returns to Juan in their jacal, she is more "womanly" in the terms her society recognizes: she is subservient and humble, and leaves the initiative to her husband. She defers to him as to her god, approaching him on her knees, and depends on him to save her. In short, she behaves not like María Concepción, but like María Rosa. She feels ineffable relief when she faces the corpse of her rival once more and sees that María Rosa is indeed dead.

The wise woman and the healer recognize that the death of María Rosa has been nothing more than the flight of an evil spirit; in fact, Soledad says she has proclaimed to María Concepción the conclusion of the battle: "Good luck to you, María Concepción, this is a happy day for you!" (pp. 19–20). Thus María Rosa's child is rightly María Concepción's child, and the easy peace with which she settles into the silent breathing of the world and the role of mother contrasts with her earlier failure to recognize either her own newborn or its subsequent death. Having absorbed eros, she is no longer simply Mary of the Conception, the virgin, but a woman who knows the fullness of love and its fruition.

On a social level, María Concepción moves from loneliness to community, from isolation and struggle outside the circle of women who wish to share her trouble to communion and peace in the circle of "reassurance, understanding, [and] a secret and mighty sympathy" (p. 20) among women whom she now recognizes as sisters. For María Concepción, blood and honey have mingled to coalesce, and she is "saturat[ed] . . . with repose" (p. 21). For Katherine Anne Porter, a seminal statement has been made, the depths of which she will probe in nearly every story to come.

"The Martyr"

Porter's next story, also set in Mexico, is "The Martyr," and it has the stuff of tragedy. It is the story of Mexico's most celebrated artist,[9] who dies of heartbreak after the beauty he loves deserts him. In this narrative, however, Porter makes the sublime ridiculous by telling the story from a detached, objective point of view. Through her use of an ironic observer-narrator, the story becomes a comic satire of sentimental excess in one man and finally in his whole society. It is a completely successful tour de force. In fact, the comedy inherent in Rubén's eating himself to death and calling himself "a martyr to love" obscures the fact that this is also Isabel's story; she is the victim of his fantasy as much as he is.

The martyr is truly a martyr to love but hardly to the love of any one woman. Rather he is in love with a romantic image of woman and projects this image onto his inamorata, Isabel, in total disregard of her real personality, wants, and needs. The objective narrator's view of Isabel is that she is a bad-tempered witch, a stereotypical Mexican spitfire, who exploits Rubén's affection for her by allowing him to support her even though she loves a rival artist. She is not,

however, dishonest. Her rude manner with visitors to Rubén's stu-
dio is not for them alone; she derisively calls Rubén "*churro*," a
Mexican nickname for a pet dog, rips up the flowers he brings her,
and shamelessly throws tantrums like a spoiled child, even to the
point of physically abusing the master. Yet he insists on interpreting
her behavior as loving.

Isabel is his Beatrice, his Laura, his inspiration; she is a goddess
before whose shrine he worships. He continually describes her as an
angel and her features and behavior as "angelic." He says more than
once, and more truly than he knows, "There is no other woman like
that woman" (p. 34). And of course he is right, for no woman, certainly not Isabel, is like the woman his imagination has created for
him: an angel of goodness, kindness, and unsurpassed beauty, a
muse who inspires the artistry of his work.

It is easy enough to recognize this woman, an ethereal creature
of light and air, placed high on her pedestal where she is unsullied by
individual personality traits or mundane human necessities: she and
Rubén often forget even to eat during the long days given to sketch-
ing her perfection. Isabel, as Rubén creates her, is an other-worldly
creature, and he recognizes his courtly role toward her: he is "deeply
in love" with her, to the point that "everyone declared Rubén would
kill on sight the man who even attempted to rob him of Isabel." He
continually pays homage to her beauty by creating sketch after
sketch of her, and when she finally leaves him for the artist she
really loves, he requites himself well by announcing that she has
taken his life with her. Then he begins, literally, to eat himself to
death. The false nature of his affection and the ludicrousness of his
pose as a soon-to-be martyred lover are caught beautifully in the far-
cical image of Rubén that the narrator supplies us after the painter
has read Isabel's farewell note:

> When Rubén read this, he felt like a man drowning. His breath
> would not come, and he thrashed his arms about a good deal.
> Then he drank a large bottle of *tequila*, without lemon or salt
> to take the edge off, and lay down on the floor with his head
> on a palette of freshly mixed paint and wept vehemently.
> (p. 34)

With characteristic hyperbole and blindness to the paradox in
his statement, Rubén declares, "I tell you, my poor little angel Isabel is a murderess, for she has broken my heart" (p. 35). The two
extremes that Rubén chooses to describe his flown idol are precisely the either/or terms which men of his kind like to apply to all
women. His friend Ramón consoles him with the fact that he knows

"how women can spoil a man's work for him"; the woman who left him was a "shameless cheat-by-night" (p. 35) who almost ruined him. Women are either angels or murderesses, good mothers or terrible mothers, virgins or harlots, and the devil take all the shades of character in between. In actuality, Isabel is neither angel nor murderess, but a human being who, frustrated with the trap in which she is enclosed, vents her anger by abusing her jailer.

Aside from her shocking behavior toward the talented and adoring Rubén, we know little of Isabel. Most readers would describe her as a flat, one-dimensional character who is nothing more than a catalyst in the author's caricature of the artist. Yet, what we do know of her suggests more of the human being than Rubén's characterization does. There are reasons for Isabel's behavior, and they in turn heighten the irony that Porter creates in characterizing the men of Mexican society.

Isabel is "bored, for sometimes she would stand all day long, braiding and unbraiding her hair while Rubén made sketches of her, and they would forget to eat until late; but there was no place for her to go until her lover, Rubén's rival, should sell a painting . . ." (p. 33). Besides posing for Rubén—a task for which she must assume the passive qualities of a statue, the image that Rubén has of her—and occasionally cooking for him, the only meaningful activity that Isabel has is quarrelling with him or pulling his hair. She is bored, but has no place to go because she depends on men for her subsistence. Thus she must stay with the man she hates until the man she loves has enough money to rescue her from her cage. There is no question of autonomy or self-sufficiency in her; she is the *real* martyr to love, idealized and typed before her individuality has asserted itself.

In fact, she undoubtedly recognizes that her beauty is her fortune. Her farewell note to Rubén says, "I am going away with someone who will . . . make a mural with fifty figures of me in it, instead of only twenty" (p. 34). Through her beauty she attracts men who will support her, and it is because of her beauty that she can bite the hand that feeds her and get away with it. When she rails at Rubén, scattering the petals of his flowers and flicking the tip of his nose with paint, she is demonstrating her worth to those who witness his tolerance, as well as punishing him for refusing to treat her like a person. She is also asserting herself in the same way that a child does: her incredible behavior makes people pay attention to her, relieving her of her statue-like stance and its attendant anonymity. Like Miranda's Aunt Amy in "Old Mortality," Isabel creates a legendary image of herself to suppress the one that society and Rubén have created for her.

She scorns his love rightly, as she scorns the bloodless image he has of her. Her own image of happiness is pathetically vague; her farewell message to Rubén indicates that she will now live with a man who thinks her truly precious: he will never allow her to cook for him, and he will paint fifty figures of her. In addition, she says, "I am also to have red slippers, and a gay life to my heart's content" (p. 34). The red slippers suggest vivacity and luxury; they are all that Isabel can imagine of the "gay life" she wishes for, but they remind us of other Porter heroines who fantasize about dancing their lives gaily away with bright flowers in their hair. Isabel's yearnings are the same. She may even find them satisfied by her new lover, if he values her for herself, but most likely she has escaped from one cage only to find another.

If Rubén has created a phantom to love, it is the phantom likewise that kills him. He succumbs, as he has made up his mind to, within a year of Isabel's departure. He dies of a heart attack induced by extreme obesity while, appropriately, dining on tamales and pepper gravy at his favorite café. The bathos of the situation is intensified by his last message to the world: "Tell them I am a martyr to love. I perish in a cause worthy the sacrifice. I die of a broken heart! . . . Isabelita, my executioner!" (p. 37). Of course, Isabel has no better fate. Already warped into stereotype, her personhood will suffer slow strangulation, constricted by a society from which she cannot escape.

"Virgin Violeta"

The protagonist of "Virgin Violeta" is another example of this sort of psychological strangulation, but this story explores the conditioning necessary to produce a feminine stereotype and illustrates its effect on emerging womanhood. "Virgin Violeta" is an interesting study because it is Porter's only attempt to focus on female puberty. In the Miranda stories, published in 1935–1936, Porter created a cycle of initiation stories from early childhood to preadolescence, but curiously wrote nothing about the experience many people would think most significant in human growth: the emotional reaction to the first sexual contact with the opposite sex. This early story of Porter's fills that gap. It is also her first characterization of the personality type that will dominate her work—a sensitive, idealistic, but inquisitive romantic. George Hendrick calls Violeta "a prototype of the character of Miranda."[10] While Violeta is, of course, very unlike Miranda in belonging to a wealthy Mexican family which shelters its females, these are superficial differences; in terms of sensibility and psychological experience, she might as well be called Miranda as Violeta, for there are substantial parallels between them that suggest Porter was learning to use autobiographical detail and was already beginning to shape the character whose viewpoint would dominate her fiction.

First, Violeta is a perceptive observer outside her family group. Her point of view dominates the story. Her position in the family is like Miranda's: she is a younger girl, growing up dominated by an older, apparently more physically attractive sister and a strong, tradition-oriented mother. Her father is a remote disciplinary voice who plays no active role in her experience. Violeta is a romantic idealist who believes she will turn into the swan she wishes to be:

> For of course everything beautiful and unexpected would happen later on, when she grew as tall as Blanca and was allowed to come home from the convent for good and all. She would then be miraculously lovely—Blanca would look perfectly dull beside her—and she would dance with fascinating young men. . . . (p. 24)

One is reminded of Miranda's romantic wish to be like the belles of her family:

> Miranda persisted throughout her childhood in believing, in spite of her smallness, thinness, her little snubby nose saddled with freckles, her speckled gray eyes and habitual tantrums, that by some miracle she would grow into a tall, cream-colored brunette, like cousin Isabel; she decided always to wear a trailing white satin gown. (pp. 176–177)

In addition, Violeta and Miranda both come from societies which revere ideal womanhood and place their women on pedestals. They share a puritanically rigid religious training and convent schooling which they hate. Violeta feels trapped by church and school, as does Miranda, whose statement that she has been "immured" in her convent school is unforgettable. Thus Violeta's experience is significant not only for the insights it offers into one girlish personality but also for its glimpse of the incipient persona of Miranda. It is as if Katherine Anne Porter, although concentrating on a culture outside her own, began her career with two stories of an emotional conflict she understood so well that it lent special authenticity to her protagonists' experience.

"Virgin Violeta," like "María Concepción," probes the inner psychology of female experience. It is a second rendering of an emotionally distraught female, torn between the romantic dream of love that her tradition has fostered in her and her innate desire for freedom, nurtured by her animal instinct. Here again we have an emotional triangle between two young women and a young man whose superficial poses are pointed out through irony. Here again is a conflict between two women that reverberates on several levels. The literal struggle is between Blanca and Violeta for beauty and male attention. On a deeper plane, however, theirs is a struggle between chastity and passion and, ultimately, between woman as sacred object and woman as person.

Blanca, the older sister, is, as her name suggests, the "white" one, a pale beauty who "blooms like a lily" and, as she has been taught, "conducts herself like one" (p. 23). Dressed in gray with only the yellow embroidery of her shawl to relieve the paleness of her image, Blanca is a porcelain piece set on a shelf. She is to be admired, but not touched. Trained to control every particle of her appearance and behavior, Blanca is demure to the point of preciosity. Her voice is "thin, with a whisper in it." Her "nod, her smile, were the perfection of amiable indifference" (p. 22), an indifference that is belied by the quaver of excitement in her voice as she reads poetry with handsome Carlos at her side. Her narcissism has reached a point where "she really didn't think of anything but the way she had her hair fixed or whether people thought she was pretty" (p. 27). One suspects she values Carlos because his attentions to her affirm her beauty and desirability.

Significantly, it is Blanca who is the real virgin in this story, and much of her value lies in her remoteness. In fact, this reality is underscored by the painting, *Pious Interview between the Most Holy Virgin Queen of Heaven and Her Faithful Servant St. Ignatius Loyola*, which Carlos gazes at and which is an emblem of his courtly evenings with Blanca:

> The Virgin, with enameled face set in a detached simper, forehead bald of eyebrows, extended one hand remotely over the tonsured head of the saint, who groveled in a wooden posture of ecstasy. Very ugly and old-fashioned, thought Violeta, but a perfectly proper picture. (p. 23)

Like the "enameled" Virgin Mary, Blanca is chaste and pure, a model before which Carlos genuflects. She is also bloodless. In addition, the allusion to Ignatius Loyola invokes the idea of discipline, since he originated the rigorous spiritual exercises practiced by those who followed him. In families like Violeta's, particularly in courtship rituals, discipline is practiced rigidly. Porter's ironic point, of course, is that this rigor was intended for virgins and celibate saints, not for lovers or those who would marry.

In contrast, Violeta has not yet learned to control her emotions; she is passionate, the color of her personality running to violets, at the deepest edges of the spectrum. Distressed by the thick-soled brown sandals and dark blue clothes she must wear, she longs to dress in bright blue dresses, to have red poppies in her hair, and to dance gaily down the carpet of life in utter disregard of any restraint or restriction. Naturally like a "young wild animal," Violeta must obey authority figures who establish difficult standards for her. At the convent, she is taught "modesty, chastity, silence, obedience"—a litany of Blanca's perfect womanhood—"with a little French and music and some arithmetic." She is confused because the outside world is so different from her inner emotional turmoil.

In many ways, Violeta is a typical adolescent. Extremely self-conscious and emotionally quixotic, she moons about and has romantic daydreams in which she is the sought-after prize who will be claimed by the true prince: "She would appear on the balcony above, wearing a blue dress, and everyone would ask who that enchanting girl could be. And Carlos, Carlos!" (p. 25). Her simmering sexuality is sublimated into a passionate attachment to Carlos's sentimental love poems, through which she can simultaneously nurture her desire for her prince and her idealized image of love. The trouble with idealized dreams like Violeta's is the trouble she already senses in her life: they conflict sharply with the reality of the physical world. In fairy tales, the climax in the relationship between the prince and his princess is at best a very asexual kiss.

A further conflict burdens her, for, like Isabel, Violeta has only narrow avenues open to her. Her mental image of herself reflects this; her sense of oppression is symbolized in the gaily-colored "parrots in the markets, stuffed into tiny wicker cages so that they bulged through the withes, gasping and panting, waiting for someone to come and rescue them" (p. 26). Other images in her daydreams reflect her ambivalence toward herself and her future life as a woman. The huge carpet she sees unrolled before her becomes the ceremonial carpet used for a large wedding service:

> Life was going to unroll itself like a long, gay carpet for her to walk upon. She saw herself wearing a long veil, and it would trail and flutter over this carpet as she came out of church. There would be six flower girls and two pages, the way there had been at cousin Sancha's wedding. Of course she didn't mean a wedding. Silly! (p. 24)

The image she identifies with most eagerly, however, betrays the real dimensions of her conflict. The passionate Violeta is not, like Blanca, an enameled virgin. She does, however, see herself as a nun—but a nun who has sinned by loving, after the image in one of Carlos's poems. She takes it to church with her and reads

> about the ghosts of nuns returning to the old square before
> their ruined convent, dancing in the moonlight with the
> shades of lovers forbidden them in life, treading with bare feet
> on broken glass as a penance for their loves. Violeta would
> shake all over when she read this, and lift swimming eyes to
> the delicate spears of candlelight on the altar. (p. 24)

Violeta would surely not be the first sentimental adolescent to be reduced to tears reading love poetry, but the conjunction of images here suggests that her tears are an emotional release from repression of sexual desire that surfaces as she reads about chaste nuns who should not but nevertheless have loved. The titillation inherent in that image of forbidden pleasure for Violeta is only enhanced by her masochistic pleasure in the nuns' punishment: "dancing with bare feet/On broken glass in the cobbled street." She finds the words "thrilling" and she "shake[s] all over" when she reads it, finally seeing herself as one of these nuns, "the youngest and best-loved one, ghostly silent, dancing forever and ever under the moonlight to the shivering tune of old violins" (p. 25).

Without ever having sinned sexually, Violeta feels she is guilty, and the story carefully exposes the seeds of repression and guilt that are Violeta's response to the standard of modesty and chastity held up before her. She self-consciously assumes that everyone can see her sexual thoughts (although she doesn't assume they know what else she is thinking). It sticks in her memory that Papacito, the voice of ultimate authority in their household, has proclaimed, "It is your fault without exception when Mamacita is annoyed with you. So be careful" (p. 26). Like a disease, sin is in Violeta; in addition to feeling guilty, she must ever guard against its eruption.

It is easy enough to see that the combination of romantic illusion, repressed sexual energy, a sense of guilt, and a desire for punishment for secret sin sets Violeta up for her disillusioning encounter with Carlos in the climax of the story. Contrary to what Violeta thinks, Carlos is very aware of her burgeoning womanhood. Far from being unconscious of her, he either deliberately avoids looking at Violeta by gazing at the picture of the Virgin or uses it as a ruse to watch her, since the picture hangs over her head. When she leaves the room, he follows her "as if he had thought of something interesting." In a darkened room he kisses her by surprise. Like Keats's Madeline, she wakes to find her dream a reality and is understandably startled by it. She pulls away. Unfortunately, Carlos's behavior impresses on her the shame rather than the thrill of what has happened.

He muffles her mouth with his hand, and his bright, shallow eyes, too close to hers, are threatening. She is reminded of Pepe, the macaw, and we are reminded of Violeta's earlier image of herself as a parrot in a confining cage. Since macaws are the most powerful species of parrot, it is clear not only that Violeta is caught in a trap, but that she is too weak, both physically and psychologically, to defend herself. Powerless to change the situation and already sensing guilt, she feels as she does when "called up to explain things to Mother Superior." She recognizes that she and Carlos are "allies in some shameful secret" (p. 29). In her mind, this does not equalize them, because Carlos is male, older, and authoritative. It doesn't occur to her to seize the advantage; she feels complete vulnerability.

What she is too narcissistic to recognize is that Carlos has taken advantage of her and will do so again by shifting blame for the situation to her. When she chides him for kissing her, he derides her foolish assumption that he has given her anything other than a "brotherly kiss," thus destroying any possibility of her taking pleasure in the thought that he has been attracted to her. He then heaps insult onto her injury with a cruel "Shame on you, Violeta." Not only is she not attractive enough for him to desire; if he toys with her, she must bear the blame and the shame to boot. He concludes the damage by becoming cold and overbearing when she expresses her sense of guilt:

> "Nonsense!" said Carlos. "Come with me this minute. What did you expect when you came out here alone with me?"
> He turned and started away. She was shamefully, incredibly in the wrong. *She had behaved like an immodest girl.*
> (p. 30, italics added)

In Violeta's world, someone's saying you are an immodest girl is tantamount to being one.

Carlos's assurance that his kiss meant nothing, his derision, and the burden of shame he heaps on her leave Violeta unbearably frustrated. When he comes to wish her goodnight, the sight of his face bearing down on her literally forces her to the wall. She screams hysterically, finally releasing her pent-up desire, anxiety, and frustration.[11]

Interestingly, Mamacita doesn't punish her daughter for her outburst (perhaps because she understands), but tells her she must learn to control her "nerves." In actuality, Violeta denies and represses her sexual nature, which has left her so vulnerable, even more deeply than before. Those thoughts which are her "very hidden thoughts— those thoughts that *were not true at all* and could never be talked about with anyone" (p. 31, italics added)—will stay hidden. She is left with "brooding" questions and with her major conflict unresolved: her attraction to "fascinating" young men threatens her modesty, her principal claim to worth. Like other Porter heroines, she recognizes that she can never love a man and retain her virtue. Instead of rescuing her from her cage, Carlos has ruined her self-esteem and destroyed her hope for the future. In the end, she has completely reversed herself; she hates Carlos, his poetry, and the convent altogether, recognizing that there is "nothing to be learned" in an institution that teaches modesty, chastity, silence, and obedience.

In her refusal to reaffirm the values of her family and society, she rejects integration with them, preferring to remain isolated and "unrenovated." While she fails to see, as Miranda eventually does, that she must be the agent of her own freedom, she has taken the first step toward personal integrity by recognizing sharply that her happiness cannot be invested in another person.

Porter's first three stories illustrate that integration and freedom are difficult for women of any class in Mexican society. In her next three stories she will demonstrate that they are virtually impossible at any level of American society.

"He"

"He," like "María Concepción," focuses on a primitive woman whose only proper role can be motherhood. Unlike María Concepción, however, Mrs. Whipple, the poor white farmwoman whose conflict is at the center of the story, has no sense of her own identity. Lacking talent and self-knowledge, she has no direction and thus lacks the grit by which Porter women survive.

Her society casts her in the role of a mother, but again in contrast to the women of María Concepción's village, Mrs. Whipple's neighbors don't value motherhood in and of itself. A mother must demonstrate her worth by being able, as is Granny Weatherall. Of course, Mrs. Whipple is anything *but* able, as her coupling with her idiot son, known only as "He," suggests. In the absence of personal identity or a talent that might help her create one, Mrs. Whipple is particularly susceptible to self-delusion and moral blindness. Her inadequacy is aptly captured in the image of her idiot son, who, cumbersome, lumbering, and ubiquitous, is the perfect and concrete visualization of his mother's own inner and outer poverty. Like Him, she is stupid and dumb, senseless as to how she got where she is and as to how to change her situation. He symbolizes the hard, uncontrollable realities that Mrs. Whipple is unable to acknowledge: her poverty, her personal inadequacy, and, most of all, her insufficiency as a mother.

Like other Porter women, however, Mrs. Whipple has to contend with a romantic—even sentimental—ideal; thus she likes to put a good face on things, fooling herself into believing that appearance is reality. She is pleased, for instance, when the preacher romanticizes her idiot son's condition by saying that He "walks with God." She herself romanticizes the image of Whipple family life, thinking of her other two children working together with her on the farm in some communal idyll, when all either of them hopes for is to leave as quickly as possible. But most of all, she sentimentalizes her motherly role as the guardian of a handicapped child. Thus she purports to love Him better than her other two children put together: "You know yourself it's more natural for a mother to be that way. People don't expect so much of fathers some way," she tells her husband (p. 49).

Of course, she fools no one but herself. Her neighbors are convinced "there's bad blood and bad doings somewhere . . ." (pp. 49–50) among the Whipples because they have produced this idiot boy. And Mrs. Whipple's public sentiments do not belie her true attitude toward this huge child she cannot control; to her, He is nothing more than an animal. He destroys the clean clothes she puts on Him and skitters through trees "like a monkey." He eats like an animal, and she fears that if she does not control Him, He will devour a whole roast pig Himself. She cannot "keep Him out of mischief" because "He's always into everything . . ." (p. 50). But most of all, her inability to reconcile His animal-like behavior with any human sensibility is evidenced in the fact that she is unable to call Him by any given name.

Ironically, it is she who is grossly insensitive to His demonstrations of human feeling. When He bolts from the sight of her butchering a suckling pig, she ignores it. When He refuses to come to the dinner table when the roasted piglet is set out, she brushes it off. Ignoring His humanity, she is able to treat Him like an ox brought in to do the heavy work, a creature impervious to pain and fatigue. He must keep the bees, lead home dangerous bulls, and steal the suckling pig from its angry sow.

When Mrs. Whipple slaughters that baby pig—one the family can ill afford to sacrifice—all for the sake of impressing her brother's family, she demonstrates not only her weak character but the poverty of her motherhood. Ultimately, she will sacrifice Him, just as she sacrifices the pig, in an attempt to make the farm appear prosperous. His reaction to the slaughtering and her refusal to see his reaction ironically point up the degree to which her own sensibility and maternal instinct are, like her son, stunted and retarded.

Finally, carelessness leads to out-and-out neglect, and He is deprived even of warmth and adequate medical care. Hard winters and Mrs. Whipple's declining fortunes begin to show in His deterioration. As they get "poorer and poorer," and the farm seems "to run down of itself," He develops latent pneumonia, begins to limp and, finally, to have seizures. The local doctor puts an end to Mrs. Whipple's maternity by admitting Him to the county home, where "He'll have good care and be off your hands" (p. 57).

Mrs. Whipple, of course, has not been changed by adversity. As she is about to relinquish her idiot child, she projects a utopian image of the family secure and united in a kind of happiness that is clearly Edenic fantasy. It is as impossible a dream as Isabel's image of romantic happiness.

Ironically, in the final scene in which He is removed to the home, Mrs. Whipple finally recognizes in His tears human pain and a sense of loss based on His love for her. She and her simple child create a mournful pietà as she cradles His head on her bosom and weeps over Him. Recalling her abuse of Him, she rationalizes that "she had loved Him as much as she possibly could. . . . there was nothing she could do to make up to Him for His life. Oh, what a mortal pity He was ever born" (p. 58).

The irony of this final sorrowful pain brings the story back to its root in Mrs. Whipple's motherhood. Having had a sentimental idea of what a mother must be, she has compounded her personal insufficiency by sacrificing her only real wealth to fill a role she thinks her society expects of her. She *has* loved Him as much as she was able, and in the sense that she could never have done much better, it is truly a mortal pity He was ever born. But Porter's stories are full of mortal pities, not the least of which is Mrs. Whipple's own psychic handicap, as uncontrollable and immutable as her son's imbecility.

"Magic"

In "Magic," as in "The Martyr," Porter focuses on a kept woman who, like Isabel, tries to escape her circumstances. A compactly ironic gem, "Magic" is about a woman who has the courage to rebel against her physical entrapment but who still ends bound to a life she hates. Although the story is told in a direct, realistic way by a black maidservant who believes in charms and magic, the reader recognizes that the title is used ironically and that the maid's rendition of the poor prostitute's return to the fancy house is meant to be balanced against the reader's own perceptions of the situation. The story, whose brevity prefigures that of some of the "Old Order" stories, appears slight, but it has been called a highly complex, "brilliant Jamesian experiment in point of view."[12] It unites the characterization of maid, mistress, the madam, and Ninette with "subtle psychological probings" as well as "bitter social criticism."[13]

Once again Porter forces us to look beyond the type suggested by the girl at the center of the story. A prostitute, she is obviously a temptress or a fallen woman, well liked by the men who visit the house. Although Violeta, Isabel, and Ninette, the prostitute, are all, irrespective of their class, in circumstances in which they must trade their sexual charm for their livelihood, Ninette is most blatantly a sex object. But she is a person as well. She is spirited and independent in challenging the madam who is cheating her of her earnings, even to the point of tolerating physical punishment in an effort to get what is due her. In effect, Ninette refuses to conform to the role her microcosmic society establishes for her.

Ironically, Ninette is overseen by an authority figure who is a woman. Again we have the paradigmatic situation in Porter: a woman who wishes to assert her integrity or identity must combat a woman who defines herself by her sex, although in this case the madam represents a larger authority, both male and female, which conspires to keep women in their "place." For her part, Ninette finds, like other Porter women, that trying to run her own life is mortally dangerous. She barely survives the madam's beating when she tries to buy her way out of the house and finally ends in the street, badly injured and penniless.

Eventually the madam wishes Ninette back and seeks charms from the black cook for the purpose. Ninette returns, supposedly irresistibly drawn by a potion made of her leftover face powder, hair, blood, and fingernail trimmings.[14] Porter's ironic implication, however, is that Ninette comes back for the same reasons she probably came in the first place: she is sick, she has no money, and she has no prospects. Furthermore, if she tries to live outside the circle where her way of life is the norm, she will be a pariah; she cannot escape what she is in the eyes of society. Nor can she be herself in the microcosm of the bordello; unless she behaves as she is expected to, all will conspire to thwart her.

The madam, her overt adversary, will violently abuse her; the cook will use incantations and hexes to disarm her; the maid, herself completely powerless, must be careful to avoid offending her mistress by so much as a pulled hair and has nothing but indifferent curiosity toward a fellow creature. Madame Blanchard, perhaps something of a whited sepulchre, who is "kept" by the legal and societal bonds of marriage, offers curiosity rather than compassion, thereby contributing through her tacit acceptance to the existence of the brothel world and the exploitation of women like Ninette. Together they weave a fine web that entraps and subjugates Ninette in a way that is not so magic after all. Ninette comes "home" to the madam because she can do nothing else.

The point of this brief story is that Ninette and Madame Blanchard are sisters under the skin. Established attitudes are the "magic" that ineffably confines both of them. The significant message here is that deviating from that confinement is deadly.

"Rope"

Porter's next story, "Rope," like "Virgin Violeta," examines the circumstances in which a woman of Porter's own class and caste might find herself. Her protagonist here demonstrates what Violeta will discover—that although it is legally and socially acceptable, marriage may be another kind of entrapment. Porter asserts again that a woman may be confined by the attitude of one who loves her; she may also be her own antagonist. This insight looks forward to the intense psychological penetration of the protagonists of "Theft," "Flowering Judas," and other complex Porter stories.

In "Rope," several critics have found an example of Porter's penchant for portraying unhappy marriages,[15] and the rope which is the center of the couple's quarrel becomes an ironic "tie that binds," an image of the constriction of their union. The man and the woman in "Rope" are unnamed and undescribed. The burden of the quarrel rests with the woman; she initiates it and she ends it. The man has to be goaded into fighting and tries several times to make peace. In the face of his patience and passivity, it is tempting to call his attacking wife a classic bitch and let it go at that.

Once again, Porter treats the conflict in the woman objectively; no omniscient narration or psychological penetration provides insight into her character. What can be said of these people must be said on the basis of their accumulated statements to each other. The story moves forward on their verbal thrusts and parries. While the quarrel does not reveal much about their background, it does reveal a great deal about their emotional states and their views of each other. In "Rope," Porter inverts the ordinary pattern of narration, making her two characters and the narrator speak in the third person and the past tense: "He thought there were a lot of things a rope might come in handy for. She wanted to know what, for instance" (p. 42).[16] This technique has a distancing effect, as if the reader were watching a film of the incident rather than experiencing the quarrel from the emotional standpoint of either husband or wife. The narrator's objectivity may suggest that the woman, removed from the time and place of the quarrel, with the advantage that hindsight always brings, is the teller of the tale. On the other hand, in the moments after the woman runs upstairs, as the man prepares to return to town, his frustration is penetrated briefly:

> He would take back the rope and exchange it for something else. Things accumulated, things were mountainous, you couldn't move them or sort them out or get rid of them. They just lay and rotted around. . . . Imagine anybody caring more about a piece of rope than about a man's feelings. (p. 47)

Since the woman's feelings are never similarly illuminated, this passage may suggest that the story is told by the husband, in which case his inability to understand his wife's frustration contrasts with the reader's comprehension of it, resulting in dramatic irony. In any case, "Rope" is the story of her frustration and his inability to comprehend it.

The wife in this story wants comfort, order in her life, and time to do the work she thinks is important. She is restricted by their lack of money, by the clutter of an unorganized household, and by the mundane chores of housework. Like other women discussed here, she cannot express her dissatisfaction plainly and directly. She deals in subterfuge, which is why the rope becomes such a bone of contention. The quarrel must reach a certain pitch before she will name her specific complaints, but a close reading of her comments reveals the way her irritation moves rapidly from one detail to the next, baffling her husband.

First, it is clear that she is generally dissatisfied with this man and their life together, and that her aggravation smolders just below the surface. Consequently, when he forgets to bring home the coffee she has been looking forward to, she takes his oversight personally, as proof that he doesn't care for her well-being. When she objects to the rope he has bought, she is objecting to a superfluous item that is tangible evidence of his carelessness toward her.

The rope then simply becomes a touchstone for all the complaints she has against him, particularly the unhappiness she has felt since they came to the country three days before. The place itself is too primitive, too disorderly, not "decently fit to live in." They have no money to spare. It is hot and they have no ice to store perishables. She doesn't want to live with "second best and scraps and makeshifts, even to the meat!" His response indicates that this is not the first time they have been in such circumstances: "He rubbed her shoulder a little. It doesn't really matter so much, does it, darling? . . . He was getting ready to say that they could surely manage somehow when she turned on him and said, if he told her they could manage somehow she would certainly slap his face" (p. 43).

What emerges in the next sequence of the argument is that she feels burdened by the clutter and chaos of the new place, hemmed in by the necessity to create order out of it, and overwhelmed by the excessive work it will require. It is only an added aggravation that her husband doesn't need the order she does. She expresses her sense of isolation by accusing him of leaving her alone to do all the work, and further suggests that he has been unfaithful to her. Feeling persecuted by her bitter remarks, he tells her that "the whole trouble with her was she needed something weaker than she was to heckle and tyrannize over. He wished to God now they had a couple of children she could take it out on. Maybe he'd get some rest" (p. 44). He thus echoes the cliché that women who are kept barefoot, pregnant, and in the kitchen are no trouble.

She is particularly stung by this remark, and her frustration mounts. Resorting to sarcasm, she evidences her bitter anger and repressed hostility. Because she needs to control her life, she feels thwarted by her husband's flexibility. When he asks her if they are going to live in the house or let it ride them to death, she turns pale, then livid. Her reaction seems an excessive response to his question, and she again substitutes the thing that is really bothering her for a direct answer to his question: " . . . she looked quite dangerous, and reminded him that housekeeping was no more her work than it was his: she had other work to do as well, and when did he think she was going to find time to do it at this rate?" (pp. 46–47).

His response is meant to put her in her place: "She knew as well as he did that his work brought in the regular money, hers was only occasional, if they depended on what *she* made—and she might as well get straight on this question once for all!" (p. 47). She brushes aside the suggestion that her work has no value or seriousness because it cannot command money. The question, she says, is their division of labor. She scoffs at the idea that he has ever been a help to her, stressing again her sense of isolation. Then she bursts into tears: " . . . her face turned slightly purple, and she screamed with laughter. She laughed so hard she had to sit down, and finally a rush of tears spurted from her eyes and poured down into the corners of her mouth" (p. 47). Her husband reacts to her hysteria by trying to douse her with water. She wrenches free and runs upstairs.

What emerges from this quarrel is a woman who is not very flexible; she needs to control, "to make her plans," to bring order out of chaos so that she can cope with living. Thus she can't manage broken eggs in the grocery basket because she has already planned to have steak for supper; she must have the rope, hammer, and nails out of the kitchen because they are underfoot; she jumps from one job to the next, saying in almost the same breath that she is going to wash windows, and then that it is important to air the mattresses. Through it all, she wishes for her husband to keep her company, to share her fears, to value her difficulty, and to remember her desire to focus on more important work.

For his part, he is an easy-going man who cannot see her dilemma; he doesn't feel the house is his responsibility and consequently doesn't feel overwhelmed by it. His role is defined since he brings in "the regular money." Furthermore, his wife's anxiety is to him a capricious display of her feminine nature. In his view, her desire for order is an "insane habit of changing things around and hiding them"; she makes "a complete fool of herself" (p. 44) by complaining to him; her comments are "silly," or else she is "raving"; she is a "hopeless melancholiac" whose coffee-drinking is making "a wreck" (p. 46) of her. Seeing her hysteria, he is not worried about what has brought it about, but thinks how she works herself "into a fury about simply nothing"; she has "not an ounce of reason," and he is tired of "humoring" (p. 47) her. He clearly thinks she has no rationality and that her emotions rule her. It is interesting to note, though, that in their exchanges, she is the one who names specific problems, even if circuitously. He resorts to name-calling and points out her "real" role to her.

When he returns from his second trip to the village that evening, she is waiting to greet him as she had that afternoon, but this time she is cool, refreshed, and expansive. She offers an apology, saying she wouldn't have behaved that way earlier if she had had her coffee. It is undoubtedly true that she wouldn't have behaved that way if there had been no match to set off the powder, but the tinder is still piled there and will ignite again easily. She asks for reassurance: "He knew how she was, didn't he?" and he replies, "Sure, he knew how she was" (p. 48).

The varieties of irony in that last line underscore the fragility of this relationship. If he means he knows how she is when she doesn't have her coffee, then he really doesn't know how she is at all, because he takes the coffee for the real issue. If he means that he knows her emotional makeup is precarious, he is right on one count, but he doesn't seem to really know why. If he means he knows how she is—a bitch who cares more about winning her point than his feelings, then he is mistaken; he really doesn't know how she is.

In any case, the story ends with the suggestion that the relationship is fated. Although husband and wife are reconciled, the cool evening will give way to another hot day in the confused household, and, like the rope the husband has carried to town and back with him, their burdens are still with them. Finally, there is the hint of things not right in the image of the lone whippoorwill, "clear out of season" and left "all by himself" by his mate (p. 48), surely the fate of the woman who insists on having things her own way. In the next group of stories, Porter begins to examine why women trapped by circumstance choose to remain so.

2 ❖ *A Closer Look*

"The Jilting of Granny Weatherall"

With "The Jilting of Granny Weatherall," Porter finds her métier. She addresses with full force her primary subject, the divided nature of female lives, but the struggle is no longer overt. It is a psychological battle, and the need to present the divided psyche of her protagonist leads Porter to her mature style. In this mode, she not only provides psychological penetration of her characters' conscious minds, but also ventures into their memories and their dreams, where, through the use of interlocking symbols, she creates the complexity of their unconscious minds as well.

An intricately woven piece, "The Jilting of Granny Weatherall" contains the components of a typical Porter story. For one thing, she focuses here on a matriarch, a major character in much of her work. Second, she again examines the relationship between birth and death, womanhood and motherhood, order and chaos. Third, she characterizes by psychic intimacy, allowing the reader profound knowledge of Mrs. Weatherall's values, hopes, and fears in each of the significant stages of her life. Fourth, time is eclipsed by the use of memory and dream so that, as in the mind, all experiences exist in one vast present. What emerges finally is a woman whose viewpoint has been and is being shaped by repeated encounters between the forces of life and the forces of death in her experience.

While on her deathbed, Mrs. Weatherall's whole life passes before her, and she is proud that she has "been strong enough for everything," despite the fact that everything she made "melted and changed and slipped under" (p. 83) her hands. Life has certainly been very different from anything she hoped or imagined; one of the great ironies of the story lies in her name and its title, for the deathbed recollections of the protagonist illustrate that although she has survived, she has not really "weathered" the storms of her experience. The repressed pain of her lover's betrayal—the jilting—has never been resolved; it surfaces from the depths of her psyche every time her controlled consciousness wanes and fades.

Dominated by the experience of that jilting, the story is a linear movement backward in time from Mrs. Weatherall's old age through her womanhood until, finally, she completes the cycle by reverting, in the last moments of her life, to a womb-like darkness. At the same time, the story moves back and forth between the concrete world of her deathbed and the world of her unconscious, where she experiences three major phases of her life and three consecutive identities simultaneously. In imitation of the mind's power of free association, Porter calls these experiences into shape by a single word and frequently juxtaposes them before they dissolve and merge into one another. Unifying all, however, is a pervasive struggle between life and order and death and chaos, characterized by the war between light and darkness which carries the story forward.

The psychological complexity of the story need not obscure thematic unity, but a frame of reference is helpful: Emily Dickinson's poem "My life closed twice before its close" serves as a perfect gloss for Porter's story, just as the story is a fictional emblem for the poem. Both stress two traumatic losses equivalent to death before the final separation from life:

> My life closed twice before its close—
> It yet remains to see
> If Immortality unveil
> A third event to me
>
> So huge, so hopeless to conceive
> As these that twice befell.
> Parting is all we know of heaven,
> and all we need of hell.   (no. 1732)[1]

The first closing in Ellen Weatherall's life comes when she is jilted. "A young woman with [a] peaked Spanish comb in her hair and [a] painted fan" (p. 83), Ellen, Mrs. Weatherall's youthful character, lives by her beauty and her delicacy. She is a prize to be claimed by a worthy man, who, by marrying her, will make of her a complete woman. She will be set down in a tidy house where the linen is starched and white, the pantry shelves are filled with neat rows of jelly glasses and crockery, and the clock is well dusted. A completely dependent person, Ellen dreams of living happily ever after; but the dream is based completely on her desirability for one man. If George loves her enough to give her his name, then order and light prevail; if he doesn't, chaos is come again:

> Such a fresh breeze blowing and such a green day with no
> threats in it. But he had not come, just the same. . . . There
> was the day . . . , but a whirl of dark smoke rose and covered

it, crept up and over into the bright field where everything was planted so carefully in orderly rows. (p. 84)

It doesn't occur to her that she may have some autonomous power to create her own happiness. Investing everything in romantic love, she loses painfully when it fails.

She suffers a terrible betrayal when the man for whom she has "put on the white veil and set out the white cake" fails to meet her at the altar. Not only does her lover reject the love she has declared for him by putting on her wedding dress, but he has left her liable to public ridicule because she stood up to be claimed, and he declined to claim her. That she is very vulnerable to this is evidenced by her relatives' response to her trouble: "Wounded vanity, Ellen. . . . Plenty of girls get jilted. You were jilted, weren't you? Then stand up to it" (p. 84). But wounded vanity is the smallest part of her misery. She has been dealt a psychic death blow from which something can be salvaged but nothing saved.

It is hard to understand the depth of this wound unless one notes a subtle but important question that echoes through the story. At the beginning Granny Weatherall thinks that things change so much that "by the time you finished you almost forgot what you were working for. What was it I set out to do? she asked herself intently . . ." (p. 83). Later, she imagines that she is giving her daughter a message for her faithless lover, George. She wishes him to know that she has forgotten him and that, furthermore, she has had husband, house, and children in spite of his abandonment: "Tell him I was given back everything he took away and more. Oh, no, oh, God, no, there was something else besides the house and the man and the children. Oh, surely they were not all? What was it? Something not given back. . . ." (p. 86).[2] At the end of the story, this sense of incompleteness reverberates in the old lady's realization that death has caught her by surprise, before she has had a chance to finish the business of assigning heirs for her possessions.

This nagging sense of something lost, incomplete, and undone is only partially answered by the fact of the jilting itself. We must not overlook the fact that Mrs. Weatherall represses her feelings about this unhappy episode; she pushes it out of her mind before she can resolve it, making it unfinished business. She keeps secrets from her children in order to protect the image of strength she projects— the sequence opens with her desire to get rid of her old love letters from George and John, so that her children will not find out "how silly" she was once. More important, though, she doesn't wish, even on her deathbed, when one would expect her to have some equanimity, to remember him herself, and she struggles against the intrusion of his memory. Thoughts of him are not only abhorrent, they are unthinkable, and we might readily wonder why. Even a completely devastated pride ought to have renewed itself to some extent over sixty years. Mrs. Weatherall's hope in a "green day" and a "bright field" is Edenic, but not totally compensatory: "there was something else besides the house and the man and the children." Eden, it appears, involves something more than a young woman's normal expectations. Ellen looks for something more than obvious advantages in this marriage; she wants fulfillment, which is translated several ways.

To some extent, she undoubtedly expects identity and individuation as a result of marrying. Significantly, Porter gives her no surname when she dramatizes her youthful character. She is simply "Ellen." After marriage, however, she will be "Ellen Weatherall" or "Mrs. Weatherall," a woman with a name, a role, and a social position, none of which can be achieved in any other reasonable way in her society. Moreover, George will help her define her sense of who she is in a far more intimate way, by introducing her to sexual experience.

What sexual experience might mean to her is significant. First of all, she is a young woman of moral upbringing to whom sex is probably largely a mystery; she undoubtedly anticipates satisfying her curiosity. Her society believed that "good" women had no sexual feelings; her Catholicism would teach that the primary purpose of sex is procreation; so that only within the context of motherhood could she have a legitimate curiosity and desire for sex. But presumably her affection for George would create a simple desire for union with him, a desire that neither her society nor her church would approve. But if her knowledge of sex came through George, she could have it both ways. She could satisfy her curiosity about the sexual side of her nature in the protected context of love, with a man who, through marriage, would be legitimized as the father of her children. Thus her normal but forbidden desires could be sanctioned through marriage to George. When the wedding is aborted, so is her sexual initiation. She is also left with the shameful—and painful—knowledge that George has not wanted her nearly as much as she has wanted him.

If her memory of George carries with it a sexual connotation, it is simple enough to understand why she has repressed it. To remember it is to think of herself as a "bad" woman, so "for sixty years she has prayed against remembering him and against losing her soul in the deep pit of hell, and now the two things were mingled in one

. . ." (p. 84). John, the man she marries, makes her a fine husband who provides her with an identity and role so powerful and consuming that she has no time to dwell on her regrets. In doing so, he protects her from George's influence. Mrs. Weatherall remembers John as a good husband and, in a telling comment, says she wouldn't have exchanged him "for anybody except St. Michael himself . . ." (p. 88). Since Saint Michael was the hero of pious legend who single-handedly fought off Satan, her reference to him again suggests that she associates memories of George with death and the devil. The faithful pray to him: "St. Michael the archangel, defend us in battle. Be our protection against the wickedness and snares of the devil. . . ."

Therefore, in terms of identity and sexuality, George's influence has been both powerful and destructive. But her worst loss is her ability to believe. The green day and the bright Edenic field are engulfed in clouds of smoke which pollute and smother everything in it, including Ellen's youthful faith and trust. It transforms potency into loss, Eden into hell, and establishes a paradigm of despair that Mrs. Weatherall will resort to at the moment of death. Thus the "something not given back" is not only the identity and the sexual initiation—which, after all, she achieves, although in a different context, with John. The something not given back is her elemental faith that "God's in His Heaven, all's right with the world." She has believed completely, and her faith has been despoiled. Never again can she put faith in any order that she has not created herself. She will spend the rest of her life lighting lamps to dispel the darkness.

On "the day the wedding cake was not cut, but thrown out and wasted" (p. 87), Ellen realizes she has been abandoned and she faints, in effect dying to the reality of the moment. As if to emphasize this symbolic death, Porter describes her falling through space where all physical limits have disappeared, the same terms she will use to describe Granny Weatherall's physical demise. When Ellen faints, "the whole bottom dropped out of the world, and there she was blind and sweating with nothing under her feet and the walls falling away" (p. 87). Later, when Granny dies, "her heart sank down and down, there was no bottom to death, she couldn't come to the end of it" (p. 88).

The death of Ellen's total personality on her spoiled wedding day is averted by the man who will eventually marry her and transform her identity by giving her children. Catching her as she swoons, he breaks her fall and saves her for the next and most significant phase of her life. But her painful loss of personal identity is not to be assuaged. "It's bitter to lose things" (p. 84), she thinks.

George's parting has been all Ellen needs of hell, for he takes with him her youthful sense of self-worth and her pride in her beauty and fragility—so deftly suggested by her Spanish comb and painted fan, and so easily destroyed in one stroke. He also takes away the possibility of her knowing sex in the context of love. Her bitter legacy from this experience is the knowledge that love is an untidy emotion which makes one exceedingly vulnerable. Love dwells in uncertainty and can lead to chaos, darkness, and death.

Although she has suffered a lethal blow, with John's help she assumes the name and identity of Weatherall and begins to assert the indomitability which "Weatherall" implies. Having learned that investing in the love of a man is ruination, even damnation, she severs the image of a dependent Ellen and moves toward the identity which marks her even as an elderly woman. By marrying John, she becomes not only Mrs. Weatherall, but Mother. Like María Concepción, Mrs. Weatherall's destiny lies in matriarchy. Unlike María Concepción, she has no primitive understanding of the cyclical unity of all things and she must grow into a knowledge of her power as a mother.

She does so during her childbearing years. By the time she has her last baby, she gives birth easily and recognizes in her role a natural fulfillment: "When this one was born it should be the last. . . . She was strong, in three days she would be as well as ever. Better. A woman needed milk in her to have her full health" (p. 86). The absence of any real love in her life, the dead part of her, is subsumed in the experiences of childbearing, just as a withered arm becomes less significant as the other arm strengthens and compensates for the inactivity of the dead limb. Another way of describing what happens to Mrs. Weatherall is that she sublimates her sexual energy by rearing children. After she has been jilted and has accepted the alternative role that marriage to John offers, she thinks how the absence of emotional love leaves her free to focus on her children: there is "nothing to worry about anymore"; having repressed her own fears, she can focus on calming the fears of her dependents (p. 87).

Her husband dies a young man, and appropriately so, for he exists, like Juan Villegas, primarily as the fecundator who allows the mother to assume her primal powers. After his function is complete, he is simply another member of her family: "She used to think of him as a man, but now all the children were older than their father, and he would be a child beside her if she saw him now." Similarly, her husband appears to be a tool for her use. She has had "fine children out of him," and after he is gone, the children are not reminders of their father, as one might expect, but reflect only their mother and her efforts to raise them: "There they were, made out of her, and they couldn't get away from that" (p. 83).

The real value of motherhood for Mrs. Weatherall, however, is that through it she learns about power. She becomes a woman who can "spread out the plan of life and tuck in the edges orderly." No longer dependent on anyone but herself, she can create her own order by cooking, sewing, and gardening; she can "have everything clean and folded away" (p. 81) without recourse to any man. She can control the chaos of fog and night by lighting lamps for her children, a small ritual by which both mother and children assert their dependence on her.

Presiding over life and death, she rides "country roads in the winter" when women have their babies and sits up nights with "sick horses and sick negroes and sick children, hardly ever losing one." Finally, she is an androgynous woman with power enough to perform a man's tasks, a person her husband wouldn't know: "She had fenced in a hundred acres once, digging the post holes herself and clamping the wires with just a negro boy to help. That changed a woman." (p. 83).

Unfortunately, that power she has enjoyed so deeply she will miss most keenly. Having achieved a vital matriarchy, Mrs. Weatherall must withstand a second death: the loss of her importance and power as her children themselves grow independent. "When she was sixty she . . . felt very old, finished . . ." (p. 82); having seen her children and her children's children, she no longer feels like the prime mover she has been in their early lives, and she attempts, unsuccessfully, to die.

She cannot accomplish this, never having been able to acknowledge death. Just as she represses the memory of her psychic death as a young woman, she also represses the thought of actual death. When she finds death in her mind, it feels "clammy and unfamiliar." Her reverie never explicitly states that her husband John and her daughter Hapsy are dead, although her thoughts about them admit no other possibility. While it is true that at the age of sixty she makes farewell visits to all her relatives, makes a will, and comes down with "a long fever," she herself says that it "was all just a notion like a lot of other things." She is not really in physical danger of her life. Her actions are more a ritual marking of the passage of her primal motherhood which in fact strengthens her, "for she had once for all got over the idea of dying for a long time" (p. 82).

Nurturing, nursing, planting, ordering, she is too much the power of light and life to admit the power of death. She represses the concept at sixty as she did at twenty, and settles down to live out her nonage. Her peace, however, is frustrated by her family's recognition of a new identity in her, even while she clings to the old. She is still Mother to them, but she is even more a Granny in their eyes. They are patient with her attempts to retain her motherly power by lecturing them and ordering them about. But this only exasperates her, and Granny nostalgically wishes for her days of power, "with the children young and everything to be done over" (p. 83). The tables are turned now, and her family sees her as childishly senile; they humor her whims to the point that she "almost made up her mind to pack up and move back to her own house where nobody could remind her every minute that she was old" (p. 82). Granny Weatherall's strength lies in her vitality, and although her children still seek her advice on some subjects, her power has clearly diminished to the point where even the family doctor condescends to her, telling her she must "be a good girl" to get well, and calling her "Missy." The old lioness has lost her teeth. Therein lies a death she has not sought, an inevitable second closing of a phase of her life.

The final closure of her experience is the literal subject of Granny Weatherall's story. It places her two earlier "deaths" in perspective; furthermore, the psychological reality of her actual death brings into final relief the symbiotic relationship of birth and death. The doubleness of these apparent opposites is inherent in the archetypal mother, and despite Mrs. Weatherall's repression of the idea of death, it continually seeps into her mind like the dark rolling clouds of fog and smoke which symbolize it.

As a mother giving life in birth, Mrs. Weatherall—like all other women—faces death. A woman in labor hovers between the death that her child may deal her and the immortality that the child bestows as her living heir, who will carry some particle of her being forward into yet unborn generations. Mrs. Weatherall recognizes the duality of this experience by saying to her husband that her "time has come," a phrase that may be used to indicate either imminent birth or imminent death. It is the phrase she uses when she recalls the labor of her favorite daughter, Hapsy, who has apparently died giving birth.

The deftness with which Porter encompasses the events of the moment with those of the past, the real and the imagined, for both the living and the dead is beautifully illustrated in a paragraph of psychological penetration which illuminates Hapsy's importance to Mrs. Weatherall:

So there was nothing, nothing to worry about any more, except sometimes in the night one of the children screamed in a nightmare, and they both hustled out shaking and hunting for the matches and calling, "There, wait a minute, here we are!" John, get the doctor now, Hapsy's time has come. But there was Hapsy standing by the bed in a white cap. "Cornelia, tell Hapsy to take off her cap. I can't see her plain." (p. 87)

The first sentence moves the reader from Ellen's jilting into her marriage to John and what both of them recognize as its most important aspect: her maternity. The thought of one of the children screaming in a nightmare becomes instantly associated with the thought of Hapsy screaming in labor, and she tells John—who would have been dead by the time Hapsy was old enough to bear a child—to get the doctor. John, in his lifetime, would have gotten the doctor for Ellen, not for Hapsy, but her calling on John to help their pregnant daughter meshes the identities of mother and daughter as childbearers. It is clear by the time the reader sees this paragraph that Hapsy is dead, so Mrs. Weatherall's phrasing, "Hapsy's time has come," implies both birth and death, as we have already noted. This almost subliminal reference to death evokes the ghost of Hapsy, which has already spoken to Mrs. Weatherall, but her faltering lucidity mistakes the nurse by the bed for her dead daughter. By the time Mrs. Weatherall complains that she "can't see her plain," the comment is ironic, because she has already unfailingly demonstrated that to the reader.

As an embodiment of motherhood, the ghostly Hapsy, "standing with a baby on her arm," is the central symbol of Mrs. Weatherall's powerful maternity. The triangle created by Mrs. Weatherall, Hapsy, and the child symbolize the universal cycle of death and its part in the generation of new life in all its doubleness. Representing three generations, taken together they are an avatar of motherhood and life poised always on the brink of death. Mrs. Weatherall takes a giant step toward death when she seeks her dead daughter and, finding her, merges with her: "She seemed to herself to be Hapsy also, and the baby on Hapsy's arm was Hapsy and himself and herself, all at once, and there was no surprise in the meeting" (p. 85).

Significantly, when Granny Weatherall tells her weeping daughter Cornelia that she is taken by surprise and that she can't go with death, it is the thought of Hapsy which leads her to the final descent into the womb-like darkness, where, crouched in a fetal position, she watches her light dwindle and sputter and waits for a sign from God. Like Dickinson, Porter proposes the skeptic's view: she makes the craftsman's decision to bring her story full circle just as birth and death come together in a final generation. Granny Weatherall is robbed of her bridegroom a second time, leaving intact the primacy of her matriarchal independence. But thus is a "third event" un-veiled to her "so huge, so hopeless to conceive" that it not only ap-proximates her previous deaths, but is a grief large enough to wipe the others away. She knows once again the parting from life that is all she needs of hell. Finally, she chooses the death that has already chosen her, blowing out the light of her life herself and asserting, even in her last moment, a final power.

But there is more than one way to read the end of this story. Un-fortunately, Mrs. Weatherall has already learned, painfully, that faith can be destroyed by betrayal. It is this ultimate destruction that she holds at bay by refusing to think of George until the last day of her life. This fear of everlasting betrayal has been repressed along with her secret pain and, not surprisingly, surfaces in her last hours. The repression of this fear and the fragility of her faith cause her final perception of nothingness. Having been arrested psychically at her first jilting, Ellen Weatherall has been locked into one perception for sixty years; it is her mentality that assumes that the paradigm re-peats itself, that she has once more been betrayed into accepting mortality. It is an unforgivable thought that even a skeptic cannot abide. Emily Dickinson knew it:

> I know that He exists.
> Somewhere—in Silence—
> He has hid his rare life
> From our gross eyes.
>
> 'Tis an instant's play.
> 'Tis a fond Ambush—
> Just to make Bliss
> Earn her own surprise!
>
> But—should the play
> Prove piercing earnest—
> Should the glee—glaze—
> In Death's—stiff—stare—
>
> Would not the fun
> Look too expensive!
> Would not the jest—
> Have crawled too far!   (no. 338)[3]

Ellen Weatherall would agree.

"Theft"

The unnamed woman who is the protagonist of "Theft" would say, with Granny Weatherall, "It's bitter to lose things." But whereas Granny Weatherall is a victim who suffers from the faithlessness of others, this woman must bear the responsibility for her losses. On the literal level, this is a story of the theft of a lovely purse and its reclamation; however, the brevity and simplicity of the story belie its intensity and psychological complexity. The protagonist in "Theft" is broke, both financially and emotionally. She is surrounded by insecure relationships which give her little or no sustenance. The only thing she apparently values is a gold purse, a bit of finery given her as a birthday present by a lover. It is the one thing she has that is not "second best," an "intolerable substitute worse than nothing" (p. 64). The purse itself symbolizes both the repressed femininity and the emotional poverty of its owner, but more importantly, in the final quarrel over ownership of the purse, the protagonist recognizes her own complicity in her losses.

The artistic rendering of this intimate shock of recognition is again deft and sure. The structure of the story is dual. The first part consists of the protagonist's memory of the events of the night before, an objective correlative which defines her psychic character; the second part tells of the next morning, when she discovers the purse missing and succeeds in retrieving it. The story begins with one sentence that is a memory: "She had the purse in her hand when she came in," and is followed by a description of the present moment: "Standing in the middle of the floor, holding her bathrobe around her and trailing a damp towel in one hand, she surveyed the immediate past and remembered everything clearly" (p. 59).

A second memory in which she visualizes herself spreading the purse to dry assures her that she had the purse when she came in and launches her into a mental reconstruction of the final events of the evening before, each of which involves some gesture related to the purse. When she has remembered details up to the moment that she emerges from the bathroom, looking for a cigarette package in the purse, she has brought the reader back to the present moment. Thus the events of the evening past are embedded in the present moments of her reclamation of the stolen purse, just as these impressions are buried in her memory. Since the reader has an open window on the events stored in the protagonist's unconscious, they reverberate for the reader just as they do for the protagonist in her moment of emotional epiphany.

The specific details the protagonist remembers communicate her emotional state. The evening is characterized by a drenching rain which ruins clothing and distorts vision, by the poverty and isolation of the characters, and by spoiled love. The whole sequence may be read as a series of transient encounters between the woman and several men, whose spending and hoarding characterize their personal worth. Besides creating an emotional ambience, these events impress us with the woman's aloofness: she parts from each of the men in turn.

The first of these is the Spaniard, Camilo, her escort for the evening. He is a man who "by a series of compromises had managed to make effective a fairly complete set of smaller courtesies, ignoring the larger and more troublesome ones" (p. 59). In short, he is a mock gentleman, a man of pretense whose reliance on a mask prevents any true communication with the heroine. That he holds back something of himself is clearly illustrated in the first image presented of Camilo: he has the habit, the heroine remembers, of seeing her up the steps to the Elevated and of "dropping a nickel in the machine before he gave the turnstile a little push and sent her through it with a bow" (p. 59). Rather than expend himself by accompanying her to her door, he makes a performance of seeing her off at the station. Gentlemanly gesture, not generosity, prevails.

In the face of the rainstorm, however, Camilo is paying for his dependence on polite ritual. His new biscuit-colored hat is being ruined by the rain, but pretense keeps him from removing it and covering it with his coat until he thinks he is beyond the view of the lady. She sees him nevertheless and feels that she has "betrayed him by seeing, because he would have been humiliated if he thought she even suspected him of trying to save his hat" (p. 60).

Undoubtedly he would be humiliated if he knew that she sees through his guise, as evidenced by her comparison of Camilo with Eddie, who not only wears shabby hats without embarrassment, but lends to them a certain flair; his hats, old and looking as if they have "been quite purposely left out in the rain," sit on his head "with a careless and incidental rightness." Camilo, however, has no such individuation. A shabby hat on him would "be merely shabby" and would depress him. It is no mistake that the image of the ineffectual but pretentious Camilo hiding his new hat under his coat is replaced by the presence of Roger, whose "long imperturbable face was streaming with water" because he has buttoned his hat into the breast of his overcoat. In addition, he provides a taxi for the protagonist to ride home in, which Camilo is too poor to do.

Because he is a weak personality, however, Camilo points up the strong character of the protagonist, who humors his need to play the gentleman's part, but who also refuses to let him extend himself beyond his means. When he insists on a taxi, she firmly refuses, knowing he hasn't the money, but she allows him to escort her to the station in the rain because she knows he must "practice . . . his little ceremonies." It might be said of Camilo that he hasn't the sense to come in out of the rain, but not so of the heroine. She is obviously practical and capable of taking care of herself, and, in her understanding of Camilo's psychology, clearly superior to him. When they finally part, she has dismissed him, but in such a way that his gallant image is preserved: "Camilo, do me the favor not to climb these stairs in your present state, since for you it is only a matter of coming down again at once, and you'll certainly break your neck" (p. 60).

With Roger, obviously a longtime friend, she need not stand on ceremony, but enjoys a comfortable companionship that requires little of her. She is free to focus on the surreal images of the storm through the cab window. What she sees is distorted by the liquor she has drunk—the tall streetlights and the torrents of rain. She observes men who are gaily colored "scarecrows" and pelican-legged girls dressed in tawdry clothing. Their snatches of conversation are the briefest outline of the emotional conflict at the heart of the story. One man calls to the other, "When I get married it won't be jus' for getting married, I'm gonna marry for *love*, see?" His friends scoff, and Roger calls them all "nuts, pure nuts." The two women who follow underscore the "crazy" idealism of the first sentiment, for they speak of love's difficulty: "Yes, I know all about *that*. But what about me? You're always so sorry for *him* . . ." (p. 61).

The only direct allusions to the protagonist's ruined love affair follow. Roger has heard from Stella, who is coming home with her mind made up. The protagonist responds, "I had a sort of letter today too. . . . making up my mind for me" (p. 61). Why she had not made up her own mind, or the nature of her vacillation, is not clear. But the rest of the conversation offers interesting clues to the puzzle.

The protagonist again opens her nearly empty purse to contribute a dime to the cab fare. Roger admires it, and she responds simply, "It's a birthday present and I like it. How's your show coming?" He replies in terms that the reader later recognizes are an apt reflection of the protagonist's aloofness and emotional retention. He stresses that he refuses to argue or compromise. "I mean to keep right on the way I'm going and they can take it or leave it. . . ." She agrees: "It's absolutely a matter of holding out, isn't it?" He assures her that "holding out's the tough part" (p. 61).

The letter she has alluded to, "making up her mind for her," in this context appears to be a response to a "take it or leave it" proposition that she herself has set up. Her easy recognition of the necessity for "holding out" supports this premise and further clarifies her character: she is a woman who, having chosen independence and separateness, refuses to compromise her freedom with emotional entanglements. She is so comfortable with Roger because they are equally dispassionate people who make no demands on each other and are therefore easy in each other's company. As he holds out, refusing to compromise the principles of his play, so she holds out emotionally, refusing to compromise her personal integrity for love. Neither of them will accept "second best" where his or her work is concerned.

Just as Roger's open practicality in protecting his hat supplants our image of Camilo's surreptitious behavior, so Roger's insistence on holding out contrasts with the behavior of Bill, the protagonist's neighbor, in the next sequence. He, too, has a play on the verge of being produced, but, unlike Roger, he is incapable of keeping his distance. By keeping himself dispassionately separate from the fracas of his play's production, Roger maintains his integrity *and* his dignity, something both he and the protagonist value. In contrast, Bill grovels, shamelessly pleading for his play to go on, even after he has been told that it "doesn't play," that it "needs a doctor" (p. 62). When he faces the reality of his bad luck, he gets drunk and cries in his cups, then begs sympathy from the protagonist. The loss of the production is not so much a loss of artistic opportunity for him as it is a loss of income. He needs money, just as he needs emotional support, because he is a spendthrift.

The details of his conversation with the protagonist illustrate that he is a prisoner not only of his emotions but of his debts as well; once one is in that position, it is easy to compromise standards and even personal pride, as Bill demonstrates. Although he is broke, he sends his ex-wife weekly checks because he "can't bear to see anybody suffer" (p. 62). He is buying on credit expensive items like a piano and a Victrola. The rug his visitor admires, however, is a bargain, which best illustrates the second-hand quality of his possessions and his character.

Its grandiose history is that it was once owned by a celebrity who payed $1,500 for it. After cigarette burns damaged it, the star discarded it, and Bill was able to buy it for only ninety-five dollars. Sodden with self-pity, Bill, too, is damaged and not worth much. Talk of money once again leads the protagonist to focus on her empty purse, and she asks Bill for money he owes her. Not only can he not pay the fifty dollars he owes her, but he hasn't the pride to honor his debt. He asks her to "have another drink and forget about it." It is at this juncture that she begins to recognize the price she is paying for repressing her emotions; she finds herself responding, despite the fact that she had meant to be firm about the debt, "Let it go, then" (p. 63).

This phrase becomes the ironic echo of the story, being the philosophical conclusion of "taking it or leaving it" and "holding out." One who practices the kind of detachment she does soon finds herself in a position where she must say "Let it go" in order to hold on to detachment. Fighting for something one wants requires emotional expenditure which the protagonist, in her poverty, is hardly capable of making.

Returning to her own apartment, she "lets it go" again, this time saying a deliberate farewell to a lover by purposefully burning his letter in the grate. The phrases of the letter she dwells on indicate that she is not being rejected but abandoned, because her lover cannot tolerate the terms she has set for their relationship: "thinking about you more than I mean to . . . yes, I even talk about you . . . why were you so anxious to destroy . . . even if I could see you now I would not . . . not worth all this abominable . . . the end . . ." (p. 63). She presumably put limits on their intimacy; perhaps she rejected emotional bonds or a partnership or in some way refused to ante up. Like Bill who owes her money, she holds out on this lover who claims an emotional debt from her. Like Roger, she holds out to gain some greater wealth; incidentally, she also saves her emotional energy for other—presumably artistic—purposes. What she fails to realize is that, like all misers, she is gradually building an inability to spend at all—that is, in the terms of the story, to love.

That the loving part of her nature, her femininity, is repressed but not completely destroyed is revealed by the second half of the story, the morning events which bracket the memory of the previous evening's encounters. Like the purse that contains small change, she still retains vestiges of another personality that allowed her to feel and to act on her emotions. This personality desired love and attachment and made her want to spend herself and to hold fast. Realizing that the purse is indeed gone, apparently stolen by the janitress, she first thinks of the emotional cost of pursuing the thief and responds characteristically, but her repressed instincts assert themselves:

> Certainly the janitress had taken the purse, and certainly it would be impossible to get it back without a great deal of ridic-

ulous excitement. Then let it go. With this decision of her mind, there rose coincidentally in her blood a deep almost murderous anger. (p. 63)

Acting on this instinct, she confronts the janitress, stating unequivocally that she doesn't want to lose the purse because it was a present; its value to her is not monetary but emotional. Its value is caught in her description: it is a "gold cloth purse" that must be incongruous in her shabby living circumstances, but is all the more to be prized for being a rose among thorns. When the janitress falsely denies the theft, the protagonist responds with a bitter variation of "let it go, then": "'Oh, well then, keep it,' she said, but in a very bitter voice; 'keep it if you want it so much'" (p. 64). In that instant three recognitions occur, one upon the other, as she sees for the first time that her rejection of attachments has been a fear of responsibility and emotional pain; she has traveled lightly to avoid obligations to any other. "She remembered how she had never locked a door in her life, on some principle of rejection in her that made her uncomfortable in the ownership of things . . ." (p. 64). She is like the biblical steward who, fearful of losing what his master has given him, buries his single talent. Her moment of insight is overwhelming as she thinks of lost goods and opportunities that ended in compromise:

> bitter alternatives and intolerable substitutes worse than nothing, and yet inescapable: the long patient suffering of dying friendships and the dark inexplicable death of love—all that she had had, and all that she had missed, were lost together, and were twice lost in this landslide of remembered losses. (p. 64)

The night before and the present moment collide in her thought of "dying friendships" and the "death of love," all of which are contained in the encounters and farewells of the previous night. But the harshest insight comes to her in the clumsy speech of the janitress, who, without knowing whereof she speaks, names the protagonist's greatest loss: her youthful femininity and her desire to love and be loved:

> "My niece is young and needs pretty things, we oughta give the young ones a chance. She's got young men after her maybe will want to marry her. She oughta have nice things. She needs them bad right now. You're a grown woman, you've had your chance, you ought to know how it is!" (p. 65)

Significantly, after the janitress has identified the purse as a "pretty thing" needed by a husband-hunting female, the protagonist rejects it for having that significance as well as its particular meaning to her: a love gift from a man she has decided not to love, a symbol of her womanly ties to a lover, who, if allowed, will become a "possession" that demands care and attention from her. Now, however, having identified the protagonist as a person who has no right to such a feminine thing, it is the janitress's turn to reject the purse. In doing so, she reverses the guilt for the theft, leading the purse's rightful owner to assert, "It wasn't really yours in the first place. . . . You mustn't talk as if I had stolen it from you." The janitress's reply and final thrust hits a deeper mark than she knows: "It's not from me, it's from her you're stealing it" (p. 65).

In the context of her epiphany, the protagonist recognizes that "her" is not just the janitress's niece, but her own other self. In her previous plea, the janitress, a generation older than her seventeen-year-old niece, has linked herself with the protagonist. They are "grown" women whose "chance" for life through love is past. For an instant, the protagonist sees herself as another sees her, washed up, the night after a storm, on the shore of her own resources, with no money, no prospects, and only the carrion comfort of her refusals: her separateness. Thus the ironic truth of the janitress's comment rings home: it is not her older self that has been deprived, but the youthful beauty in her of which the empty gold purse is the remaining visible remnant. Finally, the rightness of her original instinct to leave her door unlocked returns to her ironically also. It has been a good instinct, not because of her "general faith," but because she was right not to be afraid of any thief but herself. Thus Porter begins to assert that if traditional roles do not foster personal integration, choosing independence in matriarchy and "single blessedness" are also mined with difficulty.

"The Cracked Looking-Glass"

In the next example of her mature work, Porter reveals a woman who has not been able to choose between maidenhood and matriarchy. She zeroes in, with horrifying accuracy, on the psychic ossification of a woman who has been denied the one natural transition open to her—the movement from erotic object to mother. If Granny Weatherall achieves satisfaction in matriarchy and the protagonist of "Theft" is clear-eyed about choosing to be a virgin artist, Rosaleen O'Toole, the protagonist of "The Cracked Looking-Glass," can only be seen as a thwarted mother. In opposition to Mrs. Whipple in "He," Rosaleen has natural maternal instincts but no outlet for them. Consequently, her unsatisfied erotic energy merges falsely with the motherly instincts she is denied using, resulting in a shallow epiphany that produces no real self-knowledge for her in the end.

The conflict in "The Cracked Looking-Glass," that between maiden and mother, is one of the oldest in history, as Aztec and other mythologies demonstrate. Certainly one of the most essential statements of this struggle for vitality and potency is found in the tale "Snow White," which provides several motifs for Rosaleen O'Toole's story, as the title suggests.[4] Porter modernizes the myth by embodying the conflict in one woman and by making it a psychological struggle rather than a physical one, but the characteristics are all the same, and the final issue is still who will have love, sex, and life or death.

Focusing on an Irish farm couple, "The Cracked Looking-Glass" has all the earmarks of a Porter story: an insightful view of the woman's repressed sexuality, a utilization of dreams to provide that insight, and the overriding presence of death. Rosaleen's psychology illustrates the typical dichotomy between the figure of the romantic belle she was in her youth and the matron she ought to become. Her looking-glass symbolizes her narcissism; with "a crack across the middle" (p. 109), it is divided, as is her perception of herself. Like the wicked queen in "Snow White," Rosaleen has been accustomed to look into her mirror and confirm that she is "the fairest one of all." Now fortyish, in mid-life, with a seventy-five-year-old husband who no longer makes love to her, she must accept the rebellious message of her mirror just as the queen mother of the folktale must. The fair young maiden is no longer reflected in it, and thus at times she can't see "herself" in it. When she does see an image, her face is, significantly, "like a monster's" (p. 122). Thus, it seems there are two Rosaleens in the looking-glass: the high-stepping maiden who was a sought-after belle and the middle-aged matron who must content herself with mothering her elderly husband, Dennis, with whom she is celebrating a twenty-fifth wedding anniversary as the story opens. The missing link in Rosaleen's adult female development is motherhood. Unlike Granny Weatherall, she has had no "fine children out of" her husband, and she has no substitute activity to satisfy her need to generate and create. With language, she spins yarns and tells tall tales—folklore that is the rudimentary stuff of the primitive artist, talk that is fueled by her barely controlled, rampant libidinal energy.

Her attempt to control that sexual energy is the thrust of the story. How difficult that might be is symbolized in the frenetic activity of the several cats which keep Rosaleen company in the kitchen and which scatter "in all directions" when she raises her voice to them. Her favorite, the Billy-cat, is lost to her except for two visions she has of her old pet— a painting of him, "the Billy-cat to the life" (p. 104), and a dream she had in which the cat came to her to tell her of his death. Her dreams and her tales are the offspring of Rosaleen's twenty-five years of marriage, and she feeds her husband, and anyone else who will listen, full of both. A fascinating belle in her youth, she still hungers for male attention and sexual fulfillment although she hasn't the temerity to seek it outside her marriage. When Guy Richards, her neighbor, pays attention to her, his overt sexual appeal is completely unsettling to her. Finally, in the midst of a bitter winter, she dreams that her sister is calling her from her deathbed; consequently, Rosaleen travels to New York and then to Boston to see her. Not finding her sister, she decides that for the first time a dream has "gone back" on her. Meeting a young Irish boy in the streets of Boston, in a maternal gesture she feeds him and then offers him a home in her house. When he calls this a sexual offer, she is outraged and runs him off, but finally admits to herself that she has loved Kevin, a young house painter she sheltered five years earlier. Returning home, aware that both dreams and love are lost, she refuses to tell any stories. But in rejecting tales and dreams, she does not turn toward truth, but toward another kind of fantasy—maybe Kevin will return to her after all. That she remains fixed psychologically, despite her change in attitude, is caught in the final reference to the looking-glass. She has forgotten to replace the cracked one with a clear piece. Her trip has not yielded a new clear vision of herself; the distorted image remains.

Far from being a character with arrested sexuality, like Laura in "Flowering Judas," Rosaleen O'Toole is a spirited woman whose husband remembers her in her youth as "a great tall rosy girl, a prize dancer," who had the boys "fairly fighting over her" when she met him (p. 107). But, like Laura, she is suspended between two images of herself. The passage of time prevents her from returning to her youth, but without becoming a mother she cannot accept age gracefully. It is true enough that, in her own mind, at least, she is still the pretty belle of her youth, with nothing to concern her except dressing and dancing and teasing the boys:

We used to be the whole day getting ready for the dances, washing our hair and curling it and trying on our dresses and

> trimming them, laughing fit to kill about the boys and making
> up things to say to them. When my sister Honora was married
> they took me for the bride. . . . With my white dress ruffled to
> the heels and my hair with a wreath. Everybody drank my
> health for the belle of the ball. . . . (p. 111)

While Rosaleen insists that she is "a settled woman over her
nonsense" (p. 116), her husband thinks that she doesn't look "a year
older," which heightens their age differences now that he is visibly
aging. From the beginning, though, there have been differences in
their needs. After he marries her, Dennis finds her a lusty young
wife and almost begins to "wish sometimes he had let one of those
strong-armed boys have her." Later, "after she cooled down a little,
he knew he could have never done better. The only thing was, he
wished it had been Rosaleen he had married that first time in Bristol, and now they'd be settled together, nearer an age. Thirty years
was too much difference altogether" (p. 107).

The truth is that Rosaleen is not ready to put on age, especially
since the joy in her life lies in her maidenhood. She still behaves like
a young girl who leads the boys a merry chase. She still loves parties
and feast days, still wears bright-colored ginghams and worries
about the curl in her red hair; but it is the courtship game that she
enjoys most. Teasing the boys and playing hard to get is what she
relishes. It satisfies her ego as nothing else can.

In fact, her triumphant girlhood—which she has recreated for
Dennis so many times that he knows her youth better than his
own—is highlighted by stories of dances and young men kept dangling in hopes of a favor from the heartbreaker Rosaleen:

> I remember a boy in Ireland was a great step-dancer, the best,
> and he was wild about me and I was a devil to him. . . . He said
> to me a thousand times, "Rosaleen, why won't ye dance with
> me just once?" And I'd say, "Ye've plenty to dance with ye
> without my wasting my time." And so it went for the summer
> long . . . till in the end I danced with him. (p. 111)

Afterward she walks home with her patient suitor and a crowd of
people under "a heaven full of stars." Before God and everybody,
Rosaleen has demonstrated her worth and even increased her value
by holding out. After agreeing to "keep steady" with the boy, she
"was sorry for it the minute [she] promised." Once the chase is
ended, the climax is gone; there is no more pleasure in it. Rosaleen
repeats the pattern of tempting, withholding, and finally acquiescing
when she meets Dennis.

Having decided after the death of his first wife "never to marry again," Dennis, a man of nearly fifty, succumbs to Rosaleen's charms; characteristically, "she led him a dance then for two years before she would have him" (p. 106). It is not surprising that on the night of their twenty-fifth anniversary Rosaleen confides, "I could feel like dancing itself this night, Dennis" (p. 110), for her dancing was in her youth a sublimation of her sexual energy, an expression of her personal freedom, and the act by which she made men notice her. It is a display of energy, however, that is controlled and made acceptable by the pattern of the dance. Consequently, dancing expressed for Rosaleen youth, freedom, and desirability, while simultaneously controlling her spirit and allowing her the pleasure of feverish anticipation. One ought to be able to trade all that for something better, but Rosaleen has found that marriage does not assuage her narcissistic need for attention.[5]

Being the bride is the prize for those who play the game well, but even on one's wedding day one begins to sink into the obscurity of housewifery. At her sister's wedding, the focus is not on the bride but on Rosaleen, who will "surely be the next bride" (p. 111). While the present bride is eclipsed, her single sister is "the belle of the ball." But Rosaleen learns only through her own experience that being the belle is better than being the bride.

In addition to having traded away the attentions that courtship provides, Rosaleen's marriage bargain leaves her physically unsustained. Instead of her lusty dancing, she now has the quiet chores of the farm, most of which involve the motherly activities of feeding and comforting. Milking links her to the female symbol of the cow. Her sympathy for the animal, which will soon go into heat, contrasts with Dennis's inability to appreciate the animal's (and Rosaleen's) physical needs:

> The cow now—the creature! Pretty soon she'll be jumping the
> stone walls after the apples, and running wild through the
> fields roaring, and it's all for another calf only, the poor de-
> ceived thing! Dennis said, "I don't see what deceit there is in
> that." "Oh, don't you now?" said Rosaleen, and gathered up her
> milk pails. (p. 107)

Milking the cow to relieve its physical burden for the moment, Rosaleen speaks to her as a fellow creature. She says to the cow: "It's no life, no life at all. A man of his years is no comfort to a woman!" (p. 107). When she assures Dennis that the anniversary cake she had made for their dinner "wouldn't upset the stomach of a nursing child," we are reminded again that she is more valuable to him as a mother than as a lover. Dennis himself muses over this difficulty, wondering

> what she thought of him now he was no human good to her. Here he was, all gone, and he had been so for years, and he felt guilt sometimes before Rosaleen, who couldn't always understand how there comes a time when a man is finished, and there is no more to be done that way. (p. 110)

Rosaleen dances no longer, but is still capable of wishing for it.

She understands well enough that "once you've given your word there's nothing to think about. . . ." Marriage is irrevocable, and it is a dead end into which a girl may come dancing, never to escape: "when a young girl marries an old man, even if he has money she's bound to be disappointed . . ." (p. 113). And disappointed Rosaleen has been. Her sexual frustration is unabated, and there has been no chance to sublimate that energy into motherhood.

Her life seems in the twenty-fifth year of her marriage unfulfilled and attended by losses, most unfortunately the loss of the child that could have transformed her from maiden to mother. When Rosaleen thinks of her "half-forgotten child," dead in two days' time (the only child she has had of the aging Dennis), she weeps in fresh agony for the lost son who might have been by now "a fine grown man and the dear love of her heart" (p. 114). Undefined as a mother, Rosaleen is essentially a maiden caught on the other side of mid-life with only the dry laurels of her successful girlhood to drape about her head. Real motherhood has eluded her, and babying animals and an aging husband has proved a frustration rather than a satisfaction. The result is a double, confused identity, reflected in Rosaleen's responses to the men in the story.

With Dennis, the man with whom she can be appropriately sexual, she must not be a wife but a mother. Kevin, the young house painter, and, later, the young Irish boy she meets in Boston represent both suitors and sons to her. She offers them mothering—food and shelter—to hide her sexual attraction to their youthful masculinity. Guy Richards, her neighbor, is partly attracted to her because of her strong maternal personality. She appeals to him by telling him stories, a double gesture that is both maternal and sexual. Kevin, who is the most significant of them, is Prince Charming to Rosaleen's chaste princess. Part of the delight of their relationship is in its nonphysical nature. There is high attraction between them and the pleasure of sexual tension, but that attraction is never named or acted upon, just as the implicit sexual meanings in fairy tales are never spelled out.

As both substitute lover and son, Kevin materializes at two important junctures in Rosaleen's thoughts. When she thinks of the
"fine man" Dennis was when she first knew him, before his "getting
old . . . took the heart out of her" (p. 108), his image swiftly becomes
Kevin's; when she thinks of her lost son who might have grown into
a becoming man, the image again becomes Kevin's. As both Prince
Charming and son, he admits both sides of Rosaleen's personality—
maiden and mother. He is so much the object of her affection that
when he shows Rosaleen a picture of his girlfriend, she cries out and
tears come to her eyes. She can neither admit to herself her jealousy
nor tolerate this sexual rival, and after he leaves her house, Rosaleen
muses that he will come back apologizing for taking up with "somebody not fit to look" at Rosaleen. Like a mother whose Oedipal conflicts remain unresolved, she still waits another five years. Her only
alternative is to mother Dennis, but "it wasn't being a wife at all to
wrap a man in flannels like a baby and put hot water bottles to him"
(p. 109). On the contrary, it is easy to disguise her pining for Kevin as
motherly longing: "the darling, the darling lad like her own son"
(p. 114).

Well he might be her son, for he, like Rosaleen, is an Irish immi-
grant isolated from kin and the city by the loneliness of the Connecticut farm country among "heathen Rooshans and Polacks and
Wops with their liquor stills and outlandish lingo" (p. 114). A native
of County Sligo like her, Kevin understands immediately the conventions which will dominate their relationship and the repartee
which will sublimate their attraction to each other. He agrees readily with Rosaleen that he ought to live in her "good Irish house," an
oasis among dour natives and heathen foreigners.

> They stood there smiling at each other, feeling they had agreed
> enough, it was time to think how to get the best of each other
> in the talk from now on. For more than a year they had tried to
> get the best of each other in the talk, and sometimes it was
> one and sometimes another, but a gay easy time and such a
> bubble of joy like a kettle singing. (p. 115)

Thus Kevin not only reinforces Rosaleen's ego; he also projects
the familiarity and comfort of home that her Bristol Irish husband,
who "might as well be English," cannot give.

In addition, he tacitly understands that they make love verbally.
When he tells Rosaleen about his girlfriend in New York, he commits a double infidelity: first by having a girlfriend at all, and second
by speaking of her, thus allowing an interloper to intrude upon the
special solace of their conversation. He doesn't realize how much

irony there is in his statement "I was greatly wrong to tell ye!" (p. 108). Later, after he is gone from her house, Rosaleen is saddened by the fact that the only "word" she gets from him is a postcard picturing a tall building in New York, which suggests his phallic significance to Rosaleen. It states only: "This is my hotel. Kevin." But it is appropriate that since the relationship is ended he should no longer converse with her. After his departure, Rosaleen can do nothing but drape his picture of her Billy-cat with a strip of crocheted lace and prop it up, shrine-like, in her kitchen, as an excuse to say his name. Significantly, the mention of Kevin angers Dennis.

Presumably, Rosaleen loses her lover/son about the same time her husband loses his sexual potency. She is doubly isolated, then, a city girl in the winter countryside of Connecticut, with no native comforts except an old husband who must be bundled like a baby. She is surrounded by sly, mean neighbors, some of whom she fears for their wildness. Not the least of these is Guy Richards, a man totally unlike the others she has known: he is a man of her own age whom she can neither baby nor tease; thus she cannot control him. Consequently, he is "a great offense" to Rosaleen. She finds his appearance and bold brawling behavior alluringly dangerous. A man with "shaggy mustaches and his shirt in rags till the brawny skin showed through" (p. 115), he clearly attracts her, and she fantasizes about having to "shoot him dead" if he "lays a finger on her." He of course offers to do no such thing; he doesn't need to, for his masculine presence and his bold eyes are enough to unnerve Rosaleen.

As he becomes an occasional visitor in their house, he displays characteristics Rosaleen liked in Kevin, but, being a native of the countryside, he is only a caricature of the Irishman she could love. When he visits her he is loquacious, telling rousing stories of his life and idealizing the memory of his mother. His leisure is spent drinking and dancing, and his bold speech stops Rosaleen cold. "It was enough to make a woman wild not to find a word in her mouth for such boldness," and she spends his visits "racking her mind for some saying that would put him in his place . . ." (p. 117).

Again, the "word" metaphorically suggests sexual connotations: Richards is a bold speaker as he would be a bold lover, and Rosaleen's inability to "put him in his place" verbally underscores the fact that she could never dominate him sexually, or even control the relationship, as she has been able to do with every other lover. Both she and Richards are verbally quick and prone to storytelling, and each is engaged by the other's tales, suggesting that they are sexually quite compatible. When Richards sits "with his ears lengthened" (p. 121) while Rosaleen tells again the story of the Billy-cat, we see that, whoever might dominate, she is as sexually appealing to him as he is to her. It is almost as if she has finally met her match in him: he reveres the memory of a mother while she reveres the memory of a son; both frequently distort reality, he by his drinking and she by her fantasizing.

As the cracked looking-glass suggests, distortion of reality is the most pervasive element in the story, from the first scene in which Rosaleen beguiles the traveling salesman with the story of her Billy-cat while her husband listens at the keyhole, muttering against the "tall tales" she tells as truth, to the scene mentioned above, when Rosaleen, like some rural Scheherazade, spins the tale again for Guy Richards while Dennis himself is enough seduced to wonder if it might be true.

Through several sequences, beginning with the first, the reader has a chance to question the nature of reality in all its duplicity. The Billy-cat, for instance, is real and present by virtue of a painted picture and Rosaleen's memory of him. The picture is said to be the cat's "spittin' image" and "the Billy-cat to the life," but his legs look too stuffed "for a living cat," and he wasn't actually sitting on the table pictured, but in Rosaleen's lap, while the picture was being painted. Thus the picture is not an accurate presentation, and Rosaleen's conjuration of him seems less so, since she so frequently merges reality and fantasy in the same breath, playing, like all good raconteurs, to her audience. "He wanted a story, so I gave him a good one. It's the Irish in me" (p. 105). Of course, whether the story parallels actuality or not, it takes on substance and a nature of its own when Rosaleen tells it.

Like María Concepción, Rosaleen has a primitive mind. She thinks animistically, talking to her animals and assuming that her favorite cat is living some kind of life after death. She believes in the physical embodiment of spirits and abstractions, like "the Evil" she has seen as a girl in Ireland. She believes in the power of the word, whether it be calling on the Holy Name to disperse ghosts or uttering imaginative curses against an enemy. Finally, she regards dreams as an important means of communication, not from her unconscious mind, but usually from the world of the dead. Thus her dreams, like her tales, although untrue, have reality because, through her telling, they achieve shape, substance, and actuality.

Through language, Rosaleen is the creator she cannot be through her body. When she invokes youth and Ireland, it is like an incantation which causes events to materialize from the foggy past. The reality of the past, the present, and the imagination become equivalent in her mouth; one begins to wonder if the eighth part of what she says is true. What is more important, however, is the power she wields. Believing what she says, she acts on that belief; she convinces the gullible who like a good story, and she even brings her cynical husband to the point where he longs for tales. When she insists on traveling to Boston to see her sister on the strength of a dream that may or may not be true, Dennis is annoyed and disgusted. But when she returns, he wants the story of that trip to Boston—whether or not it is true. Ultimately, her blarney has a right to exist for its own sake, as a demonstration of the creative power of a woman too confined to realize her potential. Finally, it is another metaphor for Rosaleen's strong sexuality. While the years have put "a quietus" on Dennis, she has become garrulous. There is surely double entendre in Dennis's bitter thought that someday when he is dead "she'll find a man can keep her quiet" (p. 113).

Aside from the creative function of keeping alive loved ones who are gone from her, Rosaleen's dreams are her way of burying her dead. She eases herself of her guilt for her great-grandfather's passing by the double ritual of dreaming of him as a soul in purgatory who can speak to her and by having an extra Mass said for him. In the case of her Billy-cat, the story of his woeful end allows her to bury him psychically and experience the grief that will lead her to accept his death. Likewise, she injures and buries the dancing swain of her youth and, in his turn, Kevin. The final dream, about Honora calling from her deathbed, suggests the demise of her youth, which was so intimately shared with this sister. "My dreams never renege on me," she tells Guy Richards. "They're all I have to go by" (pp. 121–122). It is certainly significant that at the age of forty-five, living with a husband who has one foot in the grave, Rosaleen's dreams are closing chapters in her experience. Of course, it is all too true in a literal sense that the people with whom she has shared love are dead to her, just as surely as she has watched Kevin disappear from her life.

In the final segment, a present experience which neatly balances the twenty-fifth wedding anniversary in all its memories, Rosaleen boards a train to New York and feels content that she is "once more on a train going somewhere" (p. 123). She thinks that having left the frozen waste of the farm and her barren, aged husband, she can pick up the threads of her youth and move forward again, but actually the trip is a journey backward in time, a nostalgic grasping for the past.

Arriving in New York, she wishes for an "hour to visit her old flat in 164th Street" (p. 123); she eyes the delicate and youthful lingerie in shop windows; wallowing in sentiment and sweets, she cries through two movies whose titles reveal the real nature of the restlessness which has motivated her trip. Both *The Prince of Love* and *The Lover King* allow her to weep copiously over the plight of dashing heroes who must overcome tremendous obstacles to marry the unnaturally beautiful girls who are their heart's desire. The love songs go "to her heart like a dagger" (p. 124), while she munches on chocolates; after the movies, she indulges in ice cream topped with strawberry preserves, just like a child on holiday. She goes to pray for Honora in a church richly dressed in candles and flowers and the fragrance of incense. Steeped in girlish romance and emotionalism, with "that lost heathen place," Connecticut, behind her, she boards a boat which will carry her overnight to Boston.

This night sea journey, undertaken to visit the sister of her youth, has several implications. Part of the funeral rites of many cultures, such a voyage ended in the land of the dead; the possible demise of Rosaleen's sister causes her to begin this journey, but she cannot find Honora any more than she can retrieve the happy days of her maidenhood when she had many men to admire her. Rosaleen's poisoned apple is age, and, unlike Snow White, she cannot cough it up. On this voyage, Rosaleen commits her youth to the land of the dead. It might also be read as a psychic journey by which she reverts to memories of past happiness, long buried in her subconscious. Moreover, if we read this journey as a paradigm of Rosaleen's sexual experience, it becomes clear that her readiness to be fructified by a man has always come to a dead end. Significantly, like a child in the womb, she falls asleep that night to the "grand steady beat" (p. 124) of the boat's engine and sleeps a dreamless sleep.

The next morning she finds herself in "dreary, ugly" Boston, and she is unable to "remember any good times there" (p. 125). This ominous note hangs over her attempt to establish a tangible link with her vanished girlhood. She searches for Honora's flat to no avail. No one knows her sister, and even the phone book doesn't list her. Rosaleen's last tie to youth and Ireland, Honora has vanished as surely as Kevin and the Irish step-dancer, confronting Rosaleen with a sharp reality difficult to face: her dream has "gone back on her," both literally—the dream of Honora's illness—and symbolically— the dream of her maidenhood for happiness "ever after" for herself and a dashing prince. She will have to bear other harsh realities in the wake of that loss, especially a recognition of her ambivalent motherhood/seduction.

Meeting a down-and-out Irish boy on the windy street, she feels heartened and feeds him mounds of food before offering him a ten-dollar bill in the name of Kevin and her lost son. Finally, she offers him a home on the farm, but the streetwise boy ignores her motherly intention and calls her invitation as he sees it: "I was caught at it once in Dublin. . . . A fine woman like yourself she was, and her husband peeking through a crack in the wall . . ." (p. 128). Insulted, Rosaleen sends him packing, but in a flash of recognition she sees that "Kevin had loved her and she had loved Kevin, and Oh, she hadn't known it in time! . . . and now he was gone and lost and dead." In other words, her potential lover is as dead to her as the son she never raised. With all her youthful hopes gone, she retreats to the isolation of Connecticut and resolves "never [to] speak to a soul again" (p. 129). She forswears creation, like the menopausal woman she is.

On her return, she cannot forbear telling Dennis that she has "left [Honora] in health," but she tells no tales despite his eagerness to hear them, and she tells him she no longer believes in dreams. Having resolved now that the city is a "wild, heartless place" (p. 130) where she could never live, Rosaleen must still bear the rejection of her heartless neighbors. The haggard mother of the boy who does Rosaleen's chores accuses her of whoring, and Richards, half-drunk, momentarily thinks of stopping that evening but then carelessly drives on, leaving Rosaleen more hopeless than ever. Even if she gives in to the "ruined life [she would have] with such a man," she thinks she would still have to bear his indifference, one more "terrible disappointment." She is left to fantasize about New York and Boston and "places full of life and gayety she'd never seen nor even heard of, and beyond everything like a green field with morning sun on it lay youth and Ireland . . ." (p. 134). Her green field is reminiscent of Granny Weatherall's bright field, where her life is perfectly ordered through marriage to the right lover. Rosaleen has had her choice and has not lived happily ever after, either. So remote is the image that she thinks of it as a dream, as unattainable in her life as it was for Ellen Weatherall.

She has, after all, forgotten to replace the cracked looking-glass, which Dennis has always described as "good enough." A new glass would have removed the "monster" from her vision, but would also reveal an image of herself she is not able to accept, the one seen by the lad in Boston. It is the image of an aging Rosaleen who can no longer attract men through her youth and spirited dancing. If she eschews tale-telling, she will no longer attract Richards, either, as his failure to stop suggests.

Her final stance is both childish and mothering. She sits with Dennis, her head on his knee, and begs him to protect himself against the cold, for without him, she will herself be forced to face the bitter cold of loneliness.[6]

3 ❖ *Shattering Illusions*

In her last three Mexican stories, "That Tree," "Flowering Judas," and "Hacienda," Porter employs an altogether new technique to characterize the psychology of her protagonists. In the same way that T. S. Eliot uses a wasteland setting to characterize the barren lives of twentieth-century human beings, Porter utilizes the revolutionary upheaval of Mexico to communicate the violent divisions that can result in the personalities of those who choose a life outside of convention, be they artists or activists.

Of the three, only one, "Flowering Judas," achieves a perfect mesh of setting, symbol, and psychology, but "That Tree" is worth examining in contrast as a story in which similar elements fall short of perfect integration. Despite their lesser technical excellence, "That Tree" and "Hacienda" provide important thematic bridges to the second half of Porter's canon that necessitate explication.

"That Tree"

"That Tree" is Porter's first attempt to tell a story from a male point of view. This center of consciousness, however, is not so vastly different from other central characters in Porter's canon, as William Nance has pointed out in *Katherine Anne Porter and the Art of Rejection*.[1] This man thinks just like Porter women. The unnamed narrator here is particularly reminiscent of the protagonist in "Theft": he wishes to live life with "no respectability, no responsibility, no money to speak of . . ." (p. 66), free to worship at the shrine of sacred Art. He is, however, treated with much greater irony: he wishes to project a bohemian image and indulges in the worst excesses of a romantic nature, picturing himself "wearing worn-out sandals and a becoming, if probably ragged blue shirt, lying under a tree writing poetry" (p. 66). Underneath, however, lie the more practical impulses of his blood—the necessity for name, money, possessions, solid work. He spends three years suppressing these impulses before unwittingly acknowledging their power over him by marrying a wife who he knows will be the incarnation of respectable middle-class values in the romantic land of his heart's desire. After four years of marriage, he is haggard from fighting this alter ego of his, now personified in his wife Miriam:

> His old-fashioned respectable middle-class hard-working American ancestry and training rose up in him and fought on Miriam's side. He felt he had broken about every bone in him to get away from them . . . , and here he had been overtaken at last and beaten into resignation that had nothing to do with his mind or heart. It was as if his blood stream had betrayed him. (p. 77)

Duality surfaces again in the same forms Porter repeatedly uses; the masculine free spirit is hedonistic, artistic, and sexually uninhibited, while the feminine personality which opposes it is rigid, domestic, and shamelessly puritanical.

The story the protagonist narrates to an unidentified companion is a monologue which reviews this conflict and the collapse of his dream. Disruption is communicated in setting, incident, and, most pointedly, in the psychological relationship of the narrator to other characters. Dramatic monologue is a vehicle for ironic truth, and in the conclusion the narrator, like Prufrock, reveals things about himself that he himself does not recognize.

The broad setting of the story is Mexico, land of enchantment and romantic possibility where "a cheerful bum" can lie down under a tree to write poetry. It is also, paradoxically, a place of revolution, possessed of a precarious peace always on the brink of upheaval. This setting is an appropriate reflection of the narrator's psyche, although he cannot admit this to himself. As in other Porter stories, the protagonist's thinly disguised psychological conflict is personified by two women.

Before his marriage, the narrator takes his new environment to his bosom in the person of an Indian girl who lives with him in sublime simplicity. Her accepting nature requires very little of him, for she "divided her time cheerfully between the painters [for whom she posed], the cooking pot, and his bed, and she managed to have a baby without interrupting any of these occupations for more than a few days" (p. 72). When his marriage is imminent, the Indian girl claims the household furniture and moves cheerfully on to another man with her baby in tow.

In starkest contrast, Miriam, who reflects the seeds of the narrator's own culture, is "a properly brought up . . . Midwestern girl, who took life seriously" (p. 67). Whereas Mexican girls instinctively support the male ego because they enjoy sexual attention and male protection, Miriam doesn't want to be protected and is diffident toward sex. She believes that "their mutual sacrifice of virginity was the most important act of their marriage, and this sacred rite once achieved, the whole affair had descended to a pretty low plane" (p. 73).

What she does want is to be supported in a middle-class manner. Like Moll Flanders, Miriam views marriage not as a love match, but as an economic agreement. Unlike the Indian girl, who almost as an afterthought claims a dowry of the man who has kept her, Miriam spends three years saving money and accumulating household linen before she will enter into marriage. She cries constantly after her arrival because she will get the worst of a bad bargain. She has traded her maidenhead for an empty house full of wilting flowers where she must cook over a charcoal brazier and wash clothes in a stone tub with cold water. What was so recently a picnic for the narrator becomes a catastrophe: "Everything that had seemed so jolly and natural and inexpensive with the Indian girl was too damnifying and costly for words with Miriam" (p. 75). Yet again there is the dichotomy between the soft, acquiescent girl and the determined inflexible woman whose husband says of her:

> No doubt about it, Miriam had force. She could make her personality, which no one need respect, felt in a bitter, sinister way. She had a background, and solid earth under her feet, and a point of view and a strong spine: even when she danced with him he could feel her tense controlled hips and her locked knees, . . . without any yielding at all. (p. 75)

It is significant that the narrator thinks Miriam has learned her discipline as a schoolteacher, supervising children, for her relationship to her husband is that of a mother to a son. Instead of taking up her husband's way of life after marriage, she brings her way of life (which he is ostensibly trying to eschew) to him and tries to impose it on his newly adopted culture. Far from being a "sweet bird" who wishes to be liberated from her cage, Miriam wishes to make a domestic nest out of her husband's garden of earthly delights. For his part, the tree he wants to lie down under represents a kind of womblike haven where all his needs are nourished at little expense to him. Miriam is his sheltering tree during the years of their marriage in that she supports them with her savings, but aside from physical sustenance, she is hardly a benevolent mother.

She fusses about cleanliness, wholesome food, and table manners. She preaches the work ethic. She is a nagging, complaining, punitive woman who wants her husband to "walk the chalk line" for her, and when he does not, she packs up her "nest" and goes home. Unlike her husband's natural mother, who managed several children and hard work "with a quiet certainty, a happy absorbed look on her face," Miriam does not define her self through nurturing. Indeed, she succeeds in "reforming" her wayward child-husband only by leaving him, or, as he insists on thinking of it, by kicking him out. It is significant that once "kicked out" of the nest, he "suddenly resolves" to make a career for himself in journalism (p. 67). The reasons for this are interesting.

From one point of view, this marital struggle might easily be seen as a conflict between id (the poet) and superego (Miriam); because of this struggle, the poet is reformed: he becomes a "journalist." Obviously, in his poet-hedonist role he never feels complete; he fails to find his ideal tree. But perhaps he fails to find it because Miriam, with her "severe" moral standards and her judgmental comments on his lifestyle, challenges his belief that his romanticism is ultimate existence.

In any case, there is little doubt that she functions as his conscience or voice of reason, pointing out that his artistic friends are opportunists and that he is a bad poet. In a sense she confirms his worst fears about himself. He admits that "except for Miriam, he would have been a lousy failure, like those bums at Dinty Moore's, still rolling under tables, studying the native customs." Instead, he is a "recognized authority on revolutions in twenty-odd Latin-American countries" with "a prose style of his own." He is a concrete success, but he is nevertheless bitter because he has "spent a good deal of time and energy doing all sorts of things he didn't care for in the least to prove to his first wife . . . that he was not just merely a bum, fit for nothing but lying under a tree . . . writing poetry and enjoying his life" (p. 78).

He owns everything he set out to discard: he has respectability, responsibility, money, good clothes—and no poetry. The reason he acquires all this baggage when Miriam departs is also explained if we think of her as his "better half," a double or alter ego struggling for supremacy of his personality. This final interpretation of their bitter feud explains several details otherwise unaccounted for.

In the first place, it accounts for the narrator's inordinate attraction to a woman so apparently unlike himself. Despite his protestations that Miriam is "not a prissy bore, not at all," her "professional habit of primness" suggests otherwise. It is this primness that he describes over and over again throughout the story—not the "sweet and gay qualities" he says she has or the "special kind of beauty" he sees in her (p. 67).

The old cliché that opposites attract suggests itself here, but it doesn't explain why the attraction persists despite the couple's disharmony and even misery together. The narrator's self-hatred justifies a certain amount of masochism in his choice of a life's companion, but even that does not fully account for the intimate bond between them even after they are divorced. So strong is this union that the narrator might easily say—and mean—what Kevin says of his girlfriend: "Who says a word against her says it against me."

Other interesting details link the narrator and Miriam indissolubly. He makes much of the professional discipline she has acquired as a teacher; yet it has never occurred to him that he too taught school during their engagement. He attributes her depression when she arrives in Mexico to the fact that "she had come all that way . . . and she couldn't see herself going back and facing the music at home" (p. 73), which readily describes the circumstances of the expatriate narrator. Moreover, her "devilish inconsistency" describes his own inner turmoil. For three years she has complained of her "stuffy little world" and waited on his letters for a "breath of free mountain air"; however, when she enters it herself, the atmosphere is too rarefied for her to survive. She tries to displace poetry and romantic ideals with a very specific domesticity: a 200-pound trunk full of linens and silk underthings. And so they are opposites, but nevertheless two parts of one whole, for all their disparateness.

From the beginning of their marriage, Miriam refuses to compromise, signalling a fight to the death. In retrospect, the narrator wishes "he might have thought of a trick to play on her that would have finished her for life." Miriam herself becomes "an avenging fury" (p. 76), and by the time she leaves, he feels she has done him serious damage; she herself is "shabby and thin and wild-looking" from the struggle (p. 77). Miriam, personifying her husband's early training and the betrayal of his own blood, defeats the poet in him and departs, but once gone, she is hardly forgotten. Her phrases and expressions "eat into his marrow" (p. 77). Instead of being free of her, he has internalized her, with all her precepts and prohibitions. He goes about creating a career "in the hugest sort of way" (p. 78).

In his own parlance, he has finally succeeded in proving to Miriam that he is "not merely just a bum" because his new identity as "journalist" lures her back to the union she has never really left. That the journalist has effectively subsumed her shows up in the fact that despite his promise to reassert the old circumstances of the poet he was—a Mexican house with no conveniences and no marriage license—the punitive tone he assumes is completely different from his previous easygoing manner. He has become someone else, even to the point of insisting that he will now be the one to draw chalk lines, and Miriam the one to walk them. Despite the fact that he says he will not remarry Miriam, his shadowy guest recognizes that, far from disunion, this couple are indeed two in one flesh, and that a new marriage ceremony is in order. He has to restrain himself from saying, "Don't forget to invite me to your wedding."

The final sentences of the story illustrate the significance of the monologue, which has amounted to a psychological retrospective of the transformation of poet to journalist. They also reinforce in one final image the irony the reader has observed in the love/hate the narrator feels for his "better self," Miriam. To emphasize the speaker's true position, Porter ends one paragraph with the first half of a broken-up statement by the narrator: "I suppose you think I don't know—." In a new paragraph he haltingly repeats the last three words "I don't know," which accurately describe his ignorance and his malady:

> "I don't know what's happening, this time," he said, "don't deceive yourself. This time I know." He seemed to be admonishing himself before a mirror. (p. 79)

It would be too farfetched to suggest that the whole monologue has been a waking dream, the journalist's Prufrock-like explanation of his actions to his poetic psyche—an excessive defense of his decision to live Miriam's way of life, even to the point of remarrying her. However, the fact that the reader knows the journalist to be a divided man emphasizes his ironic insistence on his self-knowledge. The image of him "admonishing himself before a mirror" infallibly calls up the doubleness of the man and his reflection, the ghost of the poet and the tenuous reality of the journalist, and finally suggests the image of Dorian Gray before his portrait, which decays before his eyes.

"Flowering Judas"

In "Flowering Judas," Porter achieves her most intense rendering of the struggle between the love/sexuality/security syndrome and the choice of autonomy through art/action. What makes the story more compelling than most is the technical intricacy of its symbolic structure[2] and its use of that structure to portray the otherwise inaccessi-

ble complexity of the protagonist's simultaneous but warring and often paradoxical psychological impulses.

Porter here creates a circle of symbols, all of which are inter-
layered with each other. For instance, on the surface, "Flowering
Judas" is the story of an attempted seduction which is told in sexual
imagery and incident—thus the story of the virgin confronting her
seducer. It is also the story of the idealistic naïf confronting political
realities—thus the story of the corruption of purity of purpose. It is
ultimately the story of a woman's recognition that her attempt to
walk a thin line for the sake of integrity, autonomy, and freedom
may be impossible because of the limitations inherent in a situation
which is supposed to free her, as well as those in herself.

Each story element is separate, but each signifies the other. The
revolution itself is the marvelous psychosymbol which incorporates
at once physical violence, chaos, corruption, and its own set of rigid-
ities, as well as the psychic presence of all these confusions in the
mind of the protagonist. Laura is attracted to the revolution because
it is both exciting and idealistic and therefore speaks to her doubleness. She attempts to control these impulses in the same way that
the young woman in "Theft" does. She will hold herself aloof, hold
out, say no. Her most obvious restraint is sexual, but she is more
than a constricted virgin; she restrains herself emotionally as well as
physically, and she does both to prevent the violation of soul as well
as body.

Consequently, by understanding Laura's psychosexual position,
one can better understand the paradoxical questions she cannot answer for herself—why she has committed herself to the revolution,
why she participates so coldly, why she cannot run. It clarifies, too,
the meaning of her nightmare, in which all symbolic elements coalesce in a horrible epiphany she cannot deny.

The complex elements of "Flowering Judas" communicate
themselves so subtly and are so intricately interwoven that they are
difficult to decipher and separate. At the heart of the story is Porter's
familiar conflict—the struggle between life forces and physical or
psychic death.

The broadest manifestation of this, the revolution, is also a
struggle between idealistic purpose and physical reality. It is a war
waged in the name of the poor and oppressed, made up of hungry,
desperate men who have abandoned their ancestral religion with its
miracle-working saints and who now look to technology and the
machine for salvation. Laura, who has not lost the habit of faith despite her disappointment with the Catholicism to which she was

born, reflects the dissatisfaction of the workers with their lot in life and their idealistic belief in the possibility of millennial change.

On the other hand, she is different from them. Her passionless exterior and her repression of emotion and sexuality identify her as *norte americana*—among, but not of, the Mexicans. Her personal training and standards still characterize her and dictate her insistence on authenticity: she commits political "heresy" by wearing only handmade lace in a time and place where mechanically produced products are revered; and in a country given to dramatic flourish, she rejects the attentions of men who rely on costume and romantic convention to impress her.

Another reverberation of the life-death conflict is contained in the stalemated struggle between Laura and Braggioni which provides the plot line of the story. Braggioni represents the revolution, but he is also political reality. Since he embodies at once the revolution as a holy war and a vehicle for personal power and private gain, he is a perfect antagonist to Laura's impractical idealism and need to believe. His worldliness and obesity are the antithesis of her ascetic ways, and his coarse sexuality offends her romanticism and, of course, threatens her physical virginity. Through these interwoven layers of meaning run strands of sexual and religious imagery. Betrayal recurs like an insistent echo, and the flower motif highlighted in the story's title carries the whole forward.[3]

In an interview with the *Paris Review*,[3] Porter described the *donnée* which gave her "Flowering Judas." A friend had asked Porter to sit with her while she was being visited by a man who intimidated her. As Porter passed her friend's window she saw the tableau created by the woman, the man seated with her, and the Flowering Judas underneath the window. Porter recreates that tableau through structure and use of language. Like "Theft," "Flowering Judas" is a two-part story, and, as in the former, Porter here skillfully encloses past history within the present moment. Laura, the protagonist, returns home in the evening to find Braggioni, the revolutionary leader, waiting for her as usual. She works for the revolution, but more specifically she works for Braggioni, to whom she owes her "comfortable situation and salary"; she may not turn him out, though his visits are threatening and distasteful to her. He sings to her; she eats her rice and pretends to read while he sings to her again; and so they have done for the evenings of one month. His presence, his singing, his conversation, their actions—all have been ritualized into a repetition which halts time and solidifies these characters for our perusal. Frozen together in the repetition of this evening that is like all the other evenings of this long, spoiled month, all the parts of their psyches exist in one eternal moment.

Written in the present tense, the story powerfully evokes the alert concentration of the conscious mind. Thinking of the past, we call the thought memory; thinking of the future, imagination. But catching the present moment is difficult; by using present tense, Porter manages not only to capture that present moment in all its immediacy, but to establish its intensity by calling up the complex psychological associations behind each action and each comment.

Braggioni and Laura exist together in time only because of the revolution, a state of chaos which both supports new life and causes death. As a couple they suggest elements of both. Braggioni's hulking presence, for instance, suggests all Laura's disillusionment with the revolution; it suggests the presence of other romantic suitors she has had and her rejection of them; but the complex associations he represents also include the presence of the children she teaches, the prisoners she visits, and the dangerous errands she runs, all at Braggioni's behest. Ultimately it encompasses her repression of her sexuality and her paradoxical attraction to and fear of death.

As others have noted, "Flowering Judas" is an intimate portrait of a woman in suspension.[4] Caught between the two poles of her "early training" and the "developed sense of reality" (read "cynicism") required by the revolution, Laura is like a tightrope walker whose inability to go either forward or backward necessitates a fall. In the meantime, she maintains a precarious balance, poised above a psychological abyss.

Any consideration of Laura illustrates that she is a walking paradox. She is a virgin with the body of a voluptuary. A woman who needs faith, she cannot believe. Having chosen the revolution as an ideological framework in place of her Catholicism, she must keep company with its cynical, self-serving participants. Wishing to run, she betrays herself by staying, seduced by the constant translation of the ideal she wishes to believe in into the vulgar reality she resists, which is symbolized by the insistent presence of Braggioni in her sitting room every night. She feels these dichotomies painfully: "She cannot help feeling that she has been betrayed irreparably by the disunion between her way of living and her feeling of what life should be" (p. 91).

"What life should be" is related to the "set of principles derived from her early training" (p. 92). She worships nobility, faith, and purity. Her image of a revolutionist sounds almost Christ-like: he should be "lean, animated by heroic faith, a vessel of abstract virtues" (p. 91). Her revolutionist should be passionate but bloodless. She is disillusioned with Braggioni, "a leader of men" who is a gluttonous egoist motivated by a love of luxury, power, and the pleasure he takes in killing. Why Laura is drawn to the revolution in the first place is something of a puzzle to her. "Uninvited she has promised herself to this place . . .",; she wonders about "the nature of this devotion, its true motives, and . . . its obligations" (p. 93).

First of all, she is undoubtedly drawn, in her "romantic error," by the "abstract virtues" she attributes to the movement. That much is obvious and provides a superficial answer. It is also obvious that she substitutes the revolution and its doctrines for the religious doctrine of her childhood. But there is something more. With her own emotions in turmoil, she must be attracted to the essential chaos of a sweeping change like revolution. At the same time, she attempts to control turmoil and change in herself; she is even rigid. Thus, her placing herself in a chaotic situation like revolution paradoxically indicates both a desire to be purged of rigidity—that is, to be different from what she is—and a desire for destruction of her old self.

The revolution has the same fatal attraction for her that a flame does for a moth. She is drawn to the light and heat of the battle, and particularly to the threat of death.[5] Even after she has discovered that being a revolutionary entails a daily round of mundane duties, "Laura feels a slow chill, a purely physical sense of danger, a warning in her blood that violence, mutilation, a shocking death, wait for her with lessening patience" (p. 93). Likewise, she has "uneasy premonitions of the future" (p. 91), and she practices stoicism "against that disaster she fears, though she cannot name it" (p. 97).

Which is not to say that idealism is not a strong force in her. That idealism holds equal sway with her is manifest in her religious devotion. She tries to resurrect the power of the Catholic faith she knew as a child; the value it had for her is caught in the image of the gold rosary she has bought in Tehuantepec. However, that power is disintegrating and false for her now. She goes to pray only in "some crumbling little church" where the beauty and richness of her faith has visibly decayed: the altar is decorated with "tinsel flowers and ragged brocades," and even the principals of this worship are ludicrous, like "the battered doll-shape of some male saint whose white, lace-trimmed drawers hang limply around his ankles below the hieratic dignity of his velvet robe" (p. 92).

If the stature of her religious faith has diminished, the ideal of purity which it has nurtured in her has not. Perhaps without realizing it, she lives the abstemious life of an anchoress. She has a celibate existence, with only one female servant for help and company;

she spends her days and nights in works of mercy, teaching Indian children, visiting political prisoners, warning endangered rebels of the threat to their lives, and aiding their escape. When she returns home at the end of a long day, she frugally eats a simple plate of rice and drinks a cup of chocolate. She has "renounced vanities" and chooses to wear "the uniform of an idea": heavy blue serge dresses with confining, tight sleeves, and round white collars that are "not purposely nunlike" (p. 92). Braggioni wonders that she "covers her great round breasts with thick dark cloth, and . . . hides [her] long, invaluably beautiful legs under a heavy skirt" (p. 97). She has not only "encased herself in a set of principles," she encases her ripe sexuality in a restraining suit of armor. The only acquiescence to her femininity is the "tiny edge of fluted" (p. 92) lace on her collars, although even that has a pristine purity about it, since she will wear only handmade lace, which is therefore uncorrupted by machines.

She wishes everything about her to appear virgin. Among the Mexicans, her virtue is "notorious," since, for them, virginity is a state of arrested development. Young men pursue her, choosing to believe in the sensuality of her "soft, round under lip which promises gayety" rather than notice that she is "always grave" (p. 95). Braggioni himself lusts after her, refusing to believe that she is as cold as she seems. In his experience he has been pursued by both girls and married women, and although he scorns emotional attachments, the chase entices him. He cannot conceive that Laura has chosen celibacy:

> He cannot understand why she works so hard for the revolu-
> tionary idea unless she loves some man who is in it. "Are
> you not in love with someone?" "No," says Laura. "And no one
> is in love with you?" "No." "Then it is your own fault. No
> woman need go begging. Why what is the matter with you?
> The legless beggar woman in the Alameda has a perfectly faith-
> ful lover. Did you know that?" (p. 100)

She is such an anomaly—a cold virgin in a passionate land—that those who know her "cannot understand why she is in Mexico" (p. 95). Certainly, in an effort to retain her independence, she isolates herself, even from emotional involvement with the small children she teaches. Despite the easy affection they bestow on her, she thinks of them as strangers, although she has a sensual affection for their "tender round hands" and loves "their charming opportunist savagery" (p. 97). She is able to function so well as Braggioni's messenger because she keeps an emotional distance from prisoners and fugitives; any pity she has for them she keeps to herself. Because she has no sentimental attachments to the Roumanian and Polish agita-tors, they cannot exploit her.

While she thinks this stance is authentic, it is a masquerade that cloaks her subconscious desires; it is also a defense against her-self. Just as Laura covers her ripe breasts with heavy cloth, restrain-ing the sexuality she is afraid will burst from her, so she restrains her emotions, which keeps her from involvements whereby she might betray her values. She is not completely successful. Especially when she deals with romantic young men, she behaves guardedly, but an occasional inconsistency suggests some equivocation on her part.

For instance, the young captain formerly of Zapata's army has a noble simplicity about him that should appeal to Laura. He comes close enough to her image of the ideal revolutionist that she agrees to go riding with him. However, he proves a "rude" hero, and he is not aggressive enough in expressing his affection for her. When he tries to take her in his arms, she spurs her horse, causing it to rear and gallop away with her. In actuality, it is she, and not her horse, who has become skittish. Laura's ironic tone in thinking about the young captain asserts that while first attracted, she has succeeded in rejecting him. Ultimately she mentally equates him and his affec-tion with the children in her classroom, who brandish their emo-tions on the blackboard ("We lov ar ticher"), festooning the words with flowers drawn in colored chalks.

The romantic gesture of the youth who serenades her among the scarlet and purple blossoms of the Judas tree in her patio is ap-pealing. It is the person she is not interested in. She tosses him a flower, on her Indian housemaid's instructions, only to find that he is enough encouraged by the gesture to follow her daily through the marketplace and about the city wearing the withered flower, like a dead hope, in his hatband. Significantly, Laura is "pleasantly dis-turbed by the abstract, unhurried watchfulness of his black eyes" (p. 96) which, as long as it is only a remote threat to her, is enjoyable. But the next lines are the most notable, for they reveal that she has not thrown the flower innocently:

> She tells herself that throwing the flower was a mistake, for she is twenty-two years old and knows better; but she refuses to regret it, and persuades herself that her negation of all ex-ternal events as they occur is a sign that she is gradually per-fecting herself in the stoicism she strives to cultivate against that disaster she fears, though she cannot name it.
> (pp. 96–97)

Her understanding that she has encouraged attention by throwing the flower complicates the reader's knowledge of her; her gesture implies a willingness to entertain romance, but she is clearly unwilling to involve herself romantically. The tossed flower, then, is at best misleading, a tease whereby she flatters herself. She rationalizes that in her restraint she is building a strong stoicism which will defend her against "that disaster she fears." However, stoicism is not likely to protect her from any outer assault; stoicism will only protect her from herself.

Finally, there is another psychological reality in the slow chills she experiences in the presence of danger and in the pleasantly disturbing feelings here described. These are heightened moments of awareness for Laura precisely because danger is imminent. These situations must tempt her, or there would be no possibility of succumbing. It is the remote but implied danger which gives the moment its pique. Possessing a hidden but vital sexuality, Laura is also titillated by dealing in forbidden fruit. Like all good puritans, Laura knows how to squeeze all possible pleasure from something she must not do, while at the same time avoiding guilt for having done it.

Nevertheless, perhaps because she suspects she is capable of undoing herself, she fears losing her virginity physically, emotionally, philosophically. This is the "warning in her blood that violence, mutilation, a shocking death, wait for her with lessening patience" (p. 93). This is "that disaster she fears, though she cannot name it" (p. 97). It would be simple enough to assume that Laura suffers from morbid fear reinforced by the real prospect of treachery during a time of political upheaval. However, we are told that "she is not afraid to knock on any door in any street after midnight, and enter in the darkness. . . ." (p. 94), and that "she knocks at unfamiliar doors not knowing whether a friend or a stranger shall answer . . . , that she may walk anywhere in safety . . . [and look] at everything without amazement" (p. 97). She rightly fears most the evil in herself, and controls this by automatic rejection: "No. No. No. She draws her strength from this one holy talismanic word which does not suffer her to be led into evil" (p. 97). As long as she denies everything, she may look at everything without amazement. The unnamed disaster she fears is not the physical death it appears to be, but the death of her essential self or psyche. The disaster she fears so much that she cannot name it is the annihilation of her precarious sense of self through sexual experience, which in turn signifies destruction of her personhood and her spiritual integrity.

On the literal level, Laura has severed ties with her former home and can no longer identify with her family and its way of life. She has given up the easy role models of marriage and motherhood and life according to the norms of her childhood community. What is left after she has rejected those familial and communal roles is a fragile knowledge of her inmost self, whose defining marks are its idealism and its virginity. If she loses either, there is little left. Her cynical revolutionary comrades try to rob her of her idealism, and she resists by refusing "to surrender her will to such expedient logic" (p. 91). She resists "violence, mutilation [and] a shocking death" (p. 93)—which is simply another way of saying rape—by denial and repression of the emotions that would make her vulnerable. This is not to say that Laura fears—or fantasizes—actual rape, but rather that on one level sexual intercourse represents to her a violation of both body and soul.

This sheds light, too, on the reason she does not bolt from her situation. Three times in the course of the story she thinks about running but does not: "Still she sits quietly, she does not run." Why? She rationalizes that she has no place else to go: "she can no longer imagine herself as living in another country, and there is no pleasure in remembering her life before she came here" (p. 93). Aside from the fact that this reasoning overlooks the problem of why she chose to come to Mexico in the first place, it is obvious that she has deliberately cut herself off from her roots by placing herself in a culture so foreign to her own. She cannot go home, and she appears to reject going forward.

Like an initiate who has been cut off from her source and not yet assimilated into a new group, she exists in a state of potency which she seems to desire to maintain, rather than *become* anything else. She wishes to immobilize herself in time, like the figures on Keats's Grecian urn, to maintain the moment of anticipation by refusing to achieve it. By maintaining her liminal state, she can experience the tantalization of erotic pleasure without experiencing complete sexual knowledge and its responsibilities. Acquiring actual sexual knowledge is a dead loss in her own mind, as we have seen, and consequently she rejects that option out of hand. It does not occur to her that she might become something more than she already is through sexual experience; for Laura, it is death rather than metamorphosis. In fact, Laura is both attracted to and frightened by sex for several reasons. She has already rejected her native country, the society in which she was born, for the foreign one of Mexico because in her family's world anatomy is destiny. (This is certainly true for Mexican women, too, but Laura's position as an outsider releases her to some extent from the customs of the country for women.) Laura rightly understands that the only way she can control her life and exercise some autonomy of her own is by controlling her anatomy. By leaving her home she has eluded the necessity for marrying, bearing children, "settling down." Thus she has become something of a lay nun, a professional virgin. She can only respond with deviousness to the Mexican men who pursue her, and for the children she teaches she feels no affection, because men and children who offer her love require an emotional commitment and represent too closely the way of life she has rejected.

However, this assumed role presents her with various problems, both practical and philosophical. Having removed herself from the society in which she would naturally marry and become a mother, she has lost the simple and natural way of losing her virginity. A highly structured society like the one native to her at least provides a natural—and protected—framework wherein its women may pass out of maidenhood. Attired in her virginity as she is, and alone in the world, any change in her position must be ostentatious and scandalous, qualities her character cannot abide. She has, perhaps unconsciously, put herself in a position that precludes a sexual/emotional relationship, while at the same time she hungers for one—thus her precarious balancing act, midway between two poles of experience, and the sense of constriction and arrested development that emanates from her.

Aside from these practical considerations, a sexual act is not one that Laura could undertake casually, even if circumstances encouraged it. For her, sex is a symbolic act as well as a physical one (in this attitude she is a prototype of many other Porter heroines), for her sense of self is closely tied to her sexuality. Consequently, for her, learning to be a sexual creature is not simply a matter of learning how to use a part of the body, like learning to walk or hold a spoon. Becoming sexual, for Laura, is a matter of becoming another woman. While intercourse is an act of becoming, a union which generates new life, for a woman whose identity is tied to her sexual status, it is primarily an act of destruction. First of all, it destroys her physical integrity with pain and bloodshed; but, more important, for Laura it destroys not only maidenhood, but the person who was a maiden. After intercourse, she will no longer be a virgin, and if she is not to be transformed into a mother, like Granny Weatherall, then what she will be is completely unknown, a psychological void that cannot be explored before it is experienced. Consequently, although Laura is irresistibly drawn toward sexual acts, she restrains herself because, for her, intercourse constitutes a leap of faith into possibility—which is at best the unknown and which may turn out to be a bottomless pit.

Aside from the uncertainty lying on the other side of that act, there is yet another threat Laura might face. In her own mind, through intercourse Laura will at the very least cease to be the woman she was and will become a woman she doesn't know. Suppose this new self, released from her straitjacket, turns out to have an appetite for sex? Suppose the new Laura has a consuming passion for sex that, once begun, can't be stopped? In that case, she will certainly have brought chaos on herself, a chaos impossible for her to control. It would also be impossible for her to control, in Mexico, circa 1910, the response of her body to intercourse. An unwanted pregnancy would visit on her a final loss of control, with her body reproducing itself, inexorably, against her will.

Of course, Laura's psychological attitudes constitute a metaphor. She has ambivalent desires not only for her body, but also for her personhood. Thus, in the revolution, she can experience a proximity to chaos and danger which allows her a doubly erotic kind of pleasure. Her participation in the revolution, but on the fringes of it, is a symbolic dabbling in sexual experience and a remote indulgence of emotional idealism: in short, a way that she can live her duality.

Then there is the matter of Braggioni, whose suit is the most direct challenge to Laura's physical, emotional, and philosophical stance. While others are merely foolish in their romantic attentions, Braggioni's notice is dangerous and not to be avoided by simple stratagem. He is both vain and cruel, so that to cross him or deride him is deadly. A thousand women, he tells Laura, have paid for the insult offered him by the first woman he loved. Consequently, she "must resist tenaciously without appearing to resist" (p. 91). A strongly sexual man and a womanizer, Braggioni is a rather sinister *miles gloriosus* whose overweight body is not, like Falstaff's, comic, but threatening:

> He bulges marvelously in his expensive garments. Over his lavender collar, crushed upon a purple necktie, held by a diamond hoop: over his ammunition belt of tooled leather worked in silver, buckled cruelly around his gasping middle: over the tops of his glossy yellow shoes Braggioni swells with ominous ripeness, his mauve hose stretched taut, his ankles bound with the stout leather thongs of his shoes. (pp. 92–93)

He is repulsive, fairly oozing the putrefaction of rotten fruit and jaded decadence. For Laura he symbolizes all the "reality" with which she has had to temper her idealism. He is a "professional lover of humanity" who "will never die of it" (p. 98). He is a parasite, grown fat on the blood of the workers; when his minions have served their purpose, he forgets them, leaving them to rot in jail or die of their despair. His obesity also embodies her own fear of loss of personal control.

Thus he is a mirror of all the things Laura hates and those she fears, too, especially her own propensity for evil. She worries that she may be "as corrupt. . . . as callous, as incomplete" (p. 93) as Braggioni. Certainly she prostitutes herself by running his errands, for she is in tacit collusion with him. The taint of his corruption is bound to rub off on her, but "still she sits quietly, she does not run." Thus Laura, the unlikely revolutionary, idealistic but compromising, dissembles with Braggioni the killer.

Having established these several layers of meaning in the first part of the story through interior monologue, Porter braids them together for fullest impact in the climax. As in previous stories, she returns us to the present moment by repeating phrases which began the story and therefore reminds us that we are still attending that single moment:

> It is this month of separation for the sake of higher principles that has been spoiled not only for Mrs. Braggioni, whose sense of reality is beyond criticism, but for Laura, who feels herself bogged in a nightmare. . . . Laura has just come from a visit to the prison, and she is waiting for tomorrow with a bitter anxiety as if tomorrow may not come, but time may be caught immovably in this hour, with herself transfixed, Braggioni singing on forever, and Eugenio's body not yet discovered by the guard. (p. 99)

The foreshadowing of Laura's nightmare is reinforced when Braggioni asks if she is going to sleep and then begins speaking hypnotically about the revolution, first in particular and then in philosophical terms. Almost every sentence highlights some motif of Laura's conflict. Braggioni emphasizes the dichotomy in Laura that is the center of the story when he tells her of the impending conflict between the Catholics and the Socialists in Morelia: "There will be two independent processions, starting from either end of town, and they will march until they meet, and the rest depends . . ." (p. 99). Inadvertently he describes the struggle between an irresistible force and an immovable object that is going on in the psyche of the protagonist.

Asking Laura to oil and load his pistols, Braggioni chides her for the absence of lovers in her life. As she fondles and lubricates his guns, Braggioni makes love to his guitar in the symbolic seduction which is the only rightful climax of this evening, to their month of evenings together. Laura says nothing, but what she feels as she peers down the pistol barrel recalls the quasi-fearful "slow chills" and the feeling of pleasant disturbance with which she responds to danger and sexual circumstances: "A long, slow faintness rises and subsides in her: Braggioni curves his swollen fingers around the throat of the guitar and softly smothers the music out of it" (p. 100).

Finally, in mesmerizing tones, as if chanting a ritual litany, Braggioni recounts the apocalyptic climax to the revolution, symbolically calling up the chaos and death of individuality Laura fears from intercourse:

> Some day this world, now seemingly so composed and eternal, to the edges of every sea shall be merely a tangle of gaping trenches, of crashing walls and broken bodies. Everything must be torn from its accustomed place where it has rotted for centuries, hurled skyward and distributed, cast down again clean as rain, without separate identity.... No one shall be left alive except the elect spirits destined to procreate a new world cleansed of cruelty and injustice, ruled by benevolent anarchy. (p. 100)

"A tangle of gaping trenches, of crashing walls and broken bodies" is not only an apt description of Armageddon, but also a description of what a woman who fears the breaking of her hymen expects to happen to her physically. Laura says goodnight by suggesting that Braggioni will feel better if he goes to Morelia and kills someone. Then, made bold by "the presence of death in the room" (p. 100), she confesses that she has failed to rescue Eugenio from his attempted suicide in the jail. Where Braggioni will commit murder, Laura sins by omission; the calloused leader refuses to be concerned and goes home to the comfort of his wife. A third time Laura thinks that she must run; a third time she denies her instinct and does not go, betraying herself.

As she drops off to sleep, burdened with the thought of her betrayal of Eugenio's life and her betrayal of self, she sees the children she teaches as prisoners bringing flowers to her, their jailer. As her consciousness recedes, the warring concepts in her psyche run together: "it is monstrous to confuse love with revolution, night with day, life with death—ah, Eugenio!" (p. 101). In that passage to sleep and the unconscious mind, Eugenio, the dead rebel, embodies her lost hope, her failed nerve, and her stifled sexuality. He beckons her as demon lover to accompany him to death; then, in a marvelous conjunction of images, sexuality, destruction, and betrayal reverberate against the life forces of nourishment, for both body and soul:

> Then eat these flowers, poor prisoner, said Eugenio in a voice of pity, take and eat: and from the Judas tree he stripped the warm bleeding flowers, and held them to her lips. She saw that his hand was fleshless, a cluster of small white petrified branches, and the eye sockets were without light, but she ate the flowers greedily for they satisfied both hunger and thirst. Murderer! said Eugenio, and Cannibal! This is my body and my blood. (p. 102)

In an inverted paradigm of the Last Supper, Eugenio offers flowers of betrayal from the Judas tree, recalling the crucifixion and his death at the hands of a betrayer. He appears at once as revolutionary, lover, priest, accuser, dead man, and death. He offers up his body and blood as a rebel willing to die for his cause, as a lover willing to use both sexually, and as a priest offering sacrifice. Laura accepts greedily, for he embodies simultaneously her hunger for both spiritual and sexual nourishment and her irrational compulsion to expose herself to destruction.

Much has been made of the superficial issue of Laura's betrayal of Eugenio, but her dream makes clear that there are many layers of betrayal in the story. First of all, it is Eugenio who entices Laura, not she him; and the apparent nourishment he offers is a stratagem. She is not deluded by him, since she sees that he is skeletal and recognizes that the food he presents is bleeding Judas blossoms. Since she is not taken in, when she accepts, she is not innocent but culpable. Eating greedily, she signifies her collusion and guilt and allows Eugenio to call her a murderer.

But her "betrayal" of Eugenio should not overshadow the far more significant self-betrayal which is the real stuff of the story. Aside from all the other things he represents, Eugenio is also a suicide, who first betrays himself. He is a rebel who has wanted a better life but who has not had the courage to survive. Thus he personifies at once the circular structure of Laura's psychic dilemma: her own idealism and death wish, her wish to participate in life even if it means death, and her simultaneous wish for survival at any expense —which, of course, necessitates spiritual death.

Thus Eugenio is the perfect embodiment of the maelstrom of conflicting desires which engulf Laura and prevent her acting, as well as the tangible evidence of the sin of omission she has committed in failing to prevent his self-destruction. It is in this last sense that he is most important in terms of Laura's psyche. Others—Braggioni and Laura—have failed to help him; but Eugenio's suicide has been first a betrayal of self.

And so it is with Laura. Betraying Eugenio, she betrays no one so much as her own person. Like the protagonist of "Theft," Laura is her own worst enemy, a woman who, in an effort to protect her integrity, has controlled her emotions to the point of being unable to act according to her own values. In her nightmare, she confronts reality. By refusing to prevent Eugenio's suicide, she has murdered her own principles. In effect, she has become a suicide, too, a waking death-in-life figure whose image she tries to dispel by invoking her talismanic word: No. It is too late. In both body and blood, she has already raped herself.

4 ❖ *Recognition*

"Hacienda"

Katherine Anne Porter's literature is concerned with the way in which human beings—mostly women—confront and cope with chaos. For woman, the balance of chaos and order is inevitably tied to her sexuality, the use of which ties her physically to motherhood and thus, in Porter's view, limits her experience. Invariably, as Porter's stories show, using sexuality brings a woman face to face with physical death, and ultimately with psychic death, too—the death of her personhood, as the supremacy of her husband and the needs of her children usurp her individuality.

How, then, can she answer her need to generate and to create—a need most often satisfied for women of preceding generations through childbearing? The answer, of course, is through art. It becomes easy to see, in this context, why Porter has made a holy temple of art, as Lodwick Hartley has pointed out.[1] Art is salvation. Art is first of all an imposition of order on the chaos of experience. Furthermore, its pursuit provides structure and protection for the woman who seeks both independence (chaos) and security (order) simultaneously in her personal life. Art provides something for her to *be* besides a mother; it allows her to create asexually and to avoid not only the entanglement of her own identity with those of others, like husband and children, but to assert her own power and individuality. This process is accomplished not by making her mark on someone else through influence, as women have been wont to do; not by leaving her stamp on a childish personality, as Porter's own grandmother did; but by making an autonomous statement of her own personality and human integrity.

Such a statement is at the same time an awesome and frightening thing for a woman to do. It represents the theft of fire and is in itself fraught with the pain of loneliness and freedom, which is Miranda's essential story. It is eminently fitting that Porter's last published story, "Holiday," begins with Miranda's feeling of isolation and loss, and ends with her psychic wound only somewhat healed: Miranda is in the company of an idiot, observing a funeral train, but the two of them shout survival. Ultimately, it is Miranda's only text—and Porter's too.

The reasons why Porter's main persona, that Everywoman often called Miranda, arrives at that position of loneliness and survival are carefully and concretely documented in "Hacienda," a story ignored by critics because it is not technically excellent. Beside the psychological depth of "The Jilting of Granny Weatherall" or the tightly integrated symbolic structure of "Flowering Judas," "Hacienda" is a discursive and rambling story about a group of discrete personalities held together only by a momentary accident of geography: for a few days, at the hacienda, they find themselves isolated together.

However, from a thematic standpoint, the story is vitally important, both for what it shows us about the psychic progress of the Porter protagonist and for its thematically pivotal position in Porter's canon.[2] It is the link between the two segments of her career, a story that uses every detail—plot, setting, character, and incident—to create a complex metaphor for the psychic dilemma of the narrator/ protagonist in the story. When she succeeds in extricating herself from the oppressive atmosphere of the corrupt hacienda, she succeeds in reasserting a choice, for separation and for self. Seeing the finality of that choice makes us better able to understand Miranda's odyssey from the position of child within the bosom of a large interconnected family to that of an adult woman, alone and outside. This odyssey is chronicled in the stories following "Hacienda": "The Old Order," "Old Mortality," "Pale Horse, Pale Rider," and "Holiday."

"Hacienda" is a complex story, although on the surface it might constitute a film of the absurd—a series of nonevents. A woman writer, absent from Mexico for ten years, journeys to an ancient feudal estate which derives its wealth from producing pulque, a liquor drunk by the peons of the country. She makes the trip to witness the filming of a documentary of the Mexican Revolution by a trio of Russian cinematographers, but filming has been interrupted by the development of a sexual triangle involving the master and mistress of the hacienda and the leading actress in the film. Yet another disruption occurs when a young Indian woman is accidentally shot by her brother and he is jailed. The writer finds the inhabitants of the hacienda jaded; neither problem is resolved, and she departs without witnessing any of the filming she came to see.

In "Hacienda," Porter takes for her subject the psychology of a country, a whole people, a culture, which becomes an objective correlative for a psychosexual role the narrator has all but left behind her. "Hacienda" is the story of her determining the truth about the role she has chosen and about the one she still might choose. Then, unlike Laura, she makes up her mind once and for all.

The story is like a Chinese box: inside the biggest one there are smaller, more intricate and no less important issues, all of which are so interwoven as to defy logical analysis. Image clusters and symbols apply on more than one level to setting, character, and theme, all of which interact with each other. Such rich meaning does not progress in linear fashion, but evolves in concentric circles. The effect is the kind one expects of poetry rather than fiction; thus it is necessary to search out not just image, but deep image, and to examine each symbol in terms of all its simultaneous meanings. Only then can the full implications of "Hacienda" be appreciated.

Not that Porter does not employ several readily identifiable techniques to assert a clear-cut theme. "Hacienda" is one of her most finely ironic stories; by showing that human beings are eminently corruptible, it prefigures *Ship of Fools*. But the reader who stops with that understanding will miss the more profound meanings of the story.

In order to clarify those meanings, it is probably best to begin with the obvious. On the simplest level, "Hacienda" is a story about distortion, corruption, and destruction perpetuated at every level of human experience: in the physical world, in politics, in art, in society, and especially in the realm of human love. A Gulliver-like figure, the narrator journeys into this ancient and complex country, one who has come out to see and to question.

Ultimately, of course, corruption becomes death. No stranger to Mexico, the narrator knows that a "love of death" is at the core of Mexican life. She will gradually become aware that this perverse love of death is not tragic; it does not derive from an existential acceptance of the realities of a difficult life in a hard land, but rather hides a vacuousness of spirit which Mexicans seek to fill with the thrill of violence and the excitement of sex. Subterranean to this behavior in the Mexican psyche is an archetypal belief in the corruptness of female sexuality and its kinship to death. In such a culture, women can function only as playthings and victims, even though their appeal gives them apparent power.

The narrator is the protagonist, but her presence is so subtle that we must remind ourselves that this nameless, faceless woman is the only person in the story who is not a pawn in the chess game of the hacienda, and she is the only one capable of being truly affected by what goes on there. It is her perception that allows her to move from ignorance to knowledge, from the position of curious outsider to inquiring visitor to one who sees good reason to shake the dust of the place from her shoes and move on. The progressive acquisition of this knowledge is the core of the story and must not be obscured by the more obvious nature of the conditions she observes. Everything in the story exists in itself, but it also redounds to her as observer, narrator, and woman.

In the immutable and foreign world that is Mexican society, a society with a "confused veneration for and terror of, the fertility of women and vegetation" (p. 165), the narrator must assess her own values and face the reasons she has made choices that put her outside the mainstream of Mexican culture and outside an even more pervasive cultural view of woman. An androgynous person who appears female but whose independent status as writer/intellectual is masculine, she is returning after ten years' absence with something precious to Porter women: hindsight, that most valuable of visions, based on two perceptions—the memory of how things were, or seemed, and the second, immediate perception, whose reality clarifies the earlier experience.

Even so, the point of view in this story is far more objective than that used in other psychologically complex Porter stories. No psychological penetration reveals the narrator's inner conflict. Instead, it is objectified through other characters, images, and symbols. Likewise, the physical landscape of Mexico symbolizes its psychology.

Speaking to the Paris Conference of the International Exposition of the Arts in 1952, Porter called the artist a "synthesis, a sounding board, a mirror, a sieve"[3] which is the way the artist/narrator here functions for the reader. Her apparently objective view of the environment does not illustrate objective detail alone; it illustrates what she perceives to be most important about Mexican culture, which in turn reveals her own psychic concerns.

As far as Mexico is concerned, what she perceives are three planes of physical/psychic activity. The first is the microcosm, the hacienda itself, a small empire dedicated to self-delusion, decay, and corruption, as evidenced in the people who inhabit and run the place, and as symbolized in the pulque which is its product. The hacienda, of course, reflects the macrocosm, the ancient Mexican landscape with its conjunction of the "solemn valley of the pyramids" (pp. 137–138), maguey fields, and proud peons, who best image their unbowed but nevertheless humbled culture. The images of the landscape itself, like the blue-shawled women selling pulque and bags of maguey worms outside the train, reverberate with passion, self-deception, and corruption.

More important, however, this obvious physical backdrop is the artistic visualization of the psychic reality of the story. It is the objectification, like the photographs prized by Andreyev, of the Mexican psyche, wherein love, sexuality, and fertility—all associated with woman—are inscrutably and indissolubly linked to corruption and decay of various kinds and, finally, to death. In the Mexican mind, the protagonist finds, love, fertility, and doom are inextricably linked, an uroboros[4] necessarily paradoxical and unending but nonetheless real.

As in "Flowering Judas," the background of "Hacienda" reflects the psychological concerns and state of the woman at the center of the story. Laura is arrested by conflicting feelings about her own sexuality, but the narrator of "Hacienda" already knows pretty much where she stands. Feeling that the pursuit of love is fraught with the possibility of psychic death, she has already set herself apart from other women by virtue of her dress, her way of life, her occupation. But she still wishes for a real and viable womanhood.

Thus, in "Hacienda" is displayed the familiar Porter dichotomy: the intellectual woman, a loner, has chosen to be nonsexual and independent; in order to determine whether power and love can exist together, she must weigh the powerful sexuality of the women of the Mexican ruling class, as well as the victimization of the young Indian girl, Rosalita, who is much desired but ultimately no more than a sexual pawn between brother and lover.

The story proceeds in a three-part movement, with each segment focusing on definition of the narrator, her need to separate distortion from the truth, and creation of the physical/psychological environment that is Mexico—that is, the vegetation/sexuality/death syndrome. It moves forward through vegetation and camera imagery and, because of the point of view, is itself almost a verbal film: a series of cinematic scenes, on the train, at the hacienda, in the billiard room, in the vat room. The narrator observes and pieces together these scenes, creating something the Russian filmmakers are incapable of doing: a piece of truth about Mexico. Thus, it is not until the end of the story that either the narrator or the reader has the full story and the full truth.

In the first segment of the story, the distortion and corruption themes are introduced, but the real emphasis is on the narrator. Its purpose is to establish her nature, role, and problem. Significantly, Porter opens the story with a trio of characters. The narrator begins her journey to the hacienda flanked by Kennerly, the American business manager, to whom she is linked by nationality, and Andreyev, the Russian filmmaker, to whom she is tied as an artist. Their presence is important because they expose background detail and because they introduce the political, social, and artistic issues in "Hacienda." More important, however, their personalities tell us what the narrator declines to tell us about herself, for they reflect the halves of her psyche.

The image projected by Andreyev—the intellectual, the liberal, the cool and unruffled artist—is the one the narrator affects. She treats Kennerly ironically, suggesting that his nervous fretfulness and his incapacity for being at home among the Mexicans are characteristics she is separate from, when in actuality they are the ones from which she must practice detachment. In truth, there are as many correspondences between her and Kennerly as between her and Andreyev, and it is Kennerly who reveals the subconscious fears which will drive her from the hacienda a few days later.

The issue of distortion is introduced immediately and is pervasive in the first movement of the story. The narrator's ironic tone from the first asserts that everything is not as it appears, and she immediately begins to catalogue the distortions of language and attitude that have taken place since the revolution in Mexico, which has been twisted and perverted. She notes that the names of things have changed, if not the realities: third-class rail travel is still available, but it is now called second-class, to illustrate that no one in Mexico remains so poor as to require humble transportation. Now, "the names of many things are changed, nearly always with the view to an appearance of heightened well-being for all creatures" (p. 135), so that only an outsider or a realist can name what is true about this society.

The narrator is both, and her cleverly ironic portrait of Kennerly, which dominates the beginning of the journey, emphasizes the need for skepticism in this environment. Kennerly, like the Mexican government, is excessive. He exaggerates and deals in outrageous hyperbole. Nothing, nothing, says the narrator's ironic tone, should be taken at face value—not the language that is spoken, not the history of the revolution, not the appearance of social conditions, not Kennerly, and not even Andreyev. Although his awareness of his own participation in duplicity and his refusal to apologize for it earns him the narrator's respect, Andreyev is anything but open and direct. He keeps his own counsel so that what cannot be observed can only be guessed.

The narrator understands this principle, too. Everything is not as it appears with her, either, although her role as truth-teller in this tale tends to obscure the fact that she, just like the others, incorporates more in character and position than meets the eye.

Kennerly and Andreyev provide insight here. The first thing apparent is that they view her differently. Kennerly knows nothing of her and makes a quick surface judgment. She is a lady, something of a responsibility, requiring a modicum of ritual deference. She must have a decent place on the train, her skirts must be tucked in around her knees, and she must not be exposed to sexual gossip. Andreyev, on the other hand, treats her as an asexual creature and deals with her as an artist rather than a female. He discusses his film and his homeland with her and does not forbear to tell her about the sexual liaisons at the hacienda. In fact, their attitudes focus attention on the two identities she tries to keep in balance, and make it apparent that her appearance—asexual artist—is only one part of her real character. She is also a woman who feels alone and fears the lack of structure that her untraditional choices afford her, even while she chooses them. Once we recognize this, it is easy to understand that the detailed portrait of Kennerly, who is, after all, only a bit player in the drama of the hacienda, is important because it provides insight into the hidden fears and psychological needs of the narrator, who is only apparently as cool and collected as Andreyev. In actuality, she is insecure, and wants the control and a certain amount of protection that her asexuality does not afford her.

Therefore, the complex relationship among these three conveys subtle characterization. First of all, all three are aliens. This is the first suggestion we have of the alienation and separateness that informs the story, and, more particularly, it establishes the alienation of the protagonist as American and female writer. Of course, it is Kennerly's alienation that is emphasized, and the ironic tone of his portrait makes him a preposterous, if pathetic, figure.

He is a corruption of good instincts, a "walking reproach to untidiness" who has "gone astray somewhere" and "overdone it"; he wears the "harried air of a man on the edge of bankruptcy, keeping up an expensive establishment because he dare[s] not retrench" (p. 139). Although he considers himself morally superior to Mexicans of every class, the ironic truth is that he is anything but the cool, superior Anglo he would like to project. In contrast to the lively dark eyes of the Indians in the second-class car, Kennerly's "light eyes and leather-colored hair" make him seem a soulless mannequin whose voice brays, whose nerves are "bundles of dried twigs," and who mindlessly corrupts his own body with warm beer and sweet American chocolate (pp. 138–139).

This portrait suggests that the narrator has doubts about herself and her own choices. Readers of "Theft" will know why. She, too, is a corruption of good instincts. Having chosen an apparent good, her art and her freedom, she finds that in so doing she eschews the right and natural proportions of a woman, that she cannot have the easy familial role of the Mexican women around her. It is quite possible that she feels she has "gone astray somewhere" and "overdone it," or feels forced to maintain an "expensive" position because it has become too difficult at this point to "retrench." Of course, the narrator cannot apply ironic distance to herself except by objectifying her fears in another character.

Enter Kennerly, a man capable of taking possession of the train "among a dark, inferior people." He proves, on scrutiny, to be a man whose blandishments, power, and moral superiority are so much hot air. The commotion he creates derives not from strength but from weakness and fear, and is essentially not a defense against an inferior race (for that is, after all, not necessary if they are truly inferior), but the best show of courage he can muster against a society full of threats and terrors he can barely name and certainly cannot control. He feels besieged by the "mountain[s] of confusion" which constitute the family groups on the train, overwhelmed by the "clutter of wet infants and draggled turkeys . . . and food baskets and bundles of vegetables" which create odors that pour over him like "mildewed pea soup" (p. 135).

To Kennerly, Mexico is corruption: full of flies, mosquitoes, and cockroaches; it is unbearably hot and offers only base food and water, which sicken his intestines with amoebic dysentery. Graft and bribery are a necessity which even the stoniest conscience cannot overcome, so Kennerly finds himself disintegrating morally as well as physically. But it is not really health or conscience Kennerly fears losing so much as his grip, and that is what he rails about. Describing the right way to make a film, Kennerly sheds light not only on his own psychic necessity, but on the narrator's too. The standards he establishes for his work are unassailable and are similar to what the narrator must desire in her own writing.

According to Kennerly, in order to be good, his work must involve a whole series of mysterious forces coming together at once: it must be art; it must communicate with its audience (in his parlance, be a "hit"); it must touch all the right psychological chords. The process by which all this is achieved, however, is no miracle, but hard, grueling work. It is fascinating to note how his frustrated description applies equally to the effort of any true artist to control the material, to shape it into some timeless form:

> His whole life of effort and despair flickered like a film across his relaxed face, a life of putting things over in spite of hell, of keeping up a good front, of lying awake nights fuming with

schemes and frothing with beer, rising of mornings gray-faced, stupefied, pushing himself under cold showers and filling himself up on hot coffee and *slamming himself into a fight in which there are no rules and no referee and the antagonist is everywhere.* "God," he said to me, "you don't know. But I'm going to write a book about it. . . ." (p. 141, italics added)

Kennerly's description, while self-pitying and ironic when applied to the business end of managing a film (he is not, after all, an artist) is an apt and accurate description of the process of creation the narrator must be familiar with, since she shares with Kennerly a deep need for control, no matter how successfully she masks it. The supreme irony, of course, is that the narrator does indeed know what he is talking about, and she, too, is going to write a "book" about it.

Of course, it is given that the narrator will dislike Kennerly; she identifies in him all her own worst tendencies: the need for security, nests, defenses, certainties. By allying herself with Andreyev, she rejects in one emotional gesture what she feels to be the weakest part of her self and simultaneously asserts herself as the cool intellectual she chooses to be instead. Kennerly recognizes their partnership and his own separation from it, and withdraws, turning to the window "as if he wished to avoid overhearing a private conversation" (p. 137).

The theme given least emphasis in the first movement of the story is the most significant and pervasive one in terms of the narrator. It is introduced in an image woven into the furious portrait of Kennerly, where it provides contrast to his fastidiousness but appears to be nothing more than local color and landscape detail. Seen from the train, the ancient pyramids, the maguey fields, and blue clouds dissolve into rain and fade before the first sharp image of the Mexican women, indelibly linked to vegetation, fertility, and death—the central issue in "Hacienda." The women crying their wares urge "mournfully" the fresh maguey worms and the pulque they produce for sale. They cry "in despair above the clamor of the turning wheels, waving like nosegays the leaf bags, slimy and lumpy with the worms they had gathered one at a time from the cactus whose heart bleeds the honey water for the pulque" (p. 138).

In one deft sentence, Porter introduces the cluster of sexual images which dominate "Hacienda," for this cluster integrates all other disparate elements: the distortion, the corruption, and the issue of the narrator's identity. The maguey, and the worms which penetrate the heart of the cactus, beginning the process of fertilization; the production of honey water which eventually becomes pulque, the drink of forgetfulness which deadens misery and pain—all are associated with woman and with the confused respect and fear man has for her essentially mysterious power to reproduce life. In the Mexican mind, woman is the maguey, and when she is penetrated in her core by the worm/penis, the mysterious process of fertilization and growth may begin. In any case, the "honey water" of her vagina, her sexuality, produces such pleasure as to make a man forget himself entirely. It goes without saying that he loses his physical vitality and is thus, Samson-like, robbed of his strength by woman; even worse, he may be so overcome with passion that he forgets his identity, his loyalties, and his honor. In these terms, certainly, woman is at best a necessary evil, an enemy to be used and held at bay because destruction is part of her office. But, most important, because of woman, man is forced to acknowledge that life is full of dark, instinctual forces—irrationality—which at once beckon and terrify him.

In the next movement of the story, the major issues merge and develop, giving the narrator a chance to weigh the true position of the Mexican women she encounters and thus to evaluate her own choice. This segment begins with the narrator and Andreyev poring over photographs of the timeless, unchanged culture stultified in the hacienda. The picturesque portraits are images of the doom inherent in the Mexican landscape as well as the "almost ecstatic death-expectancy which is in the air of Mexico" (p. 143); in this segment of the story, this critical theme and its links to love and sex will be developed through a pastiche of nonevents.

Andreyev's photos, the making of the film itself, and the camera imagery used here ironically emphasize the degree of distortion possible in this society even in the face of the camera, an instrument which doesn't lie, according to considered wisdom. The Indians, says Andreyev, are so picturesque "we shall be accused of dressing them up" (p. 143). Yet another irony inheres in the fact that despite their being unable to "dress up" like their masters, they nevertheless are not exactly what they appear to be.

Apparently proud and arrogant, the Indians suggest classical art: lovers are "two sculptured figures inclining towards each other"; young girls seem like caryatids, walking in rows "like dark statues . . . their mantles streaming from their smooth brows, water jars on their shoulders"; faces are "smoothed out and polished" like marble (pp. 142–143). But the central and most telling image of the Indian is of the man "in his ragged loose white clothing, weathered and molded to his flat-hipped, narrow-waisted body, leaning between the horns of the maguey, his mouth to the gourd, his burro with the casks on either side waiting with hanging head for his load . . ." (p. 142). This image projects, too, a "formal traditional tragedy," which is beautiful but "hollow" (p. 142). Like the maguey and all that it represents, the Indians are, despite appearances, hollow and corrupt precisely because they are enthralled to the servile work of farming the cacti and enslaved by their passions for sex, for violence, for "senseless excitement."

If there is tragedy in "the closed dark faces . . . full of instinctive suffering" (p. 142) or in the servitude of such a proud race, it is without substance, because while they suffer, they do so with "only the kind of memory animals may have, which is "a common memory of defeat" (p. 143). Their proud posture is a "mockery" not only because they have been in pain and subjection for so long that they have made of their doom a god, but because they participate in the duplicity which keeps them subservient. They manufacture their own opiate, pulque, which keeps economic power in the hands of their masters. In addition, as we shall see, because they give themselves up totally to their sexuality, they lack the common discipline and restraint such pride implies. It is a position the narrator recognizes as equally true for women. Those who become wives and mothers acquiesce in their own subservience, create their own economic dependence, and hand over power to the men who support and therefore control them. This is the natural outcome of using one's sexuality, a force that may be controlled with the kind of proud restraint the protagonist utilizes.

Within the hacienda itself, another hollow and corrupted space, the Spanish ruling class lacks even the semblance of tragic pride the peons manage. Hubris here is reduced to grasp, greed, and power; the physical emptiness of the place is captured in the cold temperature, inadequate lighting, the "chill gloom" of empty room after empty room, and the "vast incurable boredom" which is the very air of the place. Attempting to assuage their own ennui, the people who inhabit the place chase thrills with fast cars, the "excitement" of the film, and sexual games which assert their real decadence (p. 151).

All of this is imaged in the effete, fragile, and theatrical appearance they affect. In yet another way, things are not what they appear. This is especially true of the women. Lolita, the actress from the Jewel Theater and "the typical Mexican mixed-blood beauty" (p. 143), is the embodiment of female Mexican sexuality. Significantly, she is first mentioned following the narrator's observations on "the almost ecstatic death-expectancy which is in the air of Mexico" (p. 143), and as personified female sexuality, she has mythic overtones.

On a simpler level, however, she is merely an actress, who makes her living by adopting the appearance of another time and person. Doña Julia, in spite of being the lady of the hacienda, be-haves and looks like a lady of the theater (read whore). Affecting Chinese dress fashioned by a Hollywood costumer, she does not fool her grandfather-in-law, a gentleman of the old school who knows a loose woman when he sees one. Doña Julia may sit at the head of her table, but she nevertheless looks like "a figure from a Hollywood comedy, in black satin pajamas adorned with rainbow-colored bands of silk, loose sleeves falling over her babyish hands with pointed scarlet finger ends" (p. 154).

In fact, the ruling class as a group are "theatrically luxurious" persons. The Spanish overseer has commissioned an expensive new costume for himself made of deerskin with silver embroidery. And Betancourt, the half-breed Mexican who is French-educated, affects "the correct costume for a moving picture director . . ." (p. 154).

The Russians occupy a more equivocal position for the narrator. They are fellow artists, capable, as she is, of observing the duplici-ties in Mexican society. Their presence connotes a certain revolu-tionary idealism, although they are all obviously men of the world capable of accommodating Mexican censorship and falsehood to ac-complish their own propaganda, and they are prepared not to quib-ble about truth along the way. Arriving on a wave of innuendo, "wild rumor," and outright lies, the Russian filmmakers essentially take the Mexicans as their bedfellows, acquiescing in the corruption of reality into falsehood. Although their dress reflects their proper per-sonalities, they are capable of creating their own brand of illusion with camera, light, and film.

All of this cultivation of distortion and falsehood, of course, cor-rupts in every visible way. Against the larger background of grand extortion, bribery, and exploitation practiced by Velarde, the local courts demand payoffs from Don Genaro. Uspensky is visibly ill, and the air of the hacienda is rotten with the smell of pulque, which is being relentlessly produced, around the clock, in the vat room next to Doña Julia's bedroom, appropriately enough. But the true level of deterioration in this society is shown in the sexual perver-sion it not only tolerates but accepts, and with which it even amuses itself. Within the walls of the hacienda, the narrator will encounter promiscuity, infidelity, lesbianism, and even incest. It is no wonder that she will also encounter death.

The sexual games of the decadent and jaded Spanish ruling class are typified in the "gay" story of Lolita and Doña Julia. Don Genaro is expected, of course, to make love to Lolita. Doña Julia feels abused by her husband's infidelity, not out of love or even pride, since she is very "modern" and expects him to be promiscuous, but because he has abused her territorial rights by bringing Lolita into his wife's house. The hypocrisy in this attitude is lost on virtually everyone, and they are prepared to be entertained when Julia and Lolita seize control of the situation.

Interestingly, the story of these two women is the sophisticated version, in small, of María Concepción and María Rosa. But instead of fighting with each other, they join in complicity, thereby thwarting their common adversary, Don Genaro, and fulfilling the mythic necessity of their roles in this peculiarly Mexican triangle. Thus it is not surprising that their competition for Don Genaro ends in their joining forces. Nor is it surprising that Don Genaro cannot "get them separated"; they are essentially one and the same woman, alike in dress, attitudes, and values, both adept at playing roles and affecting theatrical images. What they project—walking and talking under the trees, "affectionately entwined, heads together," or "whispering together, arms lying at ease about each other's waists" (p. 144)—is the image of Siamese twins. Just as María Concepción must take on the role of her husband's mistress in order to resume her rightful position, Doña Julia must couple with Lolita, a fertility goddess of sorts, in order to become reconciled with her husband.

Lolita's masculinity in this pairing surfaces in the "deep throaty voice" with which she woos Doña Julia, in the aggressive glances she throws her way, and in the masculine way she mounts her horse, clearly forgetting her "role" (p. 144). On the surface, this is a lesbian relationship. On the mythic level, it recalls again the Aztec belief that vegetation and fertility were assured by the sacrifice of a young goddess to the Great Mother. As we have already seen in the discussion of "María Concepción," Xochiquetzal, who is goddess of marriage and patroness of harlots, is subsumed by the fertility goddess of the corn, thus ensuring her fecundity with the male and the continuation of life.

Either way, the doubling of these two women is significant. It clarifies and reinforces our understanding, and the narrator's, of woman in Mexico. If she is theatrical and frivolous on one level, she is significant and vital to life and death through her sexuality. The fact that she appears perverted points up her sharp opposition to the narrator in ways far more important than dress and behavior.

The implications of the triangle involving the hacienda's Indians are less clear, but they, too, echo the archetypal understanding of the vegetation myths. In the initial telling of the tale, only the surface details are recounted. Justino has been playing with a gun and has accidentally shot his sister. It is nobody's fault, not even Justino's. When he runs to the mountains he is inexplicably and forcibly brought back by a man who is his friend, Vicente, and because of Vicente, Justino is now in jail.

Many details here do not bear scrutiny, but it is only the narrator who asks the hard and obvious questions, such as how the gun came to be loaded in the first place. The others implicitly understand the sexual circumstances of the story, and that contributes to their great interest and pleasure in hearing about it. The narrator, too, is alert to overtones not entirely clear: the story of Justino and his sister is sandwiched in between references to the tale of Julia, Lolita, and Genaro, implying its sexual nature. Furthermore, the story is told and retold in imagery that establishes the tension between male and female sexuality. The terms of the story suggest a very obvious double entendre. As is evidenced in the pride and self-confidence of the young Indian man who has the lead in the film and who not coincidentally brings them the story, the making of the film and their parts in it lend a sense of daring and machismo to these male Indians. Thus, Justino has "borrowed" the pistol which killed his sister "from the firearms being used in the picture."

If the pistol in the story is seen for the Freudian symbol that it is, then the sexual analogy in Justino's story becomes transparent:

> It was true he was not supposed to touch the pistols, and there was his first mistake. He meant to put it back at once, but you know how a boy of sixteen loves to play with a pistol. Nobody would blame him. . . . The girl was nineteen years old. Her body had been sent already to the village to be buried. There was too much excitement over her; nothing was done as long as she was on the place. (p. 150)

Translated in terms of Mexican patriarchal mentality, then, the boy should not have touched his penis and given rein to his sexual appetite. But he did so in innocence, and of course it is not reasonable to expect a young male to control his sexuality, that is, to "put [the pistol] back." In addition, there was the added temptation of the girl, who, despite being his sister, was ripe—nineteen—and obviously so much a sex object that it superseded her being a blood relative. Now that she is a victim of her own anatomy and appetite, her body has been sent to the village for burial: she will be put into the ground like a fertile seed in imitation of some ancient Aztec sacrifice to the corn goddess. Like woman in the primal sense, like Lolita, the primary sex object in the story, the girl creates too much excitement around the hacienda and nothing can be accomplished while she is present.

So the narrator's second piece of truth is that if she cannot identify with the perverse superficiality of the upper-class Mexican woman, she finds little to embrace in the victimization of the more down-to-earth Indian women who accept sex in a hearty, if bawdy, way, sitting at night laughing among themselves at the rowdy songs sung by the men in the vat room. The hopeless position of women in the narrator's view is underscored by a seemingly inconsequential incident which follows the telling of Justino's story. On the road to the hacienda, the narrator spies a rabbit "cracking the strings of its heart in flight" from "lean hungry dogs," and she, automatically identifying with the potential victim, screams at the rabbit to run. Just as quickly, the dogs are championed by the macho male Indian riding with her, who leaves no doubt about the sexual overtones to this metaphorical contest when he turns to the narrator with blazing eyes to demand, "What will you bet, señorita?" (p. 151).

The señorita will bet nothing, because as long as she maintains her stance as an artist, she need not deal with men in obvious sexual terms. This becomes clear as the visit is played out. When the party arrive at the hacienda, they are admitted to the corral by an old woman servant, but their sight is immediately captured by the three Russian filmmakers waving from their balconies, far above ground level. Later, when it is time to retire, the narrator is taken by Doña Julia through her boudoir, a "long shallow room" like a vaginal canal. It is located between the billiard room, site of male activities where the women can only watch, and the vat room, where the pulque is readied for shipment. Doña Julia's room is

> puffy with silk and down, glossy with bright new polished
> wood and wide mirrors, restless with small ornaments, boxes
> of sweets, French dolls in ruffled skirts and white wigs. The air
> was thick with perfume which fought with another heavier
> smell. (p. 161)

The place aptly captures Julia's position as whore-priestess, who exists for and by the will of the men who surround her and who yet has some mysterious office to perform by virtue of her femaleness for the ritualistic corruption that takes place in the hacienda. Julia's perfume wars with the smell of pulque, "a thick vapor . . . sour, stale, like rotting milk and blood" (p. 161)—the smells of childbirth.

Although she has access to this female enclave, the narrator significantly moves to the stair to climb to her own room on the level where the male artists are staying. Up there, safe in her balcony, there is "no longer any perfume to disturb the keen fine wind from the mountains, or the smell from the vat-room" (p. 162). Separated from those female trappings and functions, the narrator can inhale the fresh air she needs to live and create.

Another important issue is at stake here, too. Since these female functions are corrupting and death-dealing, it is no wonder that the narrator feels suffocated by them. Among her acquaintances and experiences at the hacienda only one figure projects her values— simplicity, forthrightness, artistry, true vision. This is, of course, Carlos Montaña.

For his part, Carlos accepts her at face value and greets her warmly and with truth, giving her the first straightforward assessment of Justino's story she has heard. He also identifies a subtle truth that she understands but needs to perceive more clearly, as he sings for her his *corrido* about the affair:

Ah, poor little Rosalita
Took herself a new lover,
Thus betraying the heart's core
Of her impassioned brother . . .

Now she lies dead, poor Rosalita,
With two bullets in her heart. . . .
Take warning, my young sisters,
Who would from your brothers part.

His language not only gives her a clear version of the story, but confirms several concepts the narrator has already begun to sense, and, in doing so, it reiterates the most significant images and themes of the story.

The phrase "heart's core" links the whole sexual story to the maguey, corrupted to its heart's core for its honey water; in Carlos's song, the sexual female lies dead with bullets in her heart, so love and sexuality are irrevocably linked to death; but, most important, Rosalita is a victim. Her "impassioned brother," guilty of the same sexuality, the same incest, lives—unhappily, to be sure, but nevertheless he lives. In Mexico, men fear loss of power, that is, death, through the mysterious sexuality of women, but in reality it is the women who die as a result of being sexual.

These insights are not lost on the narrator, and she is prepared to grasp them even more firmly and finally in the last movement of the story. Once she has confirmed them in her own mind and has seen that they apply also to her, she will no longer waver, but will choose again what she has chosen before.

The same issues predominate in the last movement of the story, but the narrator's clear sense of the corruption of the hacienda and its even closer link to the woman/sexuality/death syndrome are ascendant. Amid the ritualistic chanting of the Indians who load the pulque barrels by night and the sounds of the inexorable procession of the workers to the maguey fields by morning, the narrator listens to Kennerly and Stepanov discuss Justino's part in a scene in the film that exactly parallels the shooting of his sister, his flight, and his capture by Vicente. It has been filmed, but badly; it has happened in reality; it will probably have to be filmed again. The repetitions here impose a sense of *déjà vu* and, with that, a question: What is actually real—the event or the remembered event? It is a question the narrator must ask herself: What is true—what she observes now or what she remembers? Does her double vision trick her? In these terms, can anything be considered real, accurate, true? Over all, she is impressed by the relentless cycle of everything that transpires in this place: Things change only to remain the same.

Carlos reappears to confirm what *is* real in the hacienda: the macho pursuit of excitement even if, and probably because, death is a possibility. Andreyev points out that the Spanish overseer puts on a "different pair of fancy trousers everyday, and sit[s] on that bench hoping that something, anything may happen" (p. 164). Carlos describes the excitement of the last Agrarian raid, during which "every man on the place had a rifle and a pistol" (p. 165). In metaphoric terms, asserting and using their sexuality is one of the few ways they can combine excitement with a sense of potency and power.

What is also real is the absolute corruption necessary to the functioning of the hacienda, and its linkages to female fertility. The sharp imagery in the description of the vat room, which the narrator finally sees for herself, emphasizes her observation and confirms her understanding of the male attitude toward women in this culture:

> We walked through the vat-room, picking our way through the puddles of sap sinking into the mud floor, idly stopping to watch, without comment, the flies drowning in the stinking liquor which seeped over the hairy bullhides sagging between the wooden frames. (p. 165)

All is overseen by the prim statue of María Santísima and the fresco depicting the young girl, later a half-goddess, who supposedly discovered the corrupting liquor. Aztec or Christian, it all has "something to do with man's confused veneration for, and terror of, the fertility of women and vegetation" (p. 165).

This knowledge will allow the narrator to ask the last necessary question of Andreyev: Why did Vicente not allow Justino, his friend, to escape? Andreyev answers unequivocally: "'Revenge,' said Andreyev. 'Imagine a man's friend betraying him so, and with a woman, and a sister! He was furious. He did not know what he was doing, maybe. . . . Now I imagine he is regretting it'" (p. 167). The deadliness of such an attitude, coupled with the inexorability of its repetition, is stressed in the perpetual motion of Don Genaro's trips to the judge and "the chanting and counting and the rolling of barrels down the incline . . . for the night" (pp. 167–168). In fact, the whole interlocking system has the inevitability of sunrise about it:

> The white flood of pulque flowed without pause; all over Mexico the Indians would drink the corpse-white liquor, swallow forgetfulness and ease by the riverful, and the money would flow silver-white into the government treasury; don Genaro and his fellow-hacendados would fret and curse, the Agrarians would raid, and ambitious politicians in the capital would be stealing right and left enough to buy such haciendas for themselves. It was all arranged. (p. 168)[5]

Just as is the role of woman. That night, playing cards with a Mexican youth, who is thin and dark and obviously lacks the robustness of a mature man, the narrator is defeated when she plays the dagger, a phallic symbol. There is no room for her kind in Mexico. "Now I shall play the crown, and there you are, defeated," he tells her, and immediately begins to talk about Justino in a way that applies metaphorically to the narrator's psychic situation. He asserts that the director has had to say to Justino repeatedly, "Don't laugh, Justino, this is death, this is not funny" (p. 169). And Doña Julia adds that Justino, being little more than an animal, will remember nothing, and, besides, there is a good chance he will not come back.

The whole conversation is a metaphoric reminder to the narrator that she must not take what she has learned lightly: this is not funny; this is death. Don't forget, don't take it lightly. This is death. If you mix in this, you may not return. People get shot in the film, and that is not real; it only imitates life. But in prison, where Justino is, people are actually shot, and they don't come back. Life is at stake. In the silence that follows, the narrator looks at all the "chance-gathered people" (of whom she is one) who are "imprisoned" in the room together. She can lose her life here. Some action is necessary to dispel the tension, and it is not long in coming.

Kennerly starts the whole circle rotating again by announcing his return to Mexico City. Don Genaro will go with him. Lolita will return. Kennerly will fret and argue more with the censors. Scenes will be redone. When Lolita, symbol of female sexuality and fertility returns, like some eternal earth goddess, "there will be great excitement." In this context, the Indian driver's strange parting comment to the narrator makes sense: "If you should come back in about ten days, . . . you would see a different place. It is very sad here now. But then the green corn will be ready, and ah, there will be enough to eat again!" (p. 170).

Rosalita has been sacrificed and buried, and Lolita will return, bringing the harvest in her wake and trailing man's "confused veneration for . . . the fertility of women and vegetation." It is woman's only power in Mexico, and in the narrator's now clear vision, to invite it, to accept it, is like twining an adder about the neck. There is no harvest for her in the hacienda or in Mexico either; nor is there any respite. Quite simply, she cannot "wait for tomorrow in this deathly air." Seeing the face of death, she does what Laura cannot do. She runs.

By the end of 1934, Porter had published the stories which made her reputation and brought her to the midpoint of her career. In them she repeatedly created women trapped by circumstance, divided against each other or within themselves, and always in conflict. Whether primitive Indians, farm women, or sophisticated New Yorkers, her women all struggle with their inability to integrate the virginal and sexual sides of their psyches. Their irreconcilable yearning for both personal independence and the love that necessitates dependence creates the dramatic tension in each of her stories.

PART 2

Through a Glass Darkly: Miranda

1935–1936

In 1935, having written her last story about her "familiar country," Mexico, Porter turned to an even more familiar country in the initiation stories centering on Miranda. Having chronicled, in unusual depth, the psychological division in her women characters, Porter began to examine the sources of this dichotomy and the nature of the "early training" by which her characters are compelled to repress one ideal and honor another.

Between January 1935 and the winter of 1936, she published all the "Old Order" stories except "The Source" (1941) and "The Fig Tree" (1960). "Old Mortality" and "Pale Horse, Pale Rider," along with their companion "Noon Wine," were all completed within one month, at the end of 1936. Such concentration and fruitfulness suggest that Porter found in Miranda's childhood experience not only a rich vein to mine, but a lodestar which led her to the culminating knowledge of "Old Mortality" and "Pale Horse, Pale Rider." After this she wrote no more about feminine conflicts; in fact, she wrote little fiction, except for Ship of Fools. *It is tempting to suggest that, having examined the conflict and its complex roots, she had said what she came to say. Certainly, references to this conflict in* Ship of Fools *indicate that Mrs. Treadwell and Jenny Brown have confronted the choice, chosen independence, and moved beyond it. And Katherine Anne Porter seems to have moved beyond it, too, perhaps because she had exorcised it in her writing.*

5 ❖ I Thought as a Child: The Old Order

The publication dates of the various stories in "The Old Order" suggest that they constitute thematic groups. The portraits of Uncle Jimbilly and Nannie, "The Witness" and "The Last Leaf," published together in January 1935, form one group. "The Grave," (April 1935), "The Circus" (July 1935), and "The Fig Tree"[1] constitute the child's confrontation with adult knowledge. "The Journey" (Winter 1936) and "The Source" (1941) portray in some depth the second most important character in Porter's fiction—the Grandmother. However, since Porter's preface to her *Collected Stories* refers to putting one of the stories in its "right place in the sequence called *The Old Order*" (p. v), it seems appropriate to examine these stories in the sequential order intended by the author: "The Source," "The Journey," "The Witness," "The Circus," "The Last Leaf," "The Fig Tree," and "The Grave."

Identifying this group of stories as a sequence allows us to see that together they comprise the length of one of her short novels; they move from beginning ("The Source") to end ("The Grave") and are unified by common characters and a single narrator, Miranda—although she often uses a double point of view: the hindsight of an adult projecting back to the perception of a young child.

It should be noted that the stories are not a chronological sequence, but a psychological one. "The Old Order" begins with an external event that was repeated so regularly in Miranda's childhood as to become ritualized in her memory, and ends with an internal experience—Miranda's recognition of the interrelationship between birth, decay perpetrated by time, and death—so profound that it buries itself in her mind, only to surface, like graveyard treasure, twenty years later. This psychological sequence moves, not from year to year, or event to event, but from outer experience to inner effect, recording the impressions which have made the child mother of the woman.[2] These vignettes are parts of the whole of Miranda's psyche; consequently, the "character sketches" which some critics have been loathe to call stories have a collective impact in relation to each other that they do not have separately.³ Thus, in "The Old Order" and in "Old Mortality," Porter examines the influences which made Miranda a divided adult. These vignettes tell us that there are two great mysteries for both the child and the adult Miranda: sex and death. The human beings she immortalizes in these portraits have been the powerful teachers of her infancy and childhood. Only one of them, Uncle Jimbilly, is male, and he is a servant. Miranda's father, who because he is her only parent, might be expected to exercise significant influence, seems largely ineffectual. He, like the other young men of the family, is hardly characterized, except in the apparently most important role they play, that of the swain. The epitome of this type of figure has to be cousin Gabriel in "Old Mortality," whose adult character is never realized because he, like Amy, is frozen in a romantic role—that of a suitor—and is restrained by all its narrow conventions. Thus it is the women of her extended family who are Miranda's role models; it is largely they who define for Miranda the meaning of her sexuality, the kinds of death to be endured, and, more important, which kind is actually fatal.

For instance, these stories offer several different visions of the Grandmother who dominates Miranda's childhood. Two of these, "The Source" and "The Journey," illustrate explicitly the origins of Miranda's double perception of womanhood and the unresolved conflict in her personal life. In "The Source" Miranda portrays her Grandmother as a wonder woman, a matriarch with all the strength and prerogatives of an ancient mother goddess. An equal but opposite portrait of the same Grandmother is contained in "The Journey," in which the psychology of this compellingly strong woman is made transparent. Here the Grandmother is a frightened, insecure woman who feels inadequate despite her apparent strength, who finds her romantic notions of love and marriage a delusion and her body and sexuality a trap. Unlike Granny Weatherall, whose fortunes and character are so similar to hers, the Grandmother does not seem to derive strength from her mothering in "The Journey": it might almost be said to be her ruin. The story is a careful examination of all the avenues open to a woman in the Grandmother's culture: she is portrayed as the spoiled and petted daughter of a wealthy planter; as a gay, pretty belle who teases a suitor into marriage; as a fruitful mother. Then she is a widow, the solitary head of her still-dependent family, and, finally, a matriarch. Miranda sees that her Grandmother has had "all the responsibilities of a man but . . . none of the privileges" (p. 336); none of her roles has made her happy, despite her show of strength. Miranda has clearly perceived ambivalence in the woman who has raised her, and in these two seminal stories Porter recreates the ambivalence which spells conflict for Miranda.

Miranda's understanding of womanhood, at the base of the Miranda cycle, as well as stories like "Theft," "Flowering Judas," and "The Cracked Looking-Glass," is that control is paramount. If a woman cannot control her body, she cannot control her life. Thus her sexuality is a threat to her. Lacking effective contraceptives, she must control access to her body. But in and of itself, sexual experience has enough intensity and power to make her relinquish control of herself; should that happen, at the very least it means a loss of virginity and the identity that may inhere in that, as well as a leap into a frenzied void that may be another kind of death. On the other hand, sexual experience can be transforming; through it a woman becomes a mother. But Miranda knows her Grandmother has clearly experienced great pain—both physical and psychic—from motherhood, and Miranda's own mother died in childbed. Thus she is caught between death and the devil (both of whom she will attempt to outride in "Pale Horse, Pale Rider"): she doesn't want motherhood, and she fears the void. She has no alternative but to eschew sex completely on the basis of what she has seen her Grandmother experience. Luckily, there have been other influences as well. The other stories in "The Old Order" record the impressive and sometimes traumatic experiences wherein Miranda learned to associate sex, birth, and death; "The Last Leaf" and "The Fig Tree" illustrate the positive models from whom she learned the value of feminine independence.

In order to see the significance of this group of "sketches," with which critics have rarely known what to do, one must recognize first that there is a dual point of view in each episode which unifies the whole and culminates in "The Grave." This double-layered perception is the key to the point of these brief incidents.

There is, first of all, the point of view of the childish Miranda, who characterizes the adults of her early experience as giants who left indelible marks on her psyche as well as on her memory. The objective descriptions of dress, behavior, conversation, and adult interaction belong to Miranda the child. But of course these are remembered events and impressions, and the adult Miranda who remembers is the second, selectively artistic point of view. This is the consciousness which provides ironic tone in "The Source" and "The Witness" and objective omniscience in "The Journey" and "The Last Leaf." More important, when Miranda recalls specific events of her childhood and overlooks others, this adult voice attests to their psychological significance for the grown woman she has become.[4]

This double perception belongs to any adult who has not completely abandoned the memory of what it was like to be a child, and
Porter here uses this layered viewpoint to show not only how the
child Miranda reacted to irrevocable influences, but what the adult
Miranda thinks of the child Miranda and her experiences. By the
time we reach "The Grave," we have accumulated a full catalog of
the influences that prepared Miranda for her insights into the cycle
of life and death in "The Grave." As we read on, in "Old Mortality,"
Miranda's psychological history from "The Old Order" is embel-
lished further by this second double perception of the adult Miranda
which has the effect of plumbing the depths of her subconscious. It
is her *Remembrance of Things Past.*

Each of these images from childhood is an "episode" which
leaps "before her mind's eye" as "plain and clear in its true colors as
if she looked through a frame upon a scene that had not stirred nor
changed since the moment it happened . . ." ("The Grave," p. 367).
Thus is Miranda, as her name implies, one who stares: "The scene
before her eyes [is] dimmed by the vision back of them" (p. 367). The
last page of "The Grave" is also the last page of "The Old Order," in
essence a mental retrospective of all visions capable of emerging
Lazarus-like from their burial places in Miranda's unconscious.
"The Old Order," then, provides special insights into what shaped
the adult Miranda, a spirited yet sensitive woman of sharp perception, uncompromising, if contradictory, in her insistence on both individuality and dependence on the sustenance of love.

These characterizations have the structure of a reverie or a waking dream, provoking one another through free association. They eschew complex technique in favor of graphic detail; however, the ac-
cumulation of these details eventually suggests symbolic values of
its own, which in turn illuminate the significance of these characters for Miranda's psyche. Consequently, while this series does not
always specifically project the conflict contained in Porter's more
complex stories, it is wool-gathering with a purpose, which allows
Miranda—and us—to see the soil in which the conflict was sown.

The significance of Miranda's character to Porter's work can
hardly be overstated. She is the identified center of consciousness in
fully half of Porter's short stories and the implicit narrator in *Ship of
Fools* and at least six other stories, including the most psychologically complex ones. To understand this personality is to understand
the viewpoint of much of Porter's work; its autobiographical overtones only make it more interesting.

Miranda, whose name literally means "one who sees," is first and foremost an acutely sensitive observer. Like Shakespeare's Miranda, she is rooted in a simple world whose environment and customs she understands. "The Old Order" is the setting forth of that world, and the Grandmother is its primary citizen. However, not even the wizard Prospero is able to continue an isolated island existence forever; in the face of inexplicable change, his Miranda must accommodate herself to what she sees, in her naïveté, as a brave new world. It is interesting that she utters that famous phrase when she first lays eyes on the young man who will be her lover. If his love is perfect, perhaps her vision can remain unsullied. Porter's Miranda utters her "brave new world" equivalent not for any man, but when the firmament itself is laid before her by an imposing female relative ("The Fig Tree"). By the time she reaches adulthood, Miranda recognizes that the structure of the Old Order is rotting from within its sentimental core while at the same time it must bow to "grotesque dislocations" in its society because the outside world is "heaving in the sickness of a millennial change."

Though Porter has protected her private life by withholding details of her biography, she has repeatedly stated that she writes from memory, and comparison of her experiences and Miranda's has led many writers to conclude that the persona Miranda is "thinly fictionalized autobiography."[5] A statement in Porter's essay on Willa Cather helps the reader to understand why Porter focuses on childhood from the fourth to the tenth year while ignoring pubertal experiences:

> I have not much interest in anyone's personal history after the tenth year, not even my own. Whatever one was going to be was all prepared for before that. The rest is merely confirmation, extension, development. Childhood is the fiery furnace in which we are melted down to essentials and that essential shaped for good.[6]

"The Old Order" is the record of those essentials for Miranda. The prepubertal period is the time when a child learns to distinguish between the concrete and the imagined; it is therefore appropriate that these stories reflect both the life of the body and the life of the mind. Physical environment, such as social structures, modes, and mores, and the human beings—particularly parents—with whom the child interacts shape personality, but so does the imagination, which affects a child's perception of that environment. And so does the unconscious, the receptacle of adult nonverbal communication as well as repressed instincts like infantile sexual behavior. "The Old Order" illustrates not only Miranda's society and role models, but her mental images—both conscious and unconscious—of that social reality.

This sequence of characters, then, is Porter's chronicle of the major influences in the life of her primary protagonist, Miranda. Like photographs in a family album, the portraits of her relatives are individual and distinct, but it is their collective influence which constitutes the "early training" that marks Miranda irrevocably.

"The Source"

There is no question that Miranda's paternal grandmother has primacy among these influences. She assumes center stage in the first memory of the "Old Order," really a character sketch of the Grandmother, which is unequivocally titled "The Source." Lest we miss the implications of the title, the story, narrated by a grown-up Miranda, is a simple account of the Grandmother's annual two-week visit to the family farm. As Miranda perceives it, it becomes a ritual visitation by an all-powerful Earth Mother, without whose good will the place and its people would perish. Thus the reader is served notice that, for Miranda, this Grandmother is not only a person but a symbol of her world.

It is clear from the beginning that this woman is the source of life, well-being, and favor, not only for Miranda and her other grandchildren, but for many of the adults connected to her family as well. She is a benevolent, if distant, divinity whose nature is fulfilled by taking care of others. It goes without saying that the narrator is dependent on her, even in awe of her. This attitude is betrayed in the first reference to her elderly relative, who is alluded to not as "my grandmother" or "Miranda's grandmother," but "the Grandmother." The use of the impersonal article and the capital *G* not only suggests that this grandmother is a special creature apart from merely mortal members of her family, but also indicates that the narrator snaps to attention at the thought of her. The narrator eventually refers to her simply as "Grandmother," but reverts in "The Journey" to her "title."

One can see why she provokes awe. She is an amazon of the hearth, a woman whose prodigious strength and industry demand attention and respectful distance. And all of this ability is focused on the land and the creatures on it. She wants to know "about the crops, . . . [the] gardens the Negroes were making, how the animals were faring" (p. 321). Most of all she wishes to visit the orchards she has planted to watch the fruit ripen, to see the roses coming into bloom, and to tie back the rampant honeysuckle "with her own hands." It is the "black, rich soft land" which calls her back; when she sees the peach tree near her town house begin to bloom, she is reminded of the fine orchards she has planted in her lifetime, and she stands "looking at the single tree, representing all her beloved trees still blooming, flourishing, and preparing to bring forth fruit . . ." (p. 322).

She is the author, the creator of that farm as she is of her orchards, and the black servants who work her land revere her omnipotence. They herald her return, which they have undoubtedly anticipated, and she likewise greets them "in her feast-day voice." Trusting to the wisdom her name (Sophia) implies, they catalogue their troubles and complaints of the past months so that she may set things right. Their trust is well founded, for she has a special provenance for restoration and renewal. The "frenzy" and "uproar" her visit brings to the place is a happy one, and the narrator's description suggests that the Grandmother's transforming presence enjoins swift miracles:

> Curtains came down in dingy heaps and went up again stiff
> and sweet-smelling; rugs were heaved forth in dusty confusion
> and returned flat and gay with flowers once more; the kitchen
> was no longer dingy and desolate but a place of heavenly order
> where it was tempting to linger. (p. 324)

Her ability to bring order out of chaos (even if it is chaos she has created), thereby nurturing her dependents, is her primary virtue and can be counted on like the rising sun. She is constant, she is provident, she is benevolent and just; she has the imperturbability of one in control. To her dependents she seems immutable. Particularly to her grandchildren, from whose viewpoint the story is told, she must seem to be as she has always been and always will be. In short, she is like an ancient goddess who descends to earth cyclically and with her restoring touch breathes new life into a dormant world.

It is clear that she embodies every attribute of the Earth Mother —even to androgyny. The final gesture of her visit is a display of "strength [and] unabated energy" (p. 325), as if she has not already demonstrated these qualities by her aggressive refurbishment of the farm. She spends an afternoon with Fiddler, her saddle horse, who, although he symbolizes masculinity, pays "no attention to anyone but the Grandmother" (p. 324). Although she rides sidesaddle, in the feminine manner, she gallops off with her skirts flying, asserting her vigor to the world. The day is finished with the stroll through the orchards for which she has come; it is the rest due her after she has surveyed the work of her hands. Then, with "instructions, advices, good-bys, blessings," the matriarch "would set out with that strange look of leaving forever . . ." (p. 325).

Consequently, in Miranda's memory the Grandmother is Janus-faced. She is a woman who likes feminine finery and who understands and adheres to the dress and gestures of a Southern lady. However, she is a woman who wants to control rather than acquiesce. This ambivalence is sharply impressed on Miranda by the only woman she and her sister have for a role model: the Grandmother is "the only reality to them in a world that seemed otherwise without fixed authority or refuge since their mother had died so early . . ." (p. 324). One simple way to read these comments on Miranda's matriarchal relative is to see them as a fond characterization of a person profoundly important in the narrator's life; however, the recurrence of the Grandmother figure in Porter's stories suggests that this may be a conscious attempt to understand that influence by examining the woman and all the details of her background. Perhaps it is even an attempt to exorcise her. In any case, her significance as a role model is clarified by a psychiatrist's comment on how girls learn from adult women:

> If a girl in her development has no other than the image of a woman in the domestic role, this image will be internalized and become her principal knowledge of what a woman is and does. It forms the basis of her morality, and behaving differently sets up a moral conflict. In spite of later worldly education, the earliest lessons come from all-powerful, life-giving and sustaining giants—parents—and they stick. This learning is, then, the education of how to please, how to be loved, how to survive. These earliest lessons from kin take priority and can be overcome only by vigorous self-purging efforts.[7]

"The Journey"

"The Journey," Miranda's most complete portrait of her grandmother, illustrates the profound influence this woman has for Miranda. Through her, Miranda forms her first impressions of sexuality, marriage, and motherhood, the three recurring experiences in this cycle of memory. All three experiences are supervised by men, which is perhaps the most significant point communicated to Miranda.

"The Journey" may be viewed as a journey from cradle to grave, which begins with the ancestors of whom the Grandmother is proud and ends with her dropping dead on the doorstep of her son's home.

Or it may be equivalent to the flashbacks Miranda is capable of, a journey backward in time for the Grandmother and Nannie, two ancient women who conspire together to recreate their mutual past by reciting it to each other while they busy their hands making memory quilts—"scraps of the family finery, hoarded for fifty years" and then cut "into strips and triangles and [fit] . . . together again in a carefully disordered patchwork . . ." (p. 326). This is, of course, what they are doing verbally and what Miranda does mentally; fitting together the pieces of the family quilt is an apt metaphor and moves in two generational directions.

The universality of their activity is emphasized by the fact that the Grandmother does not remember alone in this sequence, but is more than aided and abetted by Nannie, her black slave, then her servant, with whom she has grown up and then grown old. The two women seem to represent two halves of one universal female experience, the one black and indentured, the other white and free. While they are not alter egos, they certainly are sisters under the skin. When Sophia Jane is ten years old, she gives Nannie a birthdate separated from her own by only three months' time and enters it in the family Bible; they marry within a few days of each other, and bear and nurse their children together. Their similarities and cohesiveness are emphasized almost to the exclusion of their racial differences, suggesting that theirs is the experience of womankind, not that of a race or class. Nannie is a servant because she is black, but her closeness to Sophia reflects the truth of the white woman's servitude as well: Sophia is subject to "burdensome rule" because she is female.[8] Both will eventually experience a quasi-emancipation: Nannie by presidential proclamation and Sophia by the death of her husband.

Certainly men govern the intertwined lives of these two women. Their female relatives are barely mentioned. Nannie remembers vividly the man who auctioned her off as well as the tall, authoritative gentleman who bought her and her parents off the auction block. She is still offended, as a grandmother and a free woman, by the judge who remembers her as a "strip of crowbait" who brought only twenty dollars to his pocket when he sold her. Not only have men exercised life-and-death power over her as a child, but she is still enslaved to their opinion, even as an autonomous adult.

Likewise, Sophia's father, characterized as a benevolent despot and a fond father who dispenses slaves and horses to his pretty daughter with all the confidence of a man who rules his manor, tacitly influences his own little girl to care about the opinions of men. She wants his good opinion partly because she loves him, but also partly because he is powerful. Furthermore, she will accept as readily as Nannie accepts auction her place on the marriage "block"; she will use her beauty and coquetry to enhance her chances of being chosen by a desirable "buyer." Of course, what is cut-and-dried economics in Nannie's case is complex psychological response in Sophia Jane's.

So accustomed is she to male authority that it doesn't occur to her to reject the suit of her second cousin, a man who looks enough like her to be her brother. The fact that he is a member of the family undoubtedly increases his eligibility, for Sophia's world is a narrow one. The fact that he chooses her formally documents, and therefore augments, her desirability in her own eyes as well as her society's. She does not reject this cousin who woos her "at arm's length" any more than Nannie demurs at marrying the husband picked for her by her owners.

In addition to a sense of her own value, Sophia's cousin Stephen provides her with a much-needed outlet for her adolescent sexual curiosity—significantly, the one psychological experience of her grandmother which Miranda details for the reader. He becomes the keeper of the keys to the locked door of her experience; as her only possible legitimate sexual partner, he will presumably teach her what she merely conjectures at in her virginal confinement. Undoubtedly, part of the reason he seems "a mysteriously attractive young man" to her is that she has heard he is "wild" and is sure that

> he was leading . . . a dashing life full of manly indulgences, the sweet dark life of the knowledge of evil which caused her hair to crinkle on her scalp when she thought of it. Ah! the delicious, the free, the wonderful, the mysterious and terrible life of men! (p. 335)

In reveries reminiscent of Virgin Violeta's, she tantalizes herself with enticing and therefore frightening fantasies which threaten "to cast her over the edge of some mysterious forbidden frenzy"—a clear metaphor for sexual activity. But she knows that children are "conceived in sin and brought forth in iniquity," and so she must provide in her fantasy the escape hatch of remorse. Thus libido and superego contend in her subconscious:

> She dreamed recurrently that she had lost her virginity (her virtue, she called it), her sole claim to regard, consideration, even to existence, and after frightful moral suffering which masked altogether her physical experience she would wake in a cold sweat, disordered and terrified. (p. 335)

When she fantasizes about losing her "virtue," she is trying on a male role which she cannot sustain psychologically. She believes, with her society, that having given up virginity, she would also give up her only claim to care and decency from others; the power brokers, men, would no longer value her, and she is dependent on them for her sense of significance. Such a belief asserts a terrible poverty of self-worth that will affect her even as a wife and mother.

It is clear that loss of virginity for Sophia constitutes both physical and psychological separation from her world. Consequently, she hides her fantasies, and for her suitor she dons the mask of the coquette, appearing "gay and sweet and decorous, full of vanity and . . . daydreams . . ." (p. 335). Having parlayed her virginity into enough mystery to make an experienced man agree to keep her for the rest of her life, she is "married off in a very gay wedding" (p. 333).

However, that high moment is not sustained. Looking back, the Grandmother thinks she struck a bad bargain. Her day of days should have been an occasion for ivory brocade, but the flimsy dotted swiss she has had to make do with symbolizes the weakness of the fabric of her marriage. Emblematically, the crops failed that year, and it seems to her that "they failed ever afterward" (p. 336). Misled by her father, she will be sorely disappointed in her husband and sons, none of whom have one-tenth of her responsibility or power, but on whom she still depends for a worthy opinion of herself.

She is first disappointed by the reality of sex and begins to experience its liability: "a grim and terrible race of procreation" (p. 334), wherein she is even denied the pleasure of nursing her babies. Her first step toward self-determination comes in claiming her right to nurture; her reward is the sensual pleasure she has wished for and bonds with her children.

Breast-feeding gives Sophia a chance to erase her sense of inadequacy (as a nonvirgin) with her new capacity for nourishing. Marriage offers her the knowledge that "she despised men . . . and was ruled by them" (p. 337). As she feels her own power taking shape, she chafes under the rule of her husband, whose sexuality she now sees as aggressive, selfish, and exploitive. She watches him spend her inheritance on machines when it is the land that yields life and sweetness for her. She is angry with him for "deserting" her when he eventually dies of a wound sustained in a war he pursued through idealism and stubbornness.

It is only in his death that she fully realizes her own potential as a person, abandoning finally all the subterfuge of her adolescence and marriage. Forced from the home she has always known into the

Texas wilderness, she breaks from the confinement of paternalism, literally building a new place with her own hands against enormous odds:

> Not until she was in middle age, her husband dead, her property dispersed, and she found herself with a houseful of children, making a new life for them in another place, with all the responsibilities of a man but with none of the privileges, did she finally emerge into an honest life: and yet, she was passionately honest. She had never been anything else. (p. 336)

But if she has been frustrated by father and husband, it is her sons who will break her heart, running away from the home she has made in a childish effort to return to the sugarcane fields of Louisiana. The significance of this final blow can be appreciated only if we remember the lessons of Sophia's early life. Buried deep in her psyche is the entrenched notion that without virginity she is not worth keeping and is likely to be abandoned. Her husband does it, and her sons attempt it. Second, we must remember that she has sublimated her sexual energy into nurturing, and thus she sees in her sons' leave-taking an indictment of her motherhood. She has been driving them like men when she should have been feeding them like children. She immediately interprets their desire for sugarcane as a hunger she cannot assuage. Although she has performed superhuman tasks to secure the homestead for her children's well-being, she is too quick to assume she has failed in what she now regards as her most important role: nourishing. The experience reinforces her sense of inadequacy as a person, and it is more terrible because, for the first time, she feels inadequate as a mother, a devastation more complete than being rejected as a person.

Of course, the poor truth of the matter is that she can never be sufficient to them, and this knowledge makes "her heart break in her breast" (p. 339). From that day forward she spoils her children, especially her boys, refusing to demand anything of them, and giving them up to young women she disapproves of, "new" women who want to vote and who don't mind leaving home to earn a living. Ironically, although her sons seek the kind of womanhood she has demonstrated to them—an active one—she rejects the thought of women "so unsexing themselves" (p. 333). While she is appalled, her sons have their way, even when it ruins her resources. Finally, they use her up. It is fitting that she dies in the home of a son who humors her wishes while she avoids commanding him in anything. They play out, for the millionth time, the pattern of a lifetime.

"The Witness"

Anyone unfamiliar with Porter's reliance on psychic processes might find the appearance of Uncle Jimbilly in "The Witness," the third story of the sequence, somewhat sudden. In contrast to the Grandmother and her strong benevolence, this old black man is slow, irascible, and grudging, a complainer rather than a doer, who buys himself an audience for his gloomy ghost and slave stories by whittling tombstones for the dead animals the children find around the farm. Although he is Nannie's husband and therefore a contemporary of the Grandmother, as well as a colorful eccentric, Porter is not just dabbling in local color here. Uncle Jimbilly provides a definite link between the stories which precede him and those which follow because of his morbid preoccupation with death.

In "The Source," when the Grandmother leaves the farm, she "sets out" from the place "with that strange look of leaving forever" (p. 325), certainly an intimation of death despite her godlike stature. In "The Journey," of course, she actually does succumb; in the very last words of the story, where the information is most stunning, we are told that the Grandmother "dropped dead over the doorsill" (p. 340). Furthermore, the paragraph which conveys this news stresses the zest, the power, and the vitality of the woman, who moves a fifty-foot adobe wall the day of her death, so that the fact of her mortality seems all the more sudden and shocking, as it must have been for the young Miranda. Even the alliterated *d*'s of the phrase have this impact. In addition, if such a vital and impervious person as the Grandmother may be claimed by death, it surely must be inescapable. What the reader is left with at the end of the second story, then, is the curious juxtaposition of life and death in human experience. This is neatly transmitted to "The Witness" in the person of Uncle Jimbilly, who symbolizes death in life just as the Grandmother has signified life over death. The Grandmother's death and Uncle Jimbilly's daily life were the earliest and most intense manifestations of mortality for Miranda.

Porter chooses to follow the image of the Grandmother, dead on the doorsill with the flush of life still on her cheeks, with a physical portrait of Uncle Jimbilly that makes us wonder what keeps him alive. He is

> so old . . . he was bent almost double. His hands were closed and stiff . . . and they could not open altogether even if a child took the thick black fingers and tried to turn them back. He hobbled on a stick; his purplish skull showed through patches

in his wool, which had turned greenish gray and looked as if
the moths had got at it. (p. 340)

With his gnarled black body and his moth-eaten head, he is as much
the figure of a bogeyman as any child's imagination could create.
Although he is a handyman who makes things last by mending or
making them over, his real "gift" is for "carving miniature tombstones out of blocks of wood" (p. 340), complete with name and date.

It is a gift the children utilize frequently, because they are constantly staging full-blown funerals for the dead creatures of the farm:
"the cart draped as a hearse, a shoebox coffin with a pall over it, a
profuse floral outlay, and, of course, a tombstone" (p. 341). Miranda's
fascination with death in "The Old Order" might make her seem a
professional mourner at the bier were it not apparent that death is
the familiar of her turn-of-the-century household. In "Pale Horse,
Pale Rider," Miranda thinks of death not only "hanging about the
place," but "welcomed" by her grandfather, her great aunt, her cousin, her "decrepit hound," and her "silver kitten" (p. 270). Her mother
has died bearing her, and death frequently claims the farm animals,
who are much more familiar to Miranda than her dead mother. Although the Grandmother infuses her family like the source of life,
death takes its turn, even with her. And Uncle Jimbilly is its witness.

Born in slavery, he is fixated on that heritage in the same way
that Miranda will become fixated on hers. While carving a tombstone, he mutters "as if to himself; but he was really saying something he meant one to hear" (p. 341). He sometimes tells "incompre-
hensible" ghost stories but more often conjures the ghosts of his
collective past by dwelling on the horror stories of his slavery. He
paints sordid pictures of slaves with their backs ripped to shreds by
leather straps or tied down in the swamps to be eaten alive by mosquitoes. The grotesque violence of these stories leads Miranda to demand the truth—"Did they act like that to you, Uncle Jimbilly?"—
and Paul to name it: "Didn't they ever die, Uncle Jimbilly?" Unlike
Uncle Remus, of whom he is a caricature, Uncle Jimbilly does not
cloak the point of his slave stories in metaphor: "Cose dey died . . .
dey died . . . by de thousands and tens upon thousands." He finishes
his narrative with a strange benediction: "Yassuh, dat's it. Lawd, dey
done it. Hosanna!" (p. 342), which may be nothing more than a rhe-
torical flourish, but might serve also as a call on God to witness his
truth. Then he gruffly dismisses the children with threats and morbid tokens of his instruction: the tombstones.

One can hardly call Uncle Jimbilly anything less than the dooms-
day merchant of his world:

He was always going to do something quite horrible to somebody and then he was going to dispose of the remains in a re-
volting manner. He was going to skin somebody alive and nail
the hide on the barn door, or he was just getting ready to cut
off somebody's ears with a hatchet and pin them on Bongo, the
crop-eared brindle dog. He was often all prepared in his mind
to pull somebody's teeth and make a set of false teeth for Ole
Man Ronk. . . . (p. 342)

The detached tone of the narrator, Miranda, suggests that the children hardly think that Uncle Jimbilly will carry out his threats. He
is only the harbinger of doom—not doom itself. Their recognition of
the toothlessness of his threats also reflects the feeling that, as children, they are not much threatened by death. Uncle Jimbilly, however, is not without warning, nonetheless: ". . . some day, somebody
was going to get a mighty big surprise, and meanwhile everybody
had better look out" (p. 343). This unsubtle bullying is simply a ver-
nacular way of saying "Be prepared, for ye know not the day nor the
hour."

Although Uncle Jimbilly is obviously protesting his social status, his enslavement—for which he blames the white family which
employs him—can best be read as a metaphor. In the first place, Uncle Jimbilly is not a slave and has not been for most of his adult life.
Second, he has not been abused either as slave or servant through a
long life with this family. Third, even the children recognize that he
never has "done a single thing that anyone told him to do. He did his
work just as he pleased and when he pleased" (p. 341). And he repeats stories he has heard as he pleases, giving an ironic twist to the
title of his vignette.

What he actually bears witness to, by his own person, is not
physical abuse of slaves by their owners but the physical deterioration and certain death to which all humans are slaves. One may go
grumbling, like Uncle Jimbilly; one may suffer terribly or gradually
rot away under the stupor of drugs like Old Man Ronk; but as surely
as he lives, someday each person is "going to get a mighty big surprise," just as the Grandmother did and her survivors will—"and
meanwhile everybody had better look out" (p. 343).

"The Circus"

In an atmosphere charged with sexual symbolism, Miranda experiences two fateful impressions in "The Circus." Here the center of
consciousness is a younger, much more vulnerable Miranda who has

not yet learned to be blasé or even to distinguish fantasy from reality. Once again, however, it is important to remember that an adult Miranda is the observer and narrator who selects the components of the story and emphasizes some of them. In the first instance, attending a circus for the first time, Miranda is terrified by the image of a ghostly clown who pretends to fall from a high wire. In the second, she suffers separation and alienation from the protective circle of her family, without whom she has no identity of her own. The images which bracket these two impressions, interestingly, are as sexual as they are puzzling and threatening to Miranda, suggesting that from an early age Miranda associated her sexuality with vulnerability and destruction. In "The Circus," Porter skillfully uses a child's viewpoint and psychology to dramatize a situation which the older Miranda will follow like a paradigm: terror in the face of sex/death, escape, and survival as an alien.

The circus is a metaphor for the outside world. It is right that we should see it from Miranda's angle of perception, and it is important to note the things that mark her consciousness. From the beginning, her own insignificance is one feeling which deeply impresses Miranda and motivates her behavior. The first thing she notes in the circus tent is the "monstrous height" of the seats which stretch "dizzyingly in a wide oval ring" and are "packed with people." Of course, the proportions of the tent would seem enormous only to someone very small; Miranda is able to observe it all unafraid while she holds tightly to Dicey's familiar hand. She is reassured because her family occupies a whole section of the seating area. If the tent is huge, her family is large enough to contain a good part of it, and Miranda has the added comfort of being able to name all the familiar faces and to attract the attention of her namesake, Cousin Miranda Gay, whom she hopes to be exactly like when she grows up.

She is exhilarated because she has been included in a family trip to the circus for the first time, signaling that she is no longer a baby. However, at the same time that she wants the security and protection of the family group to assure her, she is thrilled at the prospect of experiencing something outside the familiar norm of family life. Her fevered attempt to take in everything at once reflects her excitement and gullibility, and presages the anxiety which overtakes her later.

Her first awareness of a threat occurs when she spies two urchins peering up at her from under their seats. Miranda locks gazes with them, but they return "a look so peculiar" that she cannot understand it. They are scruffy, streetwise boys who return a "bold grinning stare without any kind of friendliness in it." When Miranda points them out to Dicey, she immediately identifies them as peeping Toms by locking her knees together and pulling her skirts around her. She sternly tells Miranda to "stop throwin' yo' legs around that way" (p. 344), making it clear that the boys' curiosity is a sexual threat against which they must protect themselves. When the band "explode[s]" near her ear, she feels her senses also assaulted "as sound and color and smell rushed together and poured through her skin and hair and beat in her head and hands and feet and pit of her stomach" (p. 344). These perceptions are so overwhelming that they effectively interrupt her mental associations with her family, in effect separating her from her psychic support.

As the hurly-burly of the circus surrounds her, her awareness of self intensifies. Her perceptions are set on edge, but she is too inexperienced to judge anything accurately. When she sees the "creature in a blousy white overall . . . with bone-white skull and chalk-white face," he appears as a ghost or a cadaver might, and she is not surprised to think he may be "walking on air, or flying." If this otherworldly figure can do something birds can do, she is not upset, but when she realizes that "high above their heads the inhuman figure" (p. 344) is walking a slender wire, her perception of danger and possible destruction terrifies her. (In "Pale Horse, Pale Rider" Miranda feels herself poised on the brink of a bottomless pit which she identifies as "her childhood dream of danger" [p. 310]. Undoubtedly her fear of falling stems from this experience.) Of course, this is the psychological lever the clown uses to titillate the crowd. They identify with him in his precarious position, but they also know that ultimately he will be safe. When he slips, only to catch himself by a heel, they express their terrible thrill with a roar of "savage delight, shrieks of dreadful laughter like devils in delicious torment . . ." (p. 345).

Freud identified dreams of falling from heights as typical, and even associated them with "acrobatic feats in a circus" and sexual feelings.[9] Porter's description of the crowd's "savage delight" and "delicious torment" is particularly apt in this context, particularly if one notes Freud's additional assertion that, in women, dreams of falling "almost always" symbolize "surrender to an erotic temptation."[10]

Miranda, of course, does not know that the clown will be safe; she identifies too completely with his vulnerability. When the grotesque figure refuses to descend, taunting the crowd, turning "his head like a seal from side to side," and blowing "sneering kisses from his cruel mouth" (p. 345), he must seem totally inhuman in his ability to defy destruction and in his condescension to the mere mortals beneath him. It is too much for Miranda. When she bursts into tears, her father and grandmother casually dismiss her from the family circle. Thus she is not only separated from them in her terror, but also physically removed from the security of their presence. But she has yet another jolt.

As she is carried screaming from the tent, a dwarf, inevitably a male and a creature having phallic connotations,[11] looks at her "with kind, not-human golden eyes." She is confronted with a strange creature who is much the same size as she but who seems malevolent. Wearing a pointed cap and shoes with turned-up toes and carrying a thin white wand, the dwarf suggests a wizard who might banish Miranda's fear; instead, he intensifies her sense of separation when he makes a face at her and Miranda sees there "a look of haughty, remote displeasure, a true grown-up look." This recognition fills her with new fear, for "she had not believed he was really human" (p. 345). She has discovered in this brief venture into the outside world that it is filled with experiences and creatures which are much more powerful than herself and which she cannot hope to control. Moreover, she finds that strangers are not disposed to care for her, an even more painful knowledge when her own family sends her away. The grimace and "haughty . . . grown-up look" of the dwarf at once embody both of these unbearable separations and link them to a latent threat of sexuality.

Dicey's angry behavior, "vicious but cautious," reinforces Miranda's loneliness. When the family returns just before dark, their collectiveness increases her sense of alienation yet again. When they "troop" into the house and scatter out "all over it," one senses their number. They have shared the experience of the circus, and Miranda has been excluded through her own fault. Furthermore, she has missed an occasion made more significant by the Grandmother's presence. Miranda's silence and drooping underlip set her apart from the "illuminated faces" of the other children around the supper table. Her father says to her, "You missed it, Baby, and what good did that do you?" (p. 347)—naming her pain, calling her a baby, and underscoring her frustration. She is powerless to make any part of the afternoon's experience do her any good, just as she is powerless in the face of her overwhelming vulnerability. She bursts into tears again and has to be taken to bed.

Falling asleep over pleasant thoughts of the circus, "the sweet little furry ponies and the lovely pet monkeys in their comical clothes" (p. 347), she finds that she cannot even control her dreams: "her invented memories gave way before her real ones, the bitter terrified face of the man in blowsy white falling to his death—ah, the cruel joke!—and the terrible grimace of the unsmiling dwarf" (p.

347). Finally her experience is put in its proper context. The circus with its new knowledge has been a waking nightmare for Miranda wherein she has been forced to confront the grotesque faces of inhuman human beings whose presence in the outside world suggests alienation and destruction. With the immensity of that weighing on her, Miranda cannot bear her separation any longer. She begs Dicey not to leave her, for if she turns out the lights once more she will abandon Miranda to "the fathomless terrors of the darkness where sleep could overtake her once more" (p. 347), where the limits of the world are undefined and the phantoms of the mind ride unchecked across the heart. One cannot help but think of Granny Weatherall, and Laura.

"The Last Leaf"

In "The Last Leaf" Miranda records her first awareness of a woman functioning as something other than a mother or a coquette. Although Aunt Nannie, the family's faithful black mammy, is not someone Miranda might be expected to emulate, she is nevertheless a startling and forceful example of the fact that a woman—even in her last years—can refuse to be defined by her culture and allow her real self to emerge. Once again, Miranda must confront two apparently divergent identities in a woman close to her: the mother and the solitary independent. She must also note that it is the independent woman whose strength keeps her alive both physically and psychically.

If Uncle Jimbilly's portrait is a sober reminder of doom, the presentation of Aunt Nannie is a hymn to survival. While he is the presence of death in the lives of the grandchildren, moving about the place muttering and wraithlike, "lonely as a wandering spirit and almost as invisible . . ." (p. 350), Nannie, although prepared to die, becomes in her nonage a forceful individual whose personality seems to command respect even from death. Although she anticipates dying, particularly after parting from the Grandmother and promising to meet her in heaven, no physical death will overtake her for years. However, her old identity dies, or is perhaps subsumed in the new vital individuality she assumes.

She has been, all her life, dutiful, self-sacrificing, and maternal, using herself up in nurturing the younger generation. In that, she has been a duplicate of Sophia Jane and other women of her generation and culture. The symbiotic relationship between the Grandmother and Nannie has already been established in "The Journey"; physically and psychically Nannie is the image and likeness of Sophia:

". . . she was thin and tall also, with a nobly modeled Negro face, worn to the bone and a thick fine sooty black, no mixed blood in Nannie . . ." (p. 348). While the Grandmother is alive, Nannie is her second-in-command, her right hand, an extension of her discipline, her principles, her self. The children of the family address them both equally as "Mammy" and recognize little difference (except those incumbent on caste) between the women who have both nurtured and reared them. Like the Grandmother, Nannie is Mother, albeit a black one: she enhances our understanding of maternity in this culture, and must have kept Miranda mindful of both the slavery and tyranny of motherhood even after the Grandmother's death. Her capacity for work and self-sacrifice is her great strength, and her motherhood is the weapon with which she extracts agreement or respect. For her part, she is taken for granted by the children she serves, and she knows that their love for her is fickle, sentimental, and largely based on their dependency. When the Grandmother's death frees her individuality, she turns her back on the Old Order, breaking ties with children, husband, and her previous identity.[12] She is no longer "the faithful old servant Nannie, a freed slave," but becomes "an aged Bantu woman of independent means, sitting on the steps, breathing the free air . . ." (p. 349).

Asking for her own small house and possessions, she begins by separating herself physically from her white family, demonstrating the falsity of their sentimental assumption that she is "a real member of the family, perfectly happy with them" (p. 349). "She did not care whether they loved her or not" (p. 348), and this detachment gives her a choice between being the family's much loved and much burdened ancient, and an African sibyl whose age is her garment of wisdom. She trades black dresses and ruffled mobcaps for a blue bandanna head wrap and a corncob pipe. Instead of the housework she has always done, she braids and sells woolen rugs in her retirement. No longer content to wait on others, she is now the one who receives visits and gifts from both strangers and family. She becomes, in old age, both physically and economically independent, but her strength in her newly revealed self is demonstrated most sharply in her rejection of Uncle Jimbilly, the husband who has fathered her numerous children.

The mate decreed for her by her owners, he is first of all a remnant of her actual slavery and a reminder of the burdens of motherhood he has given her. Second, she sees him as a man, servant or not, whose sex entitled him to her service, and thus she refuses his presence in her house: "I don' aim to pass my las' days waitin on no man . . . I've served my time, I've done my do, and dat's all" (p. 351). As with her white family, she is able to stay free of servitude because she does not need the affection or the company of those who would use her, however unwittingly, in the name of custom.

More important, however, is the fact that her refusal of Uncle Jimbilly is also a refusal of death. Miranda recognizes that "there was nothing about him that suggested any connection with even the nearest future," (p. 350) and, as we have already noted, her descriptions of him inevitably suggest a ghostlike creature with his "blue mouth" and his lonely wandering. Certainly he seems to have little investment in the present moment, sleeping in the smokehouse attic and eating at odd hours in the kitchen, apart from human company. Nannie, with the solid comfort of her own cabin, her pipe, and her hard-earned ease, is right to refuse him, for their union has never renewed life for either of them, and Nannie's real identity, so lately realized, is essentially singular. She can, on occasional visits, give her efforts to her white family again, but "with a kind of satisfaction in proving to them that she had been almost indispensable" (p. 350), hardly the Nannie to whom they condescended by taking her for granted. Free of needing their love or money, Nannie can be commanded by neither whites, nor men, nor even death, for she belongs, finally, to no one but herself. A last leaf, anticipating the breeze to which she will succumb, Nannie nevertheless remains in Miranda's memory a survivor.

One last facet of this memory is worth noting. Nannie would be particularly important to Miranda because she survives the changing social order at the onset of the twentieth century. Miranda and her family can feel "the old world . . . sliding from under their feet," knowing that they have "not yet laid hold of the new one" (p. 349). Where her grandmother remains firmly entrenched in the old world, Nannie straddles the two, having been both a traditional woman and an independent one. It is appropriate that she serves as the transition figure while Miranda's consciousness is becoming more aware of independent women.

Significantly, our last image of Nannie is not that of the "aged Bantu woman of independent means" but of Nannie misusing her maternity. Miranda remembers, almost as if mentally reasserting the contrast with Nannie's new self, that "in the old days" Nannie often got her way with Harry, Miranda's father, by reminding him that she had nursed him at her breast. He always gave in to

> the smothering matriarchal tyranny to which he had been delivered by the death of his father. Still he submitted, being of that latest generation of sons who acknowledged, however re-

luctantly, however bitterly, their mystical never to be forgiven
debt to the womb that bore them, and the breast that suckled
them. (p. 351)

It is, after all, not only women who can be oppressed by familial relationships. This realization marks a shift in Miranda's perspective.

"The Fig Tree"

It is the tension of that conflict and the memory of Nannie as nursemaid that combines with her subliminal fear of death to produce the
next memory, a story of another strong woman and another kind of
survival in "The Fig Tree."

Symbolizing luck and life, the fig tree makes an interesting juxtaposition with the image of the grave which follows it in the last
story of this sequence. Once again utilizing the point of view of the
small child, Porter dramatizes pre-school-age Miranda's near hysteria when she thinks she has mistakenly buried a small chicken
alive and her joyful relief when her authoritative Great-Aunt Eliza
gives her the knowledge that erases her fear.

The first image in "The Fig Tree" functions as a transition from
the previous story about Nannie and simultaneously illustrates
what her environment is doing to Miranda's psyche. In it, the old
mammy Nannie is "gripping with her knees to hold Miranda while
she brushed her hair or buttoned her dress down the back. When Miranda wiggled, Aunt Nannie squeezed still harder, and Miranda wiggled more, but never enough to get away" (p. 352). At the behest of
Miranda's father and grandmother, Nannie is quite literally trying to
squeeze Miranda into the shape her society thinks acceptable for females: her hair is curled and confined by a rubber band; despite the
heat, her hair is "jammed" into a "freshly starched white chambray
bonnet" which covers her ears and forehead and which is itself an-
chored by a big safety pin—all so that Miranda's face will not be
"ruined" by freckles and sunburn.

Likewise, the horses are harnessed to a carriage "with boxes and
baskets tied on everywhere" (p. 352). The Grandmother walks
through the house stuffing things into the big leather bag on her
arm. Aside from the sense of containment illustrated by all this restraining and tying and stuffing, there is conflict between the Grandmother and Miranda's father, as well as the threat of continued tension in the competitive relationship between the Grandmother and
her sister Eliza.

In this confining, tense atmosphere, death is Miranda's familiar,

in spite of her ignorance about it. Dying is "something that happened all the time," to her mother and to unnumbered animals and
insects (which then demand proper burial). Clearly Miranda herself
is vulnerable. But that does not seem to frighten her. She can only
think of death in terms she knows. It means "gone away forever"; it
means a long line of slowly moving carriages and the tolling of the
bell; more specifically, it means an absence of motion. She knows
that the "sure sign" of death is an inert body, which must be quickly
buried.

Consequently, when she finds a dead chicken in the fig grove,
she rushes to bury it before they leave. She is horrified to hear a
voice calling "weep, weep" from the grave just as her family calls to
leave for the farm. Caught in a smothering environment, Miranda
understands that the bird is being stifled and projects her own fear of
being buried alive onto the chicken in its "proper" grave. She cries
hysterically when she must leave.

When they finally arrive in the country, new confusions await
Miranda in the shape of her Great-Aunt Eliza, an impressive woman
who will leave an indelible image on Miranda's psyche and forever
change what she might wish to be. Coming from her Grandmother-
dominated world, Miranda is accustomed to an insistence on lady-
like behavior and propriety, to value being placed on feminine beauty,
and to the utter necessity for controlling one's instincts and personal
desires. Great-Aunt Eliza literally turns that world topsy-turvy.

Whereas Grandmother was the pretty sister, pristinely thin and
pale with white hair, Great-Aunt Eliza has never been pretty, and so
has been able to be herself—something more closely resembling a
great bear:

> Great-Aunt Eliza loomed like a mountain with her grizzled
> iron-colored hair like a curly wig, her steel-rimmed spectacles
> over her snuff-colored eyes, and snuff-colored woolen skirts
> billowing about her, and her smell of snuff. When she came
> through the door she quite filled it up. When she sat down the
> chair disappeared under her, and she seemed to be sitting sol-
> idly on herself from her waistband to the floor. (p. 359)

Clearly the things which overwhelm Miranda are two ineradicable
and unladylike facts: Great-Aunt Eliza is huge; and Great-Aunt Eliza
dips snuff. Yet, however novel these incidental details might be for
Miranda, they are not the reasons she continues to be fascinated by
her unusual relative. Great-Aunt Eliza, after all, is not a circus freak;
she is Grandmother's sister and shares important character traits
with Miranda, who is always "watching and listening—for every-

thing in the world was strange to her and something she had to know about . . ." (p. 359). The same description might easily characterize Eliza, for when she

> was not on the roof before her telescope, always just before
> daylight or just after dark, she was walking about with a mi-
> croscope and a burning glass, peering closely at something she
> found in the grass; now and then she collected fragments that
> looked like dried leaves or bits of bark, brought them in the
> house, spread them out on a sheet of white paper, and sat
> there, poring, as still as if she were saying her prayers. (p. 360)

Miranda, "one who sees," spends all her time at the farm staring in fascination at Great-Aunt Eliza, who in turn is staring at something else; Miranda forgets the chickens and kittens she loves to pet and feed (which are, incidentally, nurturing habits) in favor of following her aunt about, "gazing, or sitting across the dining-table gazing . . ." (p. 360). Surely the fragments known as "The Old Order" are the im- ages Miranda has gleaned from a childhood of gazing, which she here spreads on a sheet of white paper.

Added to this natural affinity she has for her elder is the fascina- tion Miranda feels in seeing, for the first time, that there is someone who does not agree with Grandmother, who refuses to recognize her authority, and who, furthermore, is capable of making Grandmother quibble like a schoolgirl and even blush. At the end of their squab- bles Eliza always seems the victor, because having no embarrass- ment for anything she does, she can remain unruffled by her sister's objections to her behavior.

Most important, Eliza in her intellectual curiosity and un- abashed self-confidence momentarily replaces the influence of Mi- randa's all-important Grandmother. The Grandmother, heavily pres- ent in the early scenes of the story, recedes, and is totally absent at Miranda's intellectual initiation. It is appropriate that Eliza play Prospero to Miranda's naïveté, that she be the one to turn Miranda's eyes outward to the stars. Seeing through the telescope the "great pale flaring disk of cold light" which she knows is the moon, Mi- randa exclaims, "Oh, it's like another world!" (p. 361). She is in "rap- ture" and "dazzled by joy" as they walk back through the fig grove "much like the one in town." As Miranda touches a low-hanging branch for luck, she hears again "weep, weep" coming from the ground, and we are returned to the moment of panic in the other fig grove beside a small grave. But this time Great-Aunt Eliza assuages her fear and plants the seeds of another revelation for Miranda's ma- turity: " 'Hear them?' she said. 'They're not in the ground at all.

They are the first tree frogs, means it's going to rain,' she said, 'weep weep'—hear them?'" (p. 361). Walking on, hand-in-hand with Great-Aunt Eliza, Miranda hears the music of the spheres in those small voices. That small explanation is wonder enough to Miranda, but her next comment will germinate so that the adult Miranda can realize its greater significance:

> "Just think," said Great-Aunt Eliza . . . "when tree frogs shed
> their skins, they pull them off over their heads like little
> shirts, and they eat them. Can you imagine? They have the
> prettiest little shapes you ever saw—I'll show you one some-
> time under the microscope." (pp. 361–362)

Eliza's final gift on this evening of epiphanies is a telescopic view of the cycle of life, which is caught and held by Miranda in "The Grave." The tree frogs shedding their skins is an image of death, since it recalls Miranda's earlier musing about "lizards on rocks turned into shells, with no lizard inside at all" (p. 354). But it is also an image of rebirth, because they are new again as they emerge from the old skin. In this sense, death is only a part of a cycle, an ever-changing process of destruction and renewal. Thus the earth does not smother, it secretes; and death is not an end but a becoming.

The symbolism of the fig tree supports this idea. It is certainly primal, held by some to be the tree from which Adam and Eve ate the forbidden fruit and by others the tree from which they took leaves to clothe themselves after they sinned. In either case it is one part of the story of how human beings first moved from innocence and ignorance to knowledge, as Miranda does in this story. In the pre-Christian world, the fig tree was sacred to Bacchus, god of wine and fertility; thus knowledge and life coexist in its symbolism, although neither tradition would have said that one necessitated the other. Finally, there is the description of the fig grove at home, which is "very dark and shady," a cavelike place suggesting the subconscious, where Miranda confronts death and guilt and must perform a ritual burial, just as she represses fears and rebellions. In the last analysis, sweet abundance is held before her, and her consignment of the dead to the earth vindicated. But the fullness of meaning for all these images remains to be realized in "The Grave."

"The Grave"

In "The Grave," all the ghosts of the Old Order are gathered up and Miranda begins to understand what ancestry will require of her. In a paradigm of the separation from the bosom of her family that she will eventually achieve, this story focuses on the removal of several caskets from the family graveyard, which are then laid to rest "for eternity" in a public cemetery. After the coffins have been disinterred from the farm's graveyard, Miranda and her brother Paul play in the empty trenches and find treasure in the pungent soil, a legacy from their dead ancestors. Later, Paul shoots a rabbit, and together they discover tiny fetuses in the dead rabbit's womb.

Once again the mysteries of birth and death revolve around the matrix of sex; the conjunction of these creates an epiphany so fearsome to nine-year-old Miranda that she will repress it for many years. Once again a story is a window on a psychological trauma, although most readings emphasize the initiation itself and ignore the fact that the adult Miranda remembers the experience only with horror and dread. "The Grave" focuses on Miranda's stifled fears about her womanhood, raising a simple story about sexual knowledge to the social and philosophical level, as Cleanth Brooks has pointed out.[13] On the social level, we can observe again a fragile, traditional femininity approved by Miranda's society warring with the sturdy individualism in Miranda's psyche. Sex complicates this struggle. Miranda's dim awareness of sexuality and fertility among the farm animals expands to include an understanding of the reproduction of human life. For both her and Paul, birth is a forbidden knowledge. After carelessly intruding on this mystery they both feel guilt and shame. But Miranda is not traumatized until her quick mind sees the link between her femaleness and the precarious, bloody ritual of birth. Giving life means risking death. This is her true legacy from her grandmother and her society.

The personal story related here achieves philosophical significance because it parallels Adam and Eve's archetypal fall from innocence in the Garden of Eden. Miranda's first sexual knowledge is not only forbidden and shocking, but carries with it guilt and the danger of expulsion as well as the sure knowledge of her own mortality. Remembering that some ethnic versions of Genesis make the sin of Adam and Eve a sexual one, we can better appreciate how the primal images here create the story of one young girl's repulsion at sexual knowledge or ultimately the story of male/female disaffection.[14]

The use of symbols which invoke simultaneously—and often ironically—all three levels of meaning is, as always, deft. The central symbol of the grave is a good example. It is, of course, a burial place and most often associated with death. However, placed in context with the death of the pregnant rabbit, the grave is also a womb, suggesting a beginning rather than an end. It connotes not only burying, but the possibility of unburying, of resurrecting. This becomes particularly significant in its third meaning, for the grave also suggests the subconscious, where Miranda constantly buries and unburies her secrets and fears.

Aside from the overriding significance of the grave as symbol, Porter uses the Eden archetype to underscore the primal importance of the children's experience in the graveyard. First of all, the story begins with one of the narrator's infrequent references to her grandfather, whose bones her grandmother has unearthed three times to ensure that they will be buried together. It is the only time we are reminded that Miranda is descended from a male as well as a female ancestor. This pairing reminds us therefore that "male and female He created them," as does the pairing of Miranda and her brother Paul as they play in the open graves. In every other mention of Miranda's siblings, her older sister Maria is also included. Maria's absence from the graveyard reinforces the pairing essential to the continuation of life.

In addition, the cemetery is secluded, a small plot "in a corner" of their grandmother's first farm. It is a pleasant if neglected "garden of tangled rose bushes and ragged cedar trees and cypress, [and] uncropped sweet-smelling wild grass" (p. 362), Edenic in an unpretentious way. The earth smells "sweet" and "corrupt," suggesting not barrenness and death, but fruitfulness and continued life, which the children also represent, as the second generation to issue from the dead whose graves they play in. The children are themselves ignorant of the potency of the earth and find the graves rather commonplace: "when the coffin was gone a grave was just a hole in the ground" (p. 363).

Nevertheless, Miranda and Paul find silver and gold in these graves, in the form of a dove-shaped coffin screw head and a gold wedding band, "carved with intricate flowers and leaves," redolent of the peace and natural beauty which is the real value of the garden graveyard. Miranda and Paul echo the first man and woman, too, in that they owned the garden formerly, but no longer do. Thus, when they pocket their talismans, Miranda suggests they ought to leave before somebody sees them and tells; feeling like trespassers where they were once at home, they quit the place to hunt.

The act of hunting joins the Edenic images in the first part of the story and the sexual symbolism that occurs throughout. The earth, of course, is nurturing and feminine, and the open graves in the fecund soil suggest the womb, as we have noted. When Miranda and Paul leap in and out of the holes, they unwittingly mimic the birth they have received from the ancestors whose bones have rested in the graves.

They are equally unaware of the role identity they exhibit in claiming the treasure they have found in the graves. Paul is "more impressed" with the silver dove Miranda has unearthed, while she is "smitten" by the thin gold ring he has found. His choice of the dove "with spread wings" associates him with the free flight of the bird and the hunt, since doves are one of the prey the children seek. Ambiguity of image is again utilized here since it is live birds that ordinarily entice Paul, but the silver dove he claims is not only without life itself, it is a death emblem, a screw head for a coffin.[15] Significantly, it is as lifeless as the doves Paul will shoot if he can find them.

The Winchester rifles the children carry are phallic, and the use of them an indicator of masculine potency. Paul has had more experience with the rifle, and Miranda defers to him. He wants a shot at the first dove or rabbit they see; and evoking simultaneously the primacy of Eden and the phallus, Miranda responds, "What about snakes? . . . Can I have the first snake?"

Miranda's inadequacy with the rifle ensures that she is no threat to Paul's masculinity; it demonstrates as well that her tomboyishness is not a pervasive masculinity. On the contrary, her desire for the gold ring and the fact that it fits her thumb perfectly suggest just the opposite. Miranda is a female through and through, although her appearance—in a period and culture which set store by appearance—might suggest otherwise. The overalls, shirt, and sandals she wears for play are identical to her brother's. She and her sister are accustomed to riding bareback astride their horses. All this seems agreeable and comfortable to Miranda since her father approves.

But her "powerful social sense, which was like a fine set of antennae radiating from every pore of her skin" (p. 365) makes her feel ashamed when she recognizes that her tomboy clothing shocks the old women who respected her grandmother—even if the clothes are practical and comfortable, and the old women themselves backbiting hypocrites. This is perhaps the clearest statement in Porter's fiction of the paradoxical emotions behind Miranda's warring impulses: Grandmother and her social standards can inflict shame even in the face of a rational understanding that a new standard makes more sense.

Now with the gold ring on her dirty thumb, she is linked to everything it symbolizes: the unbroken circle suggests the preciousness of her virginity as well as the security, love, and honor she will derive from a respectable marriage. She wishes to put aside her overalls in favor of a totally impractical—but ideal—femininity: "She wanted to go back to the farmhouse, take a good cold bath, dust herself with plenty of Maria's violet talcum powder . . . put on the thinnest, most becoming dress she owned, with a big sash, and sit in a wicker chair under the trees . . ." (p. 365). It is perhaps because her reverie is interrupted at precisely this point that the climactic moment has such an impact for her. In the next instant Paul kills a rabbit precipitously and with one shot. Miranda's romantic image is supplanted by the realistic one of Paul with a phallic knife, expertly skinning the rabbit's bloated, pregnant body. Miranda is too naïve to consciously register that a male has killed this special rabbit, but the point is not lost on her unconscious mind. Even if rabbits were not fertility symbols, the image of the tiny fetuses, "dark gray, their sleek wet down lying in minute even ripples, like a baby's head just washed, their unbelievably small delicate ears folded close, their little blind faces almost featureless" (p. 366), would be sufficient to suggest burgeoning life aborted.

Accustomed to seeing dead animals, Miranda reacts as she does to Great-Aunt Eliza's telescope: "She looked and looked . . . filled with pity and astonishment and a kind of shocked delight in the wonderful little creatures for their own sakes, they were so pretty" (p. 366). However, her reaction shifts abruptly and without explanation when she sees that "there's blood running over them." In that moment of pity and fear, she sees the tragic implications of birth. She begins to tremble with a new insight, understanding at once "a little of the secret, formless intuitions in her own mind and body," understanding distantly that the female prize she has wished to be could not remain dressed in organdy and seated in a wicker chair; she would be claimed in marriage to bear bloody babies who are sometimes aborted and who sometimes bring death to their mother, even as they seize life for themselves.

The story does not state that Miranda remembers the death of her own mother in childbirth, but certainly she recognizes for the first time the blood rites of womanhood, even though she does not recognize words like menstruation, intercourse, and parturition. She feels "terribly agitated" and, significantly, has taken the masculine rifle again under her arm. Whereas the fetuses were before "wonderful little creatures," they are now a "bloody heap." Miranda wants nothing to do with the rabbit skin, a prize she usually claims. Paul, whose guilt already shows in his voice, makes a grave of the mother's body for the young and furtively hides them all away. At last he makes a secret of what they have seen, adding to Miranda's agitation the sense that they have trespassed.

She worries, is confused and unhappy, and then finally represses the experience until, twenty years later, she is halted in a foreign marketplace by a vendor carrying a tray of sugar sweets shaped like baby rabbits. It triggers the image of that earlier sight and, we are told, she is "reasonlessly horrified" by the "dreadful vision," lest we doubt the psychological shock of the original experience. In repressing her earlier memory, Miranda has refused to relinquish her ghost; and, failing that, she has not been able to exorcise it.

Her reasonless horror is finally dissolved by the thought that she and Paul had, that day, "found treasure in the opened graves" (p. 367). But it is not the gold ring which hangs in her mind's eye nearly twenty years later. It is the image of Paul, his face lit by the sun, full of potency and possibility, handling the silver dove which was hers first, before she ignorantly traded it away.

This time she trades her ignorance, reclaiming the dove in its positive image: the spirit's ability to fly free. With that knowledge, Miranda expects to resurrect her own freedom, but even more complex epiphanies await her.

6 ❖ *Face to Face*

"Old Mortality"

"Old Mortality" completes the story of Miranda's role models. As Jane Flanders has noted, Miranda's Aunt Amy and her Cousin Eva, who dominate the story, have equal, if different, reasons for repudiating the Old Order.[1] Their experiences demonstrate that to be a legendary beauty like Amy in such a society one must sacrifice freedom, and even life. To be independent, a bluestocking, and a suffragist like Eva is to become ossified in bitterness. Part of the point of the story is that everybody in the family has long since decided what to think about Amy and Eva. The only person who has not is the one still capable of learning something about them: Miranda. Behind the history of these women is the curious, quizzical figure of Miranda, sifting and balancing, from the vantage point of adulthood, what she knew when she was eight, then ten, and finally eighteen. It is not Amy's life but Miranda's heritage that one learns about in the three segments of time which end with Miranda's promise to herself to find her own truth, made "in her hopefulness, her ignorance" (p. 221). Those last two words are the judgment of the older narrator on eighteen-year-old Miranda's limited view, just as they are the reader's clue that "Old Mortality" is a fiction of memory in a double sense: it is the memory of her forebears, but it is also Miranda's memory of what she has been and, therefore, what she has become.[2]

In Part I of the story, Miranda is portrayed as easily seduced by romantic illusion. It is her practical-minded sister, Maria, who disabuses her of her notions. Intent on knowing the truth, even at an early age, Miranda is hampered by her childish credulousness. As an eight-year-old, she is most susceptible to every sentiment and every bit of romantic claptrap that her society is capable of. She listens to the adults around her, consuming everything they say. At the same time, however, she always wonders what they mean, since her interpretation of family events is very much at odds with the interpretation the family places on them. When, for instance, Miranda's father announces that "There were never any fat women in the family, thank God," Miranda thinks immediately of Great-Aunt Eliza's huge frame and Great-Aunt Keziah, who weighs 220 pounds. Later she will be old enough to recognize that

> something seemed to happen to their father's memory when he thought of the girls he had known in the family of his youth, and he declared steadfastly they had all been, in every generation without exception, as slim as reeds and graceful as sylphs. (p. 174)

In truth, something seems to happen to the memory of all the members of this society when they think of their past: "their hearts and imaginations were captivated by their past," which is far more significant to them than the everyday world of the present. The Grandmother, who sits all day making memory quilts with Nannie, feels "twice a year compelled in her blood" to sit by her old trunks "crying gently and easily" over faded finery, pictures, and mementoes. The elderly relative who heard Rubinstein play frequently in the past finds Paderewski lacking in the present. However, it is not just the past but emotion and sentiment that captivate the whole family, and the story of Gabriel's unrequited love for Amy is the family's favorite—and collective—legend.

What Porter says but does not stress is that this family is Southern. Not only do they revere their past, they aggrandize it in a manner that suggests Twain was right when he accused Walter Scott's medieval romances of starting the Civil War. Miranda looks at pictures of the young men "in their high buttoned coats, their puffy neckties, their waxed mustaches, their waving thick hair combed carefully over their foreheads" and thinks no one could have taken them seriously. However, these same young men are romanticized into chivalric heroes whose nobility of purpose defines the whole race. Furthermore, while their eyes and ears tell them that Cousin Molly Parrington's charm is aggressive, bold, and sometimes even cruel or shocking, their imaginations assure them that their women are unequaled not only in their beauty and desirability, but in their purity, gentility, and sensibility. They are the fair virgins of a society whose virtue they both embody and inspire. In actuality, Amy's circumstances combine the poetry and tragedy Miranda's family love with their personal history; their pleasure in Amy's story is like the eight-year-old Miranda's pleasure in thinking what it would be like "to have the assassination of Lincoln in the family" (p. 180).

Similar in structure to "The Old Order," "Old Mortality" is a pastiche of memories, details, and emotions, "floating ends of narrative" which Maria and Miranda patch together as well as they can, the "fragments of tales that were like bits of poetry or music . . ."

(p. 176). And like the memories of the Old Order, they have been "packed away and forgotten for a great many years" (p. 193). It is ostensibly Amy's story, told from a number of points of view, but all is sifted through Miranda's perception. In actuality, the chronology of the story belongs to Miranda, and the tale depends primarily on what she will do with the legend of Amy and the bitter reality of Cousin Eva.

If "The Old Order" is a catalogue of the "giants" of Miranda's childhood who taught her what a woman might be, "Old Mortality" is the story of Miranda's confrontation with the most formidable archetype her society can offer: the Southern belle, a nineteenth-century American manifestation of the virgin love goddess.

Obviously, Amy was once a person who has now become a legend; she was "beautiful, much loved, unhappy, and she . . . died young." The mystery in her behavior encourages others to speculate aloud about her and the meaning of her actions. Enigmatic, devilish, magnetic to men, she has also been capricious, toying with Gabriel's affection, agreeing to marry two other men, and then subsequently breaking those engagements without reason. She has been the cause of a near duel and her brother Harry's flight to Mexico; and yet she never offers an explanation of the affair. Finally, after dismissing Gabriel summarily, she whimsically agrees to marry him when he is disinherited. Her family says good-bye to her after her wedding, and six weeks later she is dead, perhaps by suicide.

A more romantic and tragic combination of circumstances is not to be imagined, conjuring as they do the likes of Juliet, Madame Bovary, and Anna Karenina. Then too, Amy is a dark lady—not only Shakespeare's, but Hawthorne's, and certainly Poe's—with more sensuousness and dangerous allure than virginity would ordinarily allow.

Amy's physical beauty supposedly corresponds in every detail to her family's standard of female perfection:

> First, a beauty must be tall; whatever color the eyes, the hair must be dark, the darker the better; the skin must be pale and smooth. Lightness and swiftness of movement were important points. A beauty must be a good dancer, superb on horseback, with a serene manner, an amiable gaiety tempered with dignity at all hours. Beautiful teeth and hands, of course, and over and above all this, some mysterious crown of enchantment that attracted and held the heart. (p. 176)

But it is interesting that Miranda, studying the old-fashioned portrait of Amy with her cropped hair and "reckless smile," is left wondering what was so enticing about this compelling girl, about whom everything and nothing was known. The obvious implication is that Amy was in reality a young woman whose graces and physical charms have been exaggerated by the family, who take more pleasure in the reflected glory they receive from their relationship to this angelic mystery than they do in the accuracy of their descriptions. There is undoubtedly some of that, but there is also the persistent fact that Amy really was a charmer, with at least two other suitors who wanted to marry her. There is something more to Amy's dark beauty than an appealing prettiness. A less romantic generation would reject the term "crown of enchantment" and call it sex appeal, but it is not quite the simple matter Cousin Eva makes it, either, when she describes Victorian mating rituals as "just sex." Amy's allure is rather a complex combination of sublimated sexual energy, real allure, and personal restraint.

Like Laura in "Flowering Judas," Amy appears to be a very distinct personality who has made her choices and insists on self-determination despite the efforts of others to influence her. In actuality, however, she is, like Laura, a very ambivalent personality confronted by a now familiar dichotomy: the choice between being a sexual coquette or marrying to become a mother. The lessons of her society for young unmarried females are contained not only in their code of female beauty, but in the more concrete example of the behavior of Miranda's father toward his daughters:

> [He] held his daughters on his knee if they were prettily
> dressed and well behaved, and pushed them away if they had
> not freshly combed hair and nicely scrubbed fingernails. "Go
> away, you're disgusting," he would say. (p. 184)

Amy has long since assimilated these lessons and mastered them; in fact, if her family is to be believed, she has raised coquetry to a high art, learning not only to display her beauty, but to flaunt her sexuality while forbidding intimacy. While she probably has little understanding of sex as a physical act, she intuitively recognizes that her physical attributes attract men and that she can entice with impunity, even irresponsibility, as long as she retains her virginity. While her family acts as if she has no control over the way men respond to her, Amy herself understands and relishes the power this gives her.

Holding the prize in abeyance as long as possible allows Amy a fleeting personal autonomy she doesn't want to relinquish. She insists that she doesn't want to marry anybody, saying she prefers to be a "nice old maid like Eva Parrington." Her Uncle Bill, referring to

Eva's political activity, casually puts a finger on the sexual nature of the courtship game: "When women haven't anything else, they'll take a vote for consolation. A pretty thin bed-fellow." Significantly, Amy responds: "What I really need is a good dancing partner to guide me through life" (p. 183), which is perhaps a wish for a strong man who will make less fearsome her plunge into sexual experience. This meaning is well illustrated by the Mardi Gras party and the "scandal" which ensues after Amy's tryst there with a former fiancé.

A time of revelry and chaos preceding the mourning and fasting of Lent, Mardi Gras sets the tone for Amy's brush with sexual and social disaster. Her costume for the fancy-dress ball is a carefully copied shepherdess outfit, which underscores the *carpe diem* atmosphere, complete with low-cut bodice, short skirts which reveal her ankles, and rouge on her cheeks. Amy's father throws a fit and declares her outfit "bawdy," while, significantly, her mother sees "nothing wrong with it" and chides her husband for using "such language before innocent young girls" (p. 185). Having been a belle herself, Amy's mother recognizes that her daughter's sex appeal is one of the few cards she has to play in the courtship game. Gabriel, attired to please Amy, looks like the sentimental fop he is in a blue satin shepherd's costume and curled beribboned wig. He is no match, much less a guide, for Amy's overt sexuality, and as the other young men swarm to her like flies to a honey pot, Gabriel is hardly able to dance with her at all.

In stark contrast to Gabriel, Raymond, a former fiancé of Amy's, arrives late and alone, with all the air of a nocturnal lover come in over his lady's balcony. He appears as the daring pirate Jean Lafitte and boldly takes Amy's attention from the others. After a sojourn with Raymond on the gallery, she waltzes by "with a young man in a Devil costume, including ill-fitting scarlet cloven hoofs" (p. 187), a costume which stresses Amy's attraction to sin, passion, and a satyr-inspired sex, and the ultimate irony of her own arcadian attire.

The foils to Amy's particular brand of womanliness are only subtly characterized. Mariana, Harry's bride-to-be and eventually the mother of Miranda, projects none of Amy's sauciness, despite the fact that she wears Mexican dress, from a country where the women are said to be spitfires. Maria and Miranda remember a picture of their mother: "her lovely face without a trace of coquetry looking gravely out from under a tremendous fall of lace from the peak of the comb, a rose tucked firmly over her ear" (pp. 184–185). It is Mariana who should be wearing the simple shepherdess costume and Amy who should portray the sultry Mexican. However, part of Amy's appeal lies in the fact that although she aggressively displays her sexuality,

she puts a demure mask over it; she has some of the same tantaliz-
ing air as a Lolita: a naïf with a smoldering appetite.

She is hardly "sweet and gay and decorous" as her second foil—
her own mother—was when she was courted. Her mother, who has
found identity in nurturing, tries to tell Amy "that marriage and
children would cure her of everything" (p. 182). But offspring are not
the end she looks for; neither is marriage itself or even a particular
man. Amy's disguised sexual anxiety and wish for personal autonomy are not desires she can name herself. She knows only an intense
longing and a nagging anticipation of death which implies both the
futility of her desires within her social structure ("Mammy, I'm not
long for this world") and the physical destruction she anticipates. A
woman born to a society which saw her father as her protector until
a husband took over that necessary role, Amy is protected to a degree which destroys personal privacy, to say nothing of individuality
or initiative. The fact that she cannot momentarily leave her social
group in the company of a man without stirring up scandal, even to
the outer reaches of her community, is proof of her confinement.

It is significant, too, that although Amy curries the favor of her
brothers and undoubtedly practices feminine wiles on her suitors,
"she would not listen to her father, nor to Gabriel" (p. 183), the two
men most intent on ruling her in this life. Her response is unequivo-
cal. She ignores her father's demands that she wear a more modest
costume to the Mardi Gras ball, and when Gabriel praises her long
hair, she cuts it short both to assert her independence of his image of
her and to divest herself of a demure femininity that seems oppressive to her. Significantly, when Gabriel accuses her of having been
kissed by Raymond, she insists that he was merely complimenting
her on her hair. Her pleasure in a compliment like that is, ironically,
a greater infidelity to Gabriel than a stolen kiss—very likely an im-
pulsive gesture.

Gabriel, in his doglike devotion, is an encumbrance to Amy—
and not only because his courtship represents a serious threat to her
virginity. Since she cannot be a belle without the attentions of a
swain, however, her victimizer becomes a victim of the sentimental
society which glamorizes these roles. While her beauty is legendary,
in the best tradition of courtly love, beauty must be praised in song
and service to be considered noteworthy. Amy's legend is at least
partly dependent on the fervor of Gabriel's courtship: the presents,
flowers, telegrams, and defense of her honor are all the concrete
proof of her desirability. In truth, Gabriel plays the Southern knight
so well that he continues the role years after Amy's death, compos-

ing sentimental poetry to her memory and supervising the carving of her tombstone even after he has taken a new wife.

For her part, Amy cultivates her dramatic image, calling herself "the heroine of this novel" (p. 189). She chooses to marry Gabriel only after he is disinherited, and then tells him they must be wed before Mardi Gras because after Lent "it may be too late." For her wedding day she disdains the colorlessness and the connotations of white satin; she does not wish to look pale, angelic, bridelike, or pure, and chooses instead an individualistic gown of silver gray silk. The wintry gray of her costume is unbroken except for a "dark red breast of feathers" on her gray velvet hat, which suggests the mortal wound which is her illness, and her marriage, and her womanhood—and which she herself seems to intend: "I shall wear mourning if I like," she tells her mother, "it is *my* funeral, you know" (p. 182).

Her one letter home illustrates that she has not changed, despite her statement that she is now "a staid old married woman." On the contrary, she goes to the races daily and delights in the successes of their horses. She wants to take to the streets during Mardi Gras because she is tired of "watching the show from a balcony." Like Laura, she covets excitement. Gabriel will be her escort in the frenzied streets of the carnival if she can convince him to descend, but he "says it isn't safe." Remembering her wish for a good dancing partner to guide her through life, one cannot help but note this symbolic allusion to Gabriel's insufficiency as a husband. He has always lacked boldness and masculinity in Amy's eyes, and his ineffectual behavior at the first Mardi Gras ball as well as his reluctance to become part of the new chaos on his honeymoon suggest he is at least a reluctant or an inept lover, and very possibly an intimidated one. Amy's reiterated insistence that Gabriel is "dull" makes it clear that he is no real threat to her virginity. But a man like Raymond is, not only because he is more aggressive than Gabriel, but because Amy finds him sexually exciting. Fearing the experience of sex itself and the potential rowdiness of her own sexuality, Amy has broken her engagement to Raymond, ultimately choosing a safer Gabriel.

Why, then, does she choose to marry at all? It may be that, anticipating her death, she leaps into chaos (or certainly a world of excitement, if not frenzy); she chooses the only opportunity she has to marry quickly and experience the worldly pleasure of sex symbolized by New Orleans with its races, the parades and balls of Mardi Gras, and the "dashing" dress she chooses to wear to the Proteus Ball. It could be also that in marrying Gabriel she does not relinquish her virginity at all, since he will do anything to please her, and this leaves her psychologically free to flirt and act the part of the unmarried belle in her new gown. A third and more complicated possibility is that the confinement and restriction of her training has effected a psychology in her which values restraint more than any other physical reality. Thus even if she consummates her marriage to Gabriel, her psychic detachment from intercourse allows her to think of herself as inviolate because she has not been excited by it. Physically she may not be a virgin, but emotionally and psychologically she is intact. Thus her marriage to Gabriel would be a real rejection of sexual participation and experience, and she could continue her pattern of sexual display and restraint. True to her anticipation, six weeks after her wedding—exactly the length of Lent, which, ironically, ends in the celebration of resurrected life—Amy is dead of a combination of consumption and medicinal overdose.

The whole issue of Amy's illness and death is a compelling and complex subject. Her death and its romantic significance to the family is well established before Amy's illness is even mentioned, and her problem is never named in specific terms. Her mother assures her that all the women of their family suffered delicacy and all survived; she adds that "young girls found a hundred ways to deny they wished to be married . . ." (p. 183). The conjunction of these two conditions suggests first that this delicacy is a fear of the sexual reality of marriage, for that is the only illness that can be cured by marriage and children:

> I tried to tell her once more . . . that marriage and children
> would cure her of everything. . . . "Why when I was your age
> no one expected me to live a year. It was called greensickness,
> and everybody knew there was only one cure." (p. 182)

Only as a virgin is she "green," a sexual novice. After marriage and birth, a woman is initiated into sexual mysteries and is thereby "cured" of her illness—that is, her fears. Of course, Amy's malady is not so readily assuaged. She has tuberculosis, a debilitating, and, in Amy's day, often fatal disease. Metaphorically, however, her consumption, which forces her to go to bed and to expel blood from her body, suggests menstruation—which in the past has been called "the curse" by many women. Conversely, of course, "curse" describes consumption. Tuberculosis was also thought to enhance the beauty of its victim, since under its influence the eyes sparkled with fever and spots of color appeared in the cheeks, just as menstruation is a sign of physical maturity, which makes a female more sexually appealing. Thus, symbolically, Amy's illness must represent her womanhood, a biological and social handicap to a free spirit.

Each of the three attacks she experiences during the last year of her life occurs after some breach of feminine restraint on her part. The first serious illness is brought on by her three-day ride to the Mexican border; the second occurs after she stays up all night dancing three times in one week; and the third results from her round of races and Mardi Gras parties in New Orleans. It is blood that keeps her in bounds, and when she steps beyond the bounds of her feminine role, she pays in blood. Should she marry and bear children, she will pay in blood anyway. She is the ultimate portrait of a woman in suspension. It is supremely ironic that the only outspoken "feminist" in the family, Eva, who crusades for female suffrage, is Amy's harshest critic, with no sympathy for Amy, who is suffocating in her confined role.

It is Eva who in her bitter jealousy can only see Amy as a "bad, wild girl" who was "*too free*" and who was "sex-ridden" and "festering." She provides a warped kind of balance to the romantic image of Amy, and she focuses attention on Amy's enigmatic death. Eva implies that Amy was pregnant by another man when she married Gabriel and that she killed herself "to escape some disgrace . . ." (p. 214). In her rage to hang infamy on Amy's memory, Eva ignores the obvious facts that, once Amy had a husband, she could bear a child without "disgrace" or "exposure" and that Amy was one who sought the public eye rather than avoided it. Eva is projecting her own feelings, perhaps, but she has no understanding of Amy as a person and reacts only to what Amy represents.

Amy would not commit suicide to avoid scandal; but would she commit suicide to fulfill an image she has of herself? It is both possible and characteristic that, recognizing the limited options she has, she chooses a last whirl around the dance floor, a last moment of gaiety and glory and then rings down the curtain on her own role. Unable to choose how she will live, she chooses instead the way she will die. Instead of fading into a ragged oblivion, she dramatically snuffs out her life (whether by accident or design) so that her beauty and mystery are etched in the memory: "She ran into the gray cold . . . and called out 'Good-by, good-by!' . . . And none of us ever saw her alive again" (p. 176).

It is possible that Amy inadvertently took an overdose of medication, although she doesn't appear to have ever done anything else inadvertently. Her consistently fatalistic outlook suggests she knows she will die young. It is also possible that she is pregnant by her husband and that, recognizing that she can no longer retain her independence, she kills herself in a direct refusal to share her life or her identity with a child. Does she intuit or intend her death? Ultimately it doesn't really matter—her "prophetic" remarks may even be the interpolation of the family mythmakers. What does matter, to Miranda especially, is that her end is death. Although she is beautiful, much loved, sought after, and greatly desired—although she marries as she should—she still dies young. Although she marries with detachment and with no unseemly passion in it, she is still struck down. As to the cause, she is at least weakened by her disease, in both its physical and its symbolic sense. She is handicapped by a weakened constitution and by a sexuality she cannot come to terms with; perhaps the point is not so much that these conditions cause her death but that in the face of them she cannot live.

Ordinarily, a Porter story would end here with a death of a kind visited on a woman ill equipped to get out of its way. But the story is as much Miranda's as it is Amy's, and the second and third parts bring her back into focus, partly by extending the imagery of Amy's experience to Miranda and Maria. Like Amy, they feel "hedged and confined" by a conventional life in their boarding school. Like her, they suffer a constant surveillance by their chaperones, the nuns, and find their lives incredibly "dull" except for Saturday afternoon trips to the races, where excitement reigns.

The symbolic value of the horses to which this family is devoted is one of the significant links between Parts I and II and between Amy and Miranda. Amy loves to ride and uses horses as a vehicle for excitement and adventure. The races in New Orleans relieve her boredom and furnish her delight when one of their horses wins. More important, however, the way family members use their horses is indicative of their stature as human beings. The family has always enjoyed owning and racing horses, but among gentlemen this is a pursuit of pleasure, not a livelihood. The first inkling Miranda has that Gabriel is less than his legend lies in the episode in which he and his grandfather quarrel over his racehorses. His grandfather fears he will be a wastrel who will use his horses to make a living, and his fear is prophetic; it foreshadows Gabriel's decline and Miranda's disillusionment in Part II.[3] However, these details are only transitions to the large meaning of "Old Mortality."

In Part II, romance opens outward and the real issues of the whole story begin to take shape. Maria and Miranda, now fourteen and ten, are separated from their family circle in a convent school in New Orleans. Their romantic, penny-dreadful image of themselves does not mask the fact that they are about to experience an initiation. They are already in the midst of the first classic stage of rites of passage: separation from their communal circle. They allude to an actual initiation ceremony, the taking of the veil; the familiar image of burial, with an expected resurrection and rebirth, is suggested by the word "immured," which the girls delight in applying to themselves. In the course of events, Miranda will further experience the second stage of initiation: isolation.

As a small girl given to illusion, Miranda has aspired to be "a tall, cream-colored brunette, like cousin Isabel . . ." (p. 177). But by the age of ten, she has decided to become a jockey instead. Incongruous and humorous as it is, her choice illustrates that Miranda has already assimilated the lessons of the Old Order and the conflict that will be her adult legacy: she moves from a traditionally feminine idol to a masculine hero and eschews beauty for independence and excitement. The same division is obvious when she rejects Spanish-style riding for the jockey's bounce.

Part II focuses on a Saturday afternoon when the girls have been taken to the races by their father to watch Uncle Gabriel's horse, Miss Lucy, run. Despite bad odds, the horse wins, and Miranda has her first encounter with the real Uncle Gabriel and the reality of a horse race. Uncle Gabriel disheartens the girls immediately with his "coarse" language and loud voice, and he soon proves to be a drunkard. He abuses himself and his horses as well, for he hasn't enough pride to earn a living by some occupation. He depends on his horses for survival, and what once was a pleasure is now desperate necessity. The ignominiousness of this situation comes home to Miranda when she sees Miss Lucy as the family members descend to the winner's circle:

> Miss Lucy was bleeding at the nose, two thick red rivulets were stiffening her tender mouth and chin, the round velvet chin that Miranda thought the nicest kind of chin in the world. Her eyes were wild and her knees were trembling, and she snored when she drew her breath. (p. 199)

Miranda stares with "her heart clinched tight. . . ." She feels "instantly and completely . . . her heart reject that victory . . ." (p. 199); hating what she sees, she feels ashamed for screaming for joy when the horse came in a winner. This is the same image we have of Miranda in the forest beside her brother and the dead rabbit, saying "Oh, I want to *see*" and, seeing, rejecting the victory. Miranda is once again repelled by the reality of the horse's blood and suffering, and in rejecting that reality, she effectively isolates herself from her uncle, father, and sister. She wants nothing else to do with the painful victory of a horse that has won heroically for a heavy man with sour breath and rumpled clothing.

Uncle Gabriel effectively destroys the rest of the afternoon for them by leading them home through a seamy neighborhood to meet his ungracious second wife, who obviously can't stand the sight of Amy's relatives and won't forbear to quarrel with her husband in front of them. The whole affair is a descent into Gabriel's particular circle of hell; he lives in a run-down hotel located, ironically, in a section of town called Elysian Fields. It is indeed a land of the dead, but instead of the warmth and peace connoted by the name, an icy tension pervades this place, and Miranda and Maria are grateful to escape. Encompassing both the image of Amy on the one hand and the successful jockey on the other, Gabriel's sleaziness taints Miranda's imagination in two directions at once. Surely the image of Amy herself must waver a bit now that Miranda has seen exposed the clay feet of Amy's hero.

In Part III, Miranda, now eighteen and married herself, is returning home for Uncle Gabriel's funeral when she meets her cousin Eva Parrington, who has the same destination. Their conversation is a reminder that the more things change, the more they remain the same. Miranda still has daredevil aspirations, and Eva still bitterly nurses old wounds inflicted by the family in her youth. The ugly relative is clearly meant to balance the beautiful one, and Eva is Amy's opposite in every way. Not only does she offer a personal contrast to Amy's life and style; she also gives Miranda her own nasty version of Amy's story; but her obvious jealousy and her mercenary spirit discredit her. We wind up discovering more about Eva than we do about Amy. While Amy married for her own puzzling motives, Eva, given the chance, would have done worse: she would have married for money. She finally ends her tirade by condemning Amy and her "rivals" for playing the courting game: "It was just sex . . . ; their minds dwelt on nothing else . . . , so they simply festered inside— they festered—" (p. 216). She succeeds primarily in describing herself; when Miranda tries to assert that Eva is too extreme by suggesting that her mother was not like that, Eva retorts easily and automatically, "Your mother was a saint," and dismisses the subject.

In view of the initiation pattern established in Part II, one might expect Part III to bring about Miranda's reintegration with her family circle. She does seem hesitantly aware that she might become like Eva, and admires the courage and heroism of her crusade for women's rights. She cringes, however, at the prospect of looking so "withered and tired . . . so *old*" and finally is completely repelled by Eva's invective:

"Beauty goes, character stays" . . . It was a dreary prospect; why was a strong character so deforming? Miranda felt she truly wanted to be strong, but how could she face it, seeing what it did to one? (p. 215)

At this point Miranda clearly sees a dichotomy between beauty and character. It is not only an axiom from her childhood but a division she has absorbed from her experience among her family. Even more important, Miranda has proved herself attractive enough to "catch a husband," but her own marriage was an impetuous elopement that has given her no true home. When she mentions it to Eva, her thoughts are completely negative:

It seemed very unreal even as she said it, and seemed to have nothing at all to do with the future; . . . the only feeling she could rouse in herself about it was an immense weariness as if it were an illness that she might one day hope to recover from. (p. 213)

It will not take her life as it has Amy's, but then Miranda will not exactly recover from it, either. So Miranda is caught between the negative image of one alternative and her own dissatisfying experience of the second.

As children do, Miranda hopes her father will make it right by welcoming her home, but she is beyond that and he rejects her. She realizes that "It is I who have no place" and feels "her blood [rebel] against the ties of blood," those "bonds that smothered her in love and hatred" (pp. 219–220). She resolves characteristically that she will stay in no place and with no person that might forbid her making "her own discoveries." Ultimately she promises herself that, barring all else, she will know the truth about her own experiences. Unfortunately, the truth she has yet to know will not make her free, either.

"Pale Horse, Pale Rider"

"Pale Horse, Pale Rider" is the story of the death not only of love, but of its possibility. After many stories of female conflict, Porter gives us in this short novel a tragic resolution: the story of Miranda's death as a lover and her resurrection as an independent loner. It is 1918, and Miranda is working as drama critic for a small western newspaper. World War I and the influenza epidemic are raging, but life is still possible for her because she is falling in love with Adam, a young officer about to be shipped out. Then Miranda contracts the flu and nearly succumbs. She recovers only to find that Adam has died of the same disease. Told in the metaphor of the wasteland and the charnel house, the story inverts the Edenic potential of human union to dust and death and completes the cycle of Miranda's education. As always in Porter's complex stories, these three images are braided; until the end of the story the reader must consider simultaneously the oppressiveness of the wasteland, the threat of death from war and pestilence, and the possibility of love and life inherent in Eden. They move the story forward concentrically.

At the end of "Old Mortality," Miranda recognizes that, like both Amy and Eva, she is "smothered . . . in love and hatred" by family ties. She mentally rejects not only her own family but her husband's family as well, resolving to free herself of "the ties of blood" to make her own discoveries and find her own truths. She is left poised on a threshold, thinking, "I hate loving and being loved, I hate it" (p. 221). In "Pale Horse, Pale Rider," we meet a Miranda who is solitary, independent, and alone, if not completely lonely; who is nevertheless still vulnerable to love; who must yet experience the shattering destruction of love in her life and learn to live after, when "there would be time for everything" (p. 317) because there would be nothing.

While the reader of this short novel does not require Miranda's past history to understand the terms of the story, a knowledge of "The Old Order" and "Old Mortality" illuminates Miranda's last shaping experience in "Pale Horse, Pale Rider." The first pages of the story link Miranda irreversibly to the protagonists of the earlier stories by alluding to family, home, oppression, and death. The wealth of family relationships that were a comfort and a defense against the outside world to the very young Miranda have become incredibly confining: everyone is "tangled together like badly cast fishing lines." Faceless relatives ask the same questions that intimidated both the Grandmother and the younger Miranda: "Where are you going, What are you doing, What are you thinking, How do you feel, Why do you say such things, What do you mean?" (p. 269). Her sense of oppression is translated metaphorically into a physical pressure on her chest—"her heart was a stone lying upon her breast outside of her . . ." (p. 269)—which is at once the physical image of the oppression she feels from the war, a foreboding of the mortal illness to come, and an implication of the danger she faces in a love relationship. She thinks of the horses she might ride in her race with death—Fiddler, Graylie, and Miss Lucy—unwittingly invoking the presence of her grandmother, whose horse was Fiddler, and Amy, who owned Miss Lucy. Having established her link to them, she chooses Graylie, "because he is not afraid of bridges." Since it is folk belief that evil spirits will not cross water, Miranda perhaps unconsciously believes she can outrun death and the devil if she makes it to a bridge. Spurring her horse forward, she establishes the journey motif which prevails in her dream sequences; all the while, the familiar stranger rides easily beside her and passes her by when she reins in and shouts, "I'm not going with you this time—ride on!" (p. 270).

This threatening dream begins the story and sets a tone that pervades Miranda's subsequent waking hours like a fateful curse. There is no question that she is threatened by death—the 1918 influenza epidemic has made hearses a common sight in the city streets—but the Great War is an even more potent manifestation of a diseased society and its instinct for death. Not only does it kill numbers outright, it corrupts all who are touched by it: it encourages sentimental patriotism and thoughtless chauvinism; it requires senseless conformity and meaningless rhetoric. Its evil is personified not only in the "lank greenish stranger" who invades Miranda's dreams, but in the grotesque Lusk Committeemen who sell Liberty Bonds by intimidation and the "unfriendly bitter" soldier in the army hospital who refuses Miranda's candy and cigarettes.

What alleviates her sense of oppression and disgust is the presence of Adam, a young lieutenant she has known only ten days. It is plain they are in love, and it is plain that love makes them terribly vulnerable. Adam has originally come to town to make his will prior to being shipped to the front. Having met Miranda, he has more to lose than life. If it is obvious that influenza is a disease and war is a disease, the most subtle implication of the metaphor here is that in such an environment even love is a disease which debilitates and devours. This will be one of Miranda's "truths" by the end of her experience, but at the beginning she has no tragic insights and feels herself out of kilter in smaller ways. For instance, in her physical appearance: "No, she did not find herself a pleasing sight, flushed and shiny, and even her hair felt as if it had decided to grow in the other direction" (p. 278). This sense of things gone awry, however, is not only Miranda's. Barrenness and decay pervade everything.

The story takes place in autumn, amid the dying of natural life, and is set in a town at the foot of the Rocky Mountains. Miranda and Adam climb stony trails for entertainment. They drink coffee they call "swill" in dingy restaurants like "The Greasy Spoon"; they dance in tawdry bars crowded with people and smoke, attend dull plays in tacky theaters, keep "unnatural hours," and walk about among funeral processions and discordant voices. The very air they breathe is rotten, as we are reminded by the image of the "thick greasy-looking cloud" said to have spread over Boston, where the influenza began.

However, it is not only the setting that suggests a wasteland. The people who inhabit this place are for the most part grotesques like Eliot's "red sullen faces" that "sneer and snarl/From doors of mudcracked houses" (*The Waste Land*, ll.344–345). They are people without values, like her pressroom colleagues who think Miranda is a fool for trying to protect a young girl's privacy by suppressing a story. They are the self-important dollar-a-year men whose faces record nothing but "the inept sensual record of fifty years," who are "too fat, too old, too cowardly, to go to war themselves . . ." (pp. 293–294). They are the washed-up, broken-down, drab performers Miranda sees with dizzying repetition. Even the men who appear whole hide some defect, like Chuck, who has bad lungs. The rest are wounded and hospitalized or, like Adam, marked for death at the front.

The women, too, are shallow human beings, "wallowing in good works" that do nobody any good but that "keep their little minds out of mischief." These seriously frivolous young virgins, in their

> Red Cross wimples, roll cock-eyed bandages that will never reach a base hospital, and knit sweaters that will never warm a manly chest, their minds dwelling lovingly on all the blood and mud and the next dance at the Acanthus[4] Club for the officers of the flying corps. (p. 290)

Like Miranda's landlady, who threatens to put her out on the street on discovering that she has influenza, these modern women seem totally without compassion, harpies who descend on a hospital ward with "girlish laughter" that has "a grim determined clang in it calculated to freeze the blood" (p. 276). Men like Chuck, rejected by the army, are just as estranged from women as the soldiers more graphically marked by the war:

> All of them had a sidelong eye for the women they talked with about it, a guarded resentment which said, "Don't pin a white feather on me, you bloodthirsty female. I've offered my meat to the crows and they won't have it" (p. 290).

In the face of this separation of the sexes, it follows naturally that human communication is poor, distorted, or nonexistent, like the pressroom sounds that punctuate Miranda's thoughts: "Bill was shouting at somebody who kept saying, 'Well, but listen, well, but listen—' but nobody was going to listen, of course, nobody. Old man Gibbons bellowed in despair, 'Jarge, Jarge—'" (p. 286). There is no communication in the repetitive argument Miranda hears a woman telling to her friend in a pub. In a larger sense, when Miranda feels alienated from the crowds in the theater, she thinks of their inability to communicate:

> There must be a great many of them here who think as I do, and we dare not say a word to each other of our desperation, we are speechless animals letting ourselves be destroyed, and why? Does anybody here believe the things we say to each other? (p. 291)

Even Miranda and Adam engage in ironic exchanges that force them to laugh—rather than cry—over the war. Their mild cynicism and their "small talk" identify them as people with style who know how to take the "right tone" in regard to the war and who recognize that tearing their hair over it is very "unbecoming." They cloak their despair under a patina of slick talk. Their careless conversational patter not only hides their serious feelings, it eliminates the possibility of their voicing them. Miranda can jokingly suggest to Adam that they run away, but on one of her last evenings with him, she cannot bring herself to say what is in her mind:

> She wanted to say, "Adam, come out of your dream and listen to me. I have pains in my chest and my head and my heart and they're real. I am in pain all over and you are in such danger as I can't bear to think about, and why can we not save each other?" (p. 296)

Unable to voice this, she communicates her need by physically tightening her hold on his shoulder: "They said nothing but smiled continually at each other, . . . as though they had found a new language" (p. 296). Ultimately it is an insufficient language, and it takes nothing less than a mortal illness for them to declare their love for each other verbally. Unfortunately, love cannot thrive in the wasteland, and that declaration soon proves a death knell.

The third motif in "Pale Horse, Pale Rider" opposes the wasteland; it is the image of an uncorrupted Eden where a loving pair can live a life of natural happiness. In this story, meaning turns crucially upon Miranda's wish for paradise. Although she is not completely naïve, Miranda's rational arguments with herself cannot withstand her sweeping affection for Adam and the naïve dream of a happy life together which she cannot even name to herself. While she cannot recognize it, her subconscious desire to possess Eden with Adam makes her eventual loss of it all the more harsh. Both this motif and its destruction are established through the character of Adam and through the imagery in the vivid dreams induced by Miranda's fever when she falls ill.

Adam, whose pairing with Miranda is central here, is from the beginning set apart as a special individual. Of course, Miranda cannot think of him as anything less. He is the "only really pleasant thought she had" (p. 278), and as such opposes all the insidious ugliness of the war. However, there are details which separate him from the common herd, even apart from Miranda's point of view. His name as well as his solitary status indicate that he is an essential and special man, separate from all others. He is literally head and shoulders above the likes of ordinary men like the pot-bellied committeeman or even Chuck Rouncivale, who is Miranda's friend. Not only is Adam a primary man, he is the best man, a prelapsarian Adam. He has "never had a pain in his life" (p. 280) and is, Miranda thinks later, "pure . . . all the way through, flawless . . ." (p. 295). Miranda thinks that he looks like "a fine healthy apple" (p. 280), which suggests at once his well-being and his innocence, since the apple is uneaten, and, inversely, the temptation he is to Miranda, a jaded Eve who already knows a fear of love.

Growing amid the wasteland of war, Adam and Miranda's flowering love seems too fragile to survive. Miranda's desire for this love is crowded by the sense that she is sure to lose it, and she lectures herself, "I don't want to love, . . . there is no time and we are not ready for it and yet this is all we have—" (p. 292). Having met only ten days before, both temper their growing affection with reserve. When their eyes meet, both are "steady and noncommittal." Miranda feels "a deep tremor" within and sets about "resisting herself methodically as if she were closing windows and doors and fastening down curtains against a rising storm" (p. 292). Although she tries to reestablish the control threatened by her emotional and physical response to Adam, her protective stance is too like what she sees in the fearful eyes around her, people who look "as if they had pulled down the shutters over their minds and their hearts . . ." (p. 294).

But all this is before she is taken ill, with only Adam to care for her. Her defenses are weakened by the onslaught of the influenza, and in an unsettling dream her subconscious desires and fears are revealed, yoked in the rich descriptive imagery of a baroque Eden so awesomely attractive and threatening that it might be lifted, along with the pale rider, from the Apocalypse. She dreams of a tall ship which beckons her to sail into an Eden that is a wild colorful antithesis to the bright green fields planted in orderly rows favored by Porter heroines. "Creeping with tangles of spotted serpents, [and] rainbow colored birds with malign eyes" (p. 299), it is a rotting Eden, an Eden after the advent of knowledge. The creatures of this place don't exist to be named, that is, to be controlled by human beings. They dwell in an Amazonian jungle from which Miranda should run lest she be devoured. Instead, she boards the ship and sails toward clamorous voices chanting "danger" and "war."

Adam makes Eden seem possible, but Miranda also senses in him a contradictory significance. Such a perfect specimen is also a perfect sacrifice; Adam in fact represents an ancient archetype: the dying and reviving god whose death assured life for his people. Usually a god of vegetation, the archetype was worshiped in the ancient world under a variety of names: Tammuz, Attis, Osiris, Adonis.[5]

The Greek myth of Aphrodite and Adonis typifies the later and more sophisticated expression of this belief. Aphrodite, goddess of love, was enamored of a beautiful youth named Adonis. Her jealous husband Ares caused Adonis to be attacked by a wild boar who killed him; but where his blood spilled, the earth produced anemones and roses of a brilliant red. In Syria, Adonis and Aphrodite were said to live on Mount Lebanon, which was sacred to them. It was the site of his birth, death, and burial, the latter evidenced by the growth of anemones among the cedars of Lebanon. In some rites the god's resurrection was simply assumed and celebrated after the lamentation and burial of his effigy. In others, his rising was dramatized by a priest who assumed the costume of a sacrificed victim. In all, his resurrection was seen in the new life of the anemone and the sprouting young corn, even after it had been previously reaped in harvest.[6] No matter what the name of the god or the manner of his ritual, the essentials—birth, death, and resurrection—result in the same meaning: new life for old.

In Adam, the only love of Miranda's ever portrayed by Porter, all the characteristics of both the Christian and pre-Christian myths are encompassed. As we have already noted, his innocence and nobility of purpose mark him as a prelapsarian Adam. But just as he is Adam, he is also Adonis. In shades of gold, tan, brown, and green— "hay colored"—he suggests simultaneously growing vegetation and the harvest time in which the story is set. True to the connotations of the name Adonis, Adam is more comely than any other man, dressed in his well-tailored uniform with the "manly smell of scentless soap, freshly cleaned leather and freshly washed skin" about him. Miranda repeatedly admires his good looks, his "extraordinary face, smooth and fine and golden . . ." (p. 295), and finally tells him specifically, "Adam, I think you're very beautiful" (p. 301). More than anything else, however, he reflects Adonis as a sacrifice. Miranda thinks of him as a "sacrificial lamb" (p. 295) being sent out to slaughter by older men who jealously want the younger ones dead. "The tom-cats try to eat the little tom-kittens, you know," she tells him (p. 294). In the largest sense, too, Adam and the other young soldiers are the human sacrifices the community is willing to pay to ensure its own security and survival. But the crucial instance of Adam's sacrificial nature will surface in yet another fevered dream of Miranda's.

After her dream of a jungle-like Eden, she is frightened into wakefulness and encourages Adam to talk with her. They remember childhood prayers and end by singing the Negro spiritual they both know: "Pale horse, pale rider, done taken my lover away . . . ," which reinstates the image of the "lank greenish stranger" from Miranda's earlier dream. He is the fourth horseman of the Apocalypse, who is, of course, death, but who is also identified in the Bible as pestilence. His greenish color links him to Adam in his olive drab uniform, both heightening our awareness of the threat he is to Miranda's welfare and of his own potential as victim. Their reserve broken down by the deadliness of Miranda's illness, they declare their love for each other as Miranda drifts into another potentially Edenic dream world, a green wood that is fraught with even more obvious danger than the previous one.

In it, Adam becomes a sacrifice who evokes both Christian and pre-Christian models, a martyr to both faith and love whose death gives life, but, ironically, a life Miranda thinks of as death because it does not include Adam. In Miranda's dream, he is struck through with arrows, falling and rising in "a perpetual death and resurrection" (pp. 304–305), suggesting Saint Sebastian, the celebrated Christian martyr who was shot with arrows, left for dead, revived, and martyred again. With his fellow believers he thought through death to find eternal life in heaven and thus his faith both kills and saves him. Likewise, Adonis figures die because they are the consorts of goddesses of love; the fact that Adam is pierced by arrows through the heart connotes Cupid's wounds as well as mortal sacrifice. It is when she tries to save him by interposing her body between him and the deadly arrow that Miranda herself is struck cleanly and Adam takes a mortal wound, in effect reversing her intention, giving his life for hers.

When she wakes again, Adam comforts her before leaving to get more coffee. Because she is taken to the hospital during his brief absence, Miranda never sees Adam again, even in her dreams. Buried in the hospital, den of pestilence and death, Miranda gives up her conscious life to hallucination and despair, caught in the image of the corpse wrapped head to foot in white which lies next to her, and in the pale rider, now translated by her delirium into a menacing German killer. Finally, in the hollow of her consciousness, she sees herself poised on a ledge above the pit of eternity and fears the fall into the unknown, a fear characteristic of Porter protagonists.

Like Granny Weatherall, Miranda sees her "self" simplified to "a minute fiercely burning particle of being" (p. 310) whose tenacity becomes a fan of radiance and rainbow which entices her into a third vision of Eden, this time rarefied beyond human imagining in return for the simple sacrifice of her self. It is a "deep clear landscape of sea and sand, of soft meadow and sky, freshly washed and glistening with transparencies of blue." The living figures who surround her are "transfigured . . . pure identities," and her apprehension becomes "ecstasy" (p. 311). Ironically, the emotional weakness that originally made her vulnerable now resurrects Miranda, cheating her of paradise. Her return from the grave is necessary because she believes she has lost or left something behind; and so she has, for Adam, left behind, is now dead and lost to her while she has life.

Brought back from the grave even after she has been shrouded in death, Miranda's revival occurs simultaneously with the Armistice. War and the sacrifice of the living are now complete; the plague is over. However, Miranda's "gift" of life after her vision of death leaves her feeling "alien"; the ravages of her ride with Death associate her with the "ragged tuneless old women" (p. 313) singing with coarse voices in the ward down the hall. Alone and isolated, they are, as she is, cast out of Eden, but now she knows it most painfully. All tenderness and emotion are leached out of her, and so she sustains the last dull blow: the news of Adam's death from influenza. Having longed for both life and love, Miranda has found them mutually exclusive. She can never again allow herself to be so vulnerable; consequently, she begins immediately and automatically to establish an ironic distance between herself and her pain. Sardonically, she thinks of herself as Lazarus coming forth from his cave in top hat and walking stick. Looking to "the art of the thing" (p. 316), she prepares to cover the ravages of her illness with cosmetics as she buries the desire for love, with Adam, in her psyche. Thus, the ghost of death at the end of the story is not the pale rider, but Adam, now as unbearably invisible and as cruelly separate from her as her vision of paradise when it slipped from her grasp. Just as she cannot will herself back, she cannot conjure his ghost, for all her desire.

If love for Adam has ended in death, for Miranda its coda is deception and treachery. She has unburied herself for love only to be buried alive by loss. Bereft of its object, her heart does not cease longing, but torments her with visions of her lost happiness. Thus reduced to the position of Tantalus, she must repress her "bitter desire" in order to own again a piece of her soul. And the reader, having watched Miranda experiencing desolation, need no longer wonder at the repression, retention, and constriction of emotion and sexuality in Porter's women.

"Holiday"

Since Katherine Anne Porter began her public career with a portrait of a peasant woman's triumphant motherhood in "María Concepción," it is fitting that one of the last two stories she published, "Holiday," records a sudden and inexplicable death blow to a matriarchal farm woman. It is as if Porter brought her stories full circle by laying the ghost of her heritage once and for all.

In "Holiday," Porter again builds a symbolically and psychologically complex story on a double point of view. The story moves forward using a triad of themes. The quickening life of the natural world in the rural Texas countryside parallels the cycle of human life in the fecund Müller family. The beauty of the burgeoning spring begins to soothe the ragged nerves of the protagonist, even though she recognizes her separateness from the solidarity and security of the family circle; she learns from the Müllers that nature is Janus-faced and that its dark side is also a part of life. And finally, from their crippled, brain-damaged daughter she learns that life *is*, even in the face of death.

Although it was not completed and published until 1960, "Holiday" was essentially written within a short time of "María Concepción" and is another examination of how a woman can survive, given the reality of family, maternity, and death. A significant difference is that it is narrated by a first-person observer who is young, impressionable, keenly sensitive, and searching for ways to outlast recent emotional ravages. In short, she is identifiable, in all but name, as the quasi-autobiographical persona Porter created repeatedly during her career: Miranda.[7]

"Holiday" is the only story other than "Hacienda" which is narrated by a first-person observer—a felicitous choice, since it distances the narrator from the Müllers, whom she observes, and at the same time lends credibility to what she says about them. It also ap-

pears to unite what are really two points of view, a similar technique
to that employed in "The Old Order." The narrator is an older Miranda than the one who experiences that rural Texas spring. She is
capable of looking back on the pain and naïveté of "that time" with
hindsight, asserting that she has since learned that we cannot escape
the troubles which belong to us, and that we are wise to run "like
. . . deer" from any others (p. 407). But she did not have that knowledge as a young woman, and her experience of the pain and renewal
in this story belonged to a younger Miranda, who records her emotions and fears with greater poignancy than the older voice might.

It is tempting to think that "Holiday" is the story which explains how Miranda eased herself past the actual rejection of the
young husband and family ties that she promises herself at the end
of "Old Mortality." It is even more tempting to read "Holiday" as a
resurrection story, the renewal of the physical and psychic ravages
Miranda sustained in "Pale Horse, Pale Rider." Even if there is no
connection, it is a fitting conclusion to the cycle of experience in
these powerful stories, whether directly related to them or simply
the resolution of some other deep hurt.

The unity of this story is impressive. "Holiday" has two narrative threads: Miranda's tale, which accounts for her coming to the
country to restore her psychic health, and the story of the Müller
family, prosperous German farmers who not only live on, but live
for, the land. The two threads are rhythmically interwoven not only
by the fact that Miranda has a place in both, but by the overwhelming presence of the natural world, which is beginning to breed lilacs
out of the dead ground of a bleak March, and by the unceasing significance of Ottilie, the Müllers' grotesquely deformed daughter
who might be the embodied specter of Miranda's psychological upheaval. They are further linked by a cycle of events—during her stay
Miranda witnesses courtship, a wedding, a birth, and a death—and a
cluster of natural images that begin and end the story.

Maternity is the mark of this tale, made in so many places that
it astounds. Imagery, symbolism, setting, time, character, even gesture communicate maternity in "Holiday." Miranda arrives inaus-
piciously enough, on a cold, bleak evening in the midst of a light rain
falling on a stark landscape in rural Texas. What she can see is mud
and bare branches, but she knows that the rain and the season are
nurturing growth:

> there was nothing beautiful in those woods now except the
> promise of spring . . . beyond this there might be something
> else beautiful in its own being, a river shaped and contained by

its banks, or a field stripped down to its true meaning,
ploughed and ready for the seed. (p. 410)

The imagery suggests the psychic barrenness of the protagonist,
but also pregnancy and fecundity. Miranda has come in hope of restoring herself, and her action underscores the material significance
of the opening pages. She expects to be nourished by the natural
world here, and she retreats, down a tunnel-like lane through the
woods to the womb of a foster family, who, although they have lived
in Texas for three generations, retain their native tongue and customs. Theirs is a "house of perpetual exile" (p. 413), which meets
her desire for isolation from the outside world, but which will also
provide her with incubating space until she is ready for rebirth. Even
in her unhappiness, Miranda believes in the inherent potency of the
barest branch and the roughest seed. The only slightly discordant
note is the view Miranda has from her window of the young Müller
boy heading off across the fields with a "lantern and a large steel
trap" (p. 412).

Miranda can understand the Müllers' commitment to the land
from her own experience with a grandmother who functioned as
they do: "[They] stuck their mattocks into the earth deep and held
fast wherever they were, because to them life and the land were one
indivisible thing ..." (p. 413). The Müllers are a family like her own
in other ways. They are a large, close-knit family, the sturdy products of a strong matriarch. In the bosom of this group, she can feel
comfortable but apart. It is interesting that one of the attractions of
the attic room the Müllers give her is an old paperback collection
of romantic novels—"*The Duchess*, Ouida, Mrs. E.D.E.N. South-
worth" (p. 408), which would, of course, emphasize the plight of the
isolated individual. Once in the midst of the strong community of
the Müller family, however, Miranda feels no need of them. Yet she
still relishes her privacy, if not her isolation.

The fact that she knows no German dispenses her from many
conversations and affords her a privacy she could only long for
among her own:

> It was good not to have to understand what they were saying. I
> loved that silence which means freedom from the constant
> pressure of other minds and other opinions and other feelings,
> that freedom to fold up in quiet and go back to my own center.
> (p. 413)

Again, Porter's imagery suggests the warmth and solace of the
womb. When Miranda arrives, the members of the younger genera-

tion are presented to her one by one. She is then introduced not to
Father Müller, but to Mother Müller, a strong old woman whose appearance at the end of that long parade of offspring suggests that she
is the author of all the hearty humanity in that house.

Among the Müllers, however, there is also a strong father who
rules his own domain. He forms his opinions on empirical evidence
and uses his own judgment regarding right behavior. He is strong-
minded, but he doesn't impose his views on his family; they seem to
share his convictions as they share his features and coloring. Father
Müller cannot be denied; his children look like him superficially, but
psychologically, they belong to their mother, who belongs to the land.

Mother Müller's strong character is singularly important to her
family, since she exercises a distinct, equal rule over this brood. She
is independent and tough, jealously guarding her female rights in
work and in the family circle. Taking care of the milking is the province of the women of the family, specifically, hers and Hatsy's. Anyone who intervenes is a trespasser, one who threatens to upset the
order of her world. Likewise, taking care of their men is the province
of these women, and that power is not to be usurped, not even by
Father Müller, whose wife has to remind him during the flooding
that it is *her* right to tend to him and not the other way around (pp.
429–430).

Directress of her whole household, Mother Müller assumes
command at dinner, introducing Miranda to the family despite the
patriarchal presence of her husband. On workdays it is she who gives
"orders right and left" to the rest of the family; she even instructs
her husband on his errands. In fact, she never defers to him, and at
dinnertime when she takes her position behind his chair in order to
serve his dinner, she is an overwhelming presence, "looming behind
him like a dark boulder" (p. 415). Her husband, by accepting her service, demonstrates his faith in her ability and his need of her partnership as well as his respect for her role. The women of this family
are not trifled with or condescended to; they are honored not only
for their intrinsic value, but for their contributions to home and
hearth. In effect, when Mother Müller and her daughters serve their
husbands dinner, they literally feed their men and symbolically assert their own importance to the well-being of others.

In fact, although this is a family of strong sons as well as strong
daughters, one hardly notices because Miranda is so fascinated with
its women. She physically describes the son who meets her at the
train station and characterizes Father Müller, but otherwise the
"two sons-in-law and three sons" (p. 415) remain a faceless group
who scarcely draw Miranda's attention. Apparently, their job is

ploughing, and they are good at it if one can judge by the prosperity of the farm and the fruitfulness of their wives. But Miranda has little interest in them. In contrast, she describes the appearance and function of each daughter, all of whom are absorbed in bearing, rearing, and nurturing life, like their mother.

Both Annetje and Gretchen, the two elder daughters, are defined by their maternity. Between them they have eight children under ten years of age; Annetje, mother of five, has recently given birth, and Gretchen is in advanced pregnancy. Both carry infants everywhere; Annetje's newborn is draped over her shoulder, and Gretchen's toddler straddles her hip. Their babies are so much a part of them that each performs other chores without ever releasing her child. Miranda marvels that these sisters care for their children "with instinctive, constant gentleness; they never seemed to be troubled by them" (p. 419).

Hatsy, the "maiden of the family," mothers her sisters' children in the absence of her own. Sitting with her nieces and nephews at dinner, she "struggled with them only a little less energetically than she did with the calves . . ." (p. 415). Even Ottilie, the crippled servant later identified as the Müllers' oldest daughter, spends her waking hours feeding the rest of the family prodigious amounts of food.

Mother Müller, whose childbearing days are over, demonstrates her maternity by presiding over her household and milking their herd of cows; her expertise in this is suggested by the ease with which she wears the yoke of milking pails, and is borne out by her actions during a flash flood. She carries a new calf on her back to the safety of the barn's loft, and then descends to methodically milk the cows despite the water rising in the stable. In contrast, her daughter Hatsy, linked to her mother by their shared chores and her mother's special regard—"Hatsy, she's a good, quick girl" (p. 421)—is only an apprentice, who carries "two tin milking pails on her arm" (p. 414) and does her mother's bidding.

In addition to all this maternity, the Müller women are tied to the natural world in which they live. Miranda observes the fragile-looking Hatsy sharing "the enormous energy and animal force that was like a bodily presence itself in the room" (p. 416), and in fact uses animal imagery to describe her hostesses. Annetje and Gretchen with their children "are as devoted and caretaking as a cat with her kittens" (p. 419); Gretchen wears "the contented air of a lazy, healthy young animal, seeming always about to yawn" (p. 416); when her new son is born, he suckles "like a young calf" (p. 428). Hatsy, who runs on thin spindly legs with "silver braids thumping on her shoulders" (p. 430) is like a young colt in her energetic movements.

But even aside from Miranda's view, there is objective evidence that the land calls to all of them. Annetje, who does her household chores quickly every morning, spends her time outdoors caring for the kittens, pigs, lambs, and calves, for whom she has a special tenderness. Occasionally, she even brings some of the outdoors in, transporting "a boxful of newly hatched chickens" to her bedroom "where she might tend them carefully on their first day" (p. 418). Hatsy plants the kitchen garden under the warm spring sun during the morning hours, and the children play their domestic games outdoors, making loaves of bread and pies in the mud.

Even the site of the family's weekly outings is the *Turnverein*, "an octagonal pavilion set in a cleared space in a patch of woods" where the young people court on Saturday nights and the families gather for gossip and picnics on Sunday afternoons. Mother Müller, who feels uneasy sitting in her own parlor, finds it possible to take "her ease after a hard week" (p. 423) at the wooded *Turnverein*.

Comfortable and at home in the bosom of their land, the Müllers appear to live in harmony with it, and easily accept its gifts. Miranda returns to the farmhouse late one evening, having been halted by a vision of the orchard trees "all abloom with fireflies." Miranda has "never seen anything . . . more beautiful":

> The trees were freshly budded out with pale bloom, the branches were immobile in the thin darkness, but the flower clusters shivered in a soundless dance of delicately woven light whirling as airily as leaves in a breeze, as rhythmically as water in a fountain. (pp. 419–420)

Hatsy, who is still hard at work scrubbing floors, is not too tired to notice "this living, pulsing fire" nor too awed by a vision which in her world makes an eternal return. She says happily to Miranda, "Now it is come spring. Every spring we have that" (p. 420).

In contrast to the women of his family, Father Müller seems more wrapped up in making money than in the land per se. He seems to have no spiritual relationship with it, nor any need of personal sustenance other than what his mind can provide. He will not go to church because time is money to him. Likewise, he thinks of his land in economic and political terms: how much he makes from it, what power it gives him. He spends his evenings in the parlor engaged in rational pursuits, playing chess and reading and rereading *Das Kapital*. His land is a commodity to be shrewdly assessed and managed wisely, not something that nurtures him, but true to his political philosophy, he uses his land to build community.

Miranda exists somewhere in between the Müller women, who are daughters of the land, and the Müller men, who use it. She is drawn to the life force of the land and hopes in its restorative power, whose effect she does experience in time. As the greening of the countryside occurs, Miranda's nerves begin little by little to settle into "the harmony of the valley rolling fluently away to the wood's edge" (p. 414). Helping Hatsy with the kitchen garden, Miranda feels the earth grow physically and metaphorically "firmer underfoot with the swelling tangle of crowding roots" (p. 418). The changes in the land, like her own healing, occur gradually, but eventually a morning dawns when everything is "quick and feathery with golden green blowing in the winds" (p. 419). Miranda loves the natural world, but wants to believe only in its benevolence. This error will eventually be corrected by the Müllers' example.

Even at best, though, Miranda is a sometime participant and a receiver of Nature's benefits, not its handmaiden, like her hostesses. This is emphasized by her frequently reiterated sense of separation from this family that takes its identity as well as its livelihood out of the land. The Müllers, too, are aware of her "difference." Because she is "a stranger and a guest," she is seated "on the men's side of the table" (p. 415), just as Hatsy is seated with the children, despite the fact that both the guest and Hatsy are adult women. In this culture, as in Miranda's childhood community, there is no real place for grown women if not behind a husband's chair, and these two have yet to be initiated into that fold. Then, too, Miranda's seat on the male side of the table suggests her ambiguous sexuality, as does another detail. Father Müller, who plays chess only with his son-in-law, proposes to teach Miranda chess, but then is "not surprised" that she cannot learn, just as he is not surprised that she knows nothing about *Das Kapital*, as if, despite his overture to her difference, he has known all along that she is a woman.

In fact, the only member of the family for whom Miranda has any real kinship is the one who seems to be no member of the family at all: Ottilie, the cruelly deformed girl who is the Müllers' oldest daughter.[8] There is no question that in the midst of this harmonious family, dwelling in the lap of nature, Ottilie represents the freakish, the abnormal, the grotesque which nature sometimes spawns in the process of spewing forth abundance. She is a caricature of a human being, with a "mutilated face," a "blurred, dark face . . . neither young nor old, but crumpled into crisscross wrinkles, irrelevant either to age or suffering; simply wrinkles, patternless blackened seams as if the perishable flesh had been wrung in a hard cruel fist" (p. 420).

Her whole body is misshapen: her knotted hands shake, her head wags, her back is bowed, her arms are withered, and she moves only in a "limping run." Significantly, she seems to Miranda "the only individual in the house," who, because she cannot really participate in the life of the family, is the only one among them separate enough to be "whole." Most important, from Miranda's point of view she is whole *because* she "belonged nowhere," in contrast to Miranda who feels she has "left or lost" a part of herself in every place she has traveled, in every life she has touched, and in every death close to her (p. 417). Actually, Ottilie occupies a very important place in the family, as her likeness to Hestia, the Greek goddess of hearth and home, suggests. She is not only the keeper of the fire but the one who, by providing food for the family, allows them their moments of community. In this sense Miranda's identification with Ottilie is ironic.

While the family seems to take no notice of her, Miranda cannot stop thinking of Ottilie, because she feels so much empathy for her. The misfit in her own family, Miranda, like Ottilie, has eyes "strained with the anxiety of . . . peering into a darkness full of danger" (p. 420). Like Ottilie, she is unable to understand and is therefore mute when the Müllers speak German. Like Ottilie, Miranda suffers muteness that is "nearly absolute" with her own family, being unable to communicate to them her fears or pain. Ottilie manages to communicate only briefly with Miranda one afternoon, illustrating that she, too, recognizes their kinship: in a moment of clear-mindedness, she shows Miranda a baby picture of herself in an attempt to say what she has been. For a moment Miranda feels united by that photograph to Ottilie, as if their lives "were kin, even a part of each other," and in that moment of recognizing the Ottilie in herself, Miranda sees "the painfulness and strangeness of her" vanish (p. 426).

From that moment, Miranda identifies not only with the suffering in Ottilie but with the insensitivity her family seems to have toward her. She thinks of Ottilie's movements as "tormented haste" and of her body as a "machine of torture," while assuming that the Müllers have forgotten her "in pure self-defense" (p. 427). Projecting her own sensitivity onto Ottilie, Miranda prays for her release through death: ". . . let us find her there like that with her head fallen forward on her knees. She will rest then. I would wait, hoping she might not come again, ever again, through that door I gazed at with wincing eyes, as if I might see something unendurable . . ." (p.

428). Of course, what is being described here is not Ottilie's but Miranda's pain, and Ottilie represents the suffering spirit of Miranda more than anything else. It is her own suffering she wishes death to release her from, which she hopes "might not come again, ever again," and the sight of which she thinks is "unendurable."

As the story progresses, Miranda's preoccupation with Ottilie increases despite the fact that the greening of the natural world indicates a healing of her spirit. Perhaps the succession of events in the Müller household conspires to agitate her, for the courtship and wedding of young Hatsy and the birth of Gretchen's son are the prominent events of Miranda's stay, and again she pays strict attention to the behavior of the women.

It is important to note that the whole community of which the Müllers are a part is, as much as any primitive tribe, geared primarily to reproducing its kind. Marriages and births are its central events. The young are expected to find partners and mate; another alternative is never even considered. In this burgeoning spring, Hatsy and Gretchen might be performing acts of sympathetic magic, inducing the fruitfulness of the earth by their own sexuality, and an encouragement of its continuance in the community.

When Hatsy marries, she runs the bride's race through the orchard, which suggests the ripening fruit and fecundity, and is finally caught by a girl who custom says will replace her as the next bride. After this, the peach blossoms in Hatsy's hair are crushed, as will be her maidenhood now that she has been "caught" by a husband. Likewise, when a baby is born, the "hard-working wives and mothers" congregate around the mother and suckling child. For them, life seems "a hearty low joke" (p. 428) in their moment of happiness over its continuance. When a birth occurs, mortality is held at bay, and the women of the community pass the baby from hand to hand as if he were a magic charm.

Ottilie, of course, is present at all these family affairs, but only Miranda seems particularly aware of her. The family takes her presence for granted, but to Miranda Ottilie is like some grim reminder of the skull beneath the skin, as she laboriously feeds the family and whoever else participates in their communal rites. Miranda assumes they have put Ottilie out of their minds to ease themselves of the pain, but this reflects what *she* would do in such circumstances. In actuality, whether they acknowledge her presence or not, the Müllers are dependent on Ottilie, and they function successfully because she is present among them. On a literal level, she cooks the food that sustains them; metaphorically they are sustained by keeping the wretched pain of her distortion among them. Ottilie's presence on the fringes of their every action is not only a sober reminder of their human frailty, but an incorporation of grief and pain into their everyday lives, and Miranda finds "great virtue and courage in their steadiness and refusal to feel sorry for anybody, least of all for themselves" (p. 428). Ottilie's presence, finally, is a sign that the Müllers can accept what Miranda cannot: the aberration, the blow a Janus-faced nature can and does periodically mete out.

The concluding events of the story demonstrate this once again to Miranda. In a sinister reversal of the motifs which have set the Müller narrative in motion, the young Müller boy who sets his steel trap for wild animals finally catches an opossum, whose mangled body he brings home to display to the family. His callousness, disapproved by Annetje, is a bad omen which is followed by a flooding rain that washes out crops, kills livestock, and ruins the peach trees and the beauty of the landscape. Mother Müller, tied so closely to her land, which has been raped by the storm, takes ill and dies unexpectedly. Her family is wild, "unnerved in panic," and demonstrates that without her it is rudderless. The Müllers will deal with the ravaging of the farm as they would with most adversity: they will redouble their efforts to meet the challenge, to repair, replant, restore. The loss of human life, which cannot be restored, is lamented with great and open grief. The value of this mourning is not lost on Miranda, who sees that "it was good to let go, to have something to weep for that nobody need excuse or explain. . . . They wept away the hard core of secret trouble that is in the heart of each separate man . . ." (p. 432).

But that release is not for Miranda. Once again she is forced to witness death and experience "the terror of dying" (p. 433). She is prostrate; despite her awareness of the recuperative power of the family's open grief, she cannot participate or release her own tension. The bare wood through which she traveled to the farmhouse has, as a result of the storm, been translated into a "violent eruption of ripe foliage of a jungle thickness, glossy and burning, a massing of hot peacock green with cobalt shadows" (p. 431), and Ottilie sits before the oven in the kitchen howling her grief. It is as if Miranda's retreat to the womb of this place must now be reversed through violent labor. Settling Ottilie into the same spring wagon in which she came to the farm, Miranda sets out to join the funeral train in a comic "lurching progress" through the mud which parallels rebirth.

As Ottilie begins to slide from the seat, Miranda grabs her by the waist, her hand inadvertently rubbing against Ottilie's skin, and she is horrified to understand, in that touch, that Ottilie is both human and female. Painful reality for Miranda is, as always, confronted and repressed; she is so shocked, she says, that "a howl . . . doglike and despairing . . . rose in me unuttered and died again, to be a perpetual ghost" (p. 434). Miranda wants to "ease" her heart of Ottilie even though she feels she has come closer to Ottilie than to anyone in her "attempt to deny and bridge the distance between" them (p. 434). She *is* closer to Ottilie than to any of the others. Miranda cannot change her ingrained view of femininity and its fulfillment; neither can she live that way. Thus in her mind she is like Ottilie, an arrested and crippled figure of a woman who will never bear life or celebrate her contribution of new life to the race. But Ottilie unwittingly reminds her that life is still worth celebrating. Suddenly comprehending the hot sun, the bright morning, and the spring-green world, Ottilie begins to laugh and clap her hands for joy. Momentarily happy over these "wonders," Ottilie loses her grief. Miranda sees that they must leave the funeral train and take a holiday ride down the mulberry lane. They are only "the fools of life, equally fellow fugitives from death" (p. 435). As such, they must do what they can do: celebrate the passing of death and the resurgence of life in the green spring air. Like Annetje, who is able to save only one lamb from the roaring flood waters near the house, they nevertheless say "Alive! Alive!"

Beyond the Looking-Glass

1942—1962

*In her only novel, Katherine Anne Porter brings to a climax a long career
of examining what appears to be a peculiarly female conflict: the need to
choose between independence and selfhood and the warm security of
love, which must necessarily impose dependence. In the stories written
before 1935, this conflict is most often played out in sexual terms—when
and how sexuality should be used and the effects of its use on selfhood.
Matriarchy and celibacy seem to be the only real alternatives in Porter's
philosophy, for both allow autonomy and power. Love given for its own
sake requires emotional readiness, susceptibilities, certainly constric-
tions, and perhaps refinement of the individual personality.*

*After 1935, Porter distances herself from this instinctive knowledge
by examining the sources of it in the Miranda stories. By this time she
was forty-five years old and had no children; her current marriage would
soon end in divorce, as would another. In effect, Katherine Anne Porter
had made her own choice—for independence—and was thus ready to
treat this issue more objectively and universally in her last major works:
in "The Leaning Tower," published in 1944, and in* Ship of Fools, *written
over a period of some twenty years before its appearance in 1962. It is no
accident that they deal with the same subject. In fact, it is interesting to
note that the only other Porter story similar in its sociopolitical criticism,
"Hacienda," also deals with a society decaying because of the pretentious
self-centeredness and aberrant love practiced by its characters. It is completely like "The Leaning Tower" and* Ship of Fools *in tone and content,
and it was written and published in 1932, the year Porter made the voyage from Mexico to Germany which inspired* Ship of Fools. *Her shipboard
experience perhaps helped her to see that aborted love might have implications for humanity as well as for individual women. In her stories
she focused either on one woman's experience or, as in "The Leaning
Tower," the broad social spectrum. Only in "Hacienda" did she balance
the two. Trying to juggle those two visions within one long work caused
her problems. In* Ship of Fools *there is no real focus on a central character
or her psychology. "Hacienda" works because it uses the broad social context to objectify what is going on in a woman's psyche.* Ship of Fools *can-*

not do that; it deals with too many issues simultaneously—without bringing them to a conclusive meaning in a given personality. No real change is possible; nothing really happens, unlike "Hacienda," where nothing appears to happen, but real change is effected in the central character, the narrator.

In Ship of Fools, Porter cannot decide whether she is writing short fiction or a novel. The frequent cinematic sequences focusing on a character or a couple, treated with more depth, might have made several short stories, while the structure of the voyage and its dramatic events necessitated the scope of a long novel. Like the men and women of the Vera, these elements never successfully merge in Porter's imagination. Her eye is on the microcosm but her mind is on the macrocosm.

This is true, too, in terms of content. On one level, she characterizes all the familiar female types from her stories in this long work; temptresses, matrons, and androgynous women dominate the ship, and she even applies aspects of their psychosexual dilemma to male characters. On a second level, she applies her understanding of that conflict in women to the universal world of the ship. To clarify meaning, she utilizes two standard motifs already familiar to readers of "Pale Horse, Pale Rider": Eden and the wasteland. But the novel ends in frustrating circularity. When human beings attempt to protect themselves by refusing to love, civilization deteriorates. Ironically, that deterioration can be halted only by people willing to risk enough to love each other purely and truly, which Porter demonstrates they find it impossible to do.[1]

Like Eliot, she feels that the failure to love quickly becomes an incestuous concern with self and, consequently, an inability to love another. In such a world, no one can communicate; rape and prostitution prevail. Sex loses its restorative power and becomes the frenzied "tickling of the nerve endings" common to nonrational animals. Few children are produced, and those who are tend to be sallow and freakish.

On a national scale, the inverted energy of aborted love can be turned into fervid nationalism and, as in Mexico, tapped for revolution. On board the Vera, energy that might have created love and human union becomes a horrifying chauvinism breeding prejudice, exclusion, and hatred. Unable to find unity and security with each other, the couples in this drought-stricken wasteland must pay passionate allegiance to fatherland—that is, to their own superiority. Such nationalism can only become totalitarian and will end in holocaust. Thus, in her last work, Porter begins with the concept of thwarted love, asserting that a society full of ruined lovers produces incest and barrenness. Such sterility can only send love-starved human beings raging toward hell.

7 ❖ Ship of Fools

In *Ship of Fools*[1] Porter uses the desert wastes of Vera Cruz, its town walls pocked with bullet holes, to establish the backdrop of the barren microcosm which the passengers will not escape, but will carry with them onto the *Vera*. Like the setting of a medieval morality play, Vera Cruz is purgatory, and it is populated by characters representing whole classes of people and human experience. The emaciated Indian, who stands for the ubiquitous starving and revolutionary masses, is opposed to the upper-class property owners and power brokers. They are joined by the grotesque, horribly maimed beggar, who seems more animal than human; and the bitter brawling of the animals of Vera Cruz, carping at each other in disparate languages, surrounds the men in the square. Amid this setting, two other crucial elements are introduced: sex and violence/death. The two essential activities of the men drinking in the square are eyeing the young women on their way to work and to church, and discussing the most recent aimless bombing by the revolutionaries, which has killed an innocent young Indian boy, cannon fodder in the grisly Mexican struggle for power.

Enter Everyman—the passengers—to suffer the aridity both of the land and the human beings in it; to be accosted, cheated, reviled, and scorned to the limits of their endurance, until "their humanity [is] nearly exhausted" (p. 22). Like Miranda, they hope to outride death and the devil, but the portents are ill. There are hurricanes along the coast, revolutions and general strikes and a smallpox epidemic in the coastal towns. They travel "at their own risk" and at individual risk, significantly refusing to make comrades of each other. Furthermore, they lack something Miranda has had: a willingness to commit themselves to another.

It is this disunity and their separateness that is the very thrust of the tale. Coming from different cultures, holding different values, and speaking different tongues, they seem to lack the most rudimentary fellow feeling. Each person functions as an island, entire to himself.

Like the initial setting in Vera Cruz, the *Vera*—the real setting of the book—is allegorical, as are the disparate pilgrims bound to it. The ship may be, as the author's note tells us, heading toward eternity, but the passengers on it are condemned to go round and round in circles. They cannot escape what they have left, and they cannot arrive at anything truly different. In this context, it is wise to remember that an earlier title of *Ship of Fools* was *No Safe Harbor*. Although this is a voyage to specific ports, there is really no place to go. Most of the passengers, like the sugar workers, are going from misery to misery. The *Vera*'s primary destination, Bremerhaven, is not really home to anyone. The German families returning there have been in Mexico so long that they will find themselves expatriates in their own country; others, like Freytag, intend to displace themselves altogether from Germany, and the businessmen and women are transients whose primary ties to their country are monetary.

Jenny Brown and David Scott, who make their home wherever they find it, do not want to go to Bremerhaven at all, but they lack the proper visas to go elsewhere. The *Vera* and its people are headed inexorably toward Germany, the leaning tower of the world's trouble in that time, which threatens to bury others in its collapse. The reader, for instance, has ironic knowledge that though Mrs. Treadwell will avoid Germany by disembarking at Boulogne, her destination, Paris, will not be safe. Even there the shock waves of destruction will be felt, and her Utopia will wind up overrun, occupied, and corrupted at its core before the destruction of world war is complete.

Among their number, the passengers count their share of misfits and outcasts, like the town of Vera Cruz: Herr Glocken, the pathetic hunchback; Herr Graf, the dying religious fanatic; Elsa Lutz, lard-like, but full of never-to-be-satisfied romantic longing; and Herr Löwenthal, the eternal scapegoat, the Jew. They adequately represent the whole of the first-class passengers, among whom the manhood is mostly hunched and dying, the womanhood stultified and unsatisfied, and where each person regards the other as a pariah. The one element that might alleviate this condition, love, struggles to survive in an environment that supports only lust: it is no mistake that the only passengers aboard when the ship docks in Vera Cruz are two Cuban "ladies of trade." But the situation is not entirely without hope. The last people to board are a Mexican bride and groom—young, beautiful, newly joined, like Adam and Eve, a potentially perfect couple.

With this pair always on the fringes of things, Porter will focus, in the body of the book, on the couplings and uncouplings necessitated on a floating wasteland where passengers must surely fear death by water. Most significantly, although she ceases to depict women with divided psyches (all the women in *Ship of Fools* have accepted their métier, for good or ill), she essentially uses her innate understanding of that conflict, projecting it into global proportions.

First of all, the passengers on the *Vera*, like her conflicted protagonists, are trapped. Physically, they are all bound to the island of the ship. Mrs. Treadwell finds the ship "like a prison, almost" (p. 248), and of course it truly functions that way for La Condesa and the deportees in steerage. Their presence beneath the grating, along with the crowded cabins and the smallness of the ship, adds to the sense of constriction all the passengers feel. Psychically, they are hemmed in by self-satisfaction, smugness, and prejudice, whether Christian or Jew.

Second, like Porter's earlier heroines, none of the characters, with the possible exception of the bride and groom, is able to use his or her sexuality to any good end. Although some reach out for unity, for one reason or the other, they all discover in the end what Mrs. Treadwell has known all along: to love, one must go naked; love is dangerous, and the best protection is an aloofness that prevents the other from coming too close. Of course, the corollary that Mrs. Treadwell is perhaps too insulated to see is that such aloofness fosters an indifference which ultimately allows evil to run rampant. Unchecked by love, evil rules the world.

And finally, of course, there is the familiar threat of death, which surfaces in a variety of forms wherever sex is indulged, but most notably in the threat posed by the incorrigible Spanish twins, Ric and Rac, self-styled demons whose symbiotic relationship opposes them to the Mexican bride and groom. Interestingly, neither pair is really characterized; their flatness suggests that they function as polar possibilities in the potential use of human sexuality. Whereas the Mexican couple are discreet and modest in their affection for each other, softly fatigued but fulfilled by their discovery of their capacity to complete each other, the twins represent sex turned in upon itself: incestuous, uncontrollable, unblinking, shameless.

Dr. Schumann calls the twins "devil-possessed"; in fact, the demonic nature of Ric and Rac seems to be the one idea in which the passengers on board the *Vera* are united. What is more significant, however, is the fact that, unlikely as it seems in the case of six-year-olds, they are creatures with sexual knowledge, and they are constantly attempting or threatening to kill by throwing things into the ocean. Their activities affect virtually every would-be couple on the ship with the exception of their own people, the Spanish dancing troupe, and the two independent and essentially asexual American women, Mrs. Treadwell and Jenny Brown, and the men associated with them. In essence, their evil, sexual presence in several instances provides a counterpoint to the developing relationships among the various men and women on the ship. Their continuous attempts to kill establish an ominous tone which culminates in the death of the innocent Etchegaray, the wood-carver, who creates the likenesses of animals while the children attempt to drown living ones. Thereafter, their elders will wreak their own havoc through their devilish fiesta, bringing to complete chaos and perdition any possible coupling on the ship.

Before we can examine these themes in detail, however, it is necessary to characterize the passengers, particularly the types of women on the *Vera* and the significance of their connection with certain men. Readers of Porter's stories have met them all before; however, although the women of the *Vera* are hardly in communion, they do not engage in overt conflict. Again, only Mary Treadwell and Jenny Brown come close to any kind of psychological conflict, as we shall see later. Although set in opposition to each other, Porter's female types in *Ship of Fools* are static, not developing. These women have already decided how to love and how to use their sexuality, and their characterization says more about the author's view of their choices than about them.

There are, first of all, the Venus figures, the temptresses. The women of the Spanish zarzuela company—Amparo, Lola, Pastora, and Concha—are a far cry from the somewhat innocent, passionate María Rosa in "María Concepción" or even the admirably independent Ninette in "Magic." Described as pretty slatterns, they are not unappealing, but their innate corruption shows in the tawdriness of their appearance, in their cheap dresses and their badly run-down shoes.

In them, something beautiful has become corrupt. The sleekness of their hair, their graceful limbs, and their glittering teeth and eyes remind the reader of nothing so much as a predatory animal. They are more than once described as having serpent's eyes, and, truly, sex on their terms has become an evil thing. We have already seen that dancing in Porter's literature is a metaphor for sexual activity, usually in a very restrained form. But these Spanish whores make their living by dancing, using it to entice the men around them. Their dancing and their "love" is something to be traded for money, and it can be fraught with violence. Concha and Amparo (and by extension, the others) not only accept but expect beatings from their pimps. Amparo shudders with masochistic pleasure when Pepe slaps her as a prelude to making love to her.

Most frightening of all, however, in Porter's terms, is that these women have so completely *become* sex that every other part of them is dead. Unlike María Rosa and Ninette, they have no personality or identity apart from their sexual natures. Pepe is interested in making love to Amparo only when her sexuality is heightened, when she has "just come from another man" (p. 221). And she herself, quarreling with Jenny Brown, slaps her inner thigh and shouts at her what she clearly thinks is the supreme insult to a woman: "'No money, no man, and nothing *here*,' she said, slapping herself again . . ." (p. 340). Even Jenny agrees that a vagina is what Amparo has. Unfortunately, she has traded her humanity for it; it is all she has.

It is no mistake that Arne Hansen, an animalistic, brutish man, is the only male who establishes a long-term business commitment with one of these women; William Denny, although crude enough, is not so powerful; he cannot wrest what he wants from Pastora, and Johann's brief sojourn with Concha is but a youthful descent into the passionate first circle of hell.

The second Venus figure, La Condesa, is far more complex. As an outcast who is being deported from her native Cuba for alleged involvement in revolutionary activities, she represents what a woman who steps outside traditional female roles can expect. As an exile, an incendiary, a prisoner, and a woman who relies on drugs which leave her in a trancelike state, she reflects not only her feelings about her own womanhood, but the psychic states of many of the women on the ship. One can believe that she "loathes" women and hates being one.

Although she is a mother, she is bored by infancy and says she found her own children interesting only after they reached the age of eighteen. In fact, she is burdened by her motherhood: she is attended everywhere by the young Cuban students whom she tolerates because they were schoolmates of her sons—the same sons whose revolutionary activities sent her into exile. Her somewhat shabby but expensive clothes make her seem not tawdry but a bit pathetic.

Yet she is not so innocent as she seems. Coming on board when the two Cuban prostitutes leave the ship, she apparently attempts to entice young sailors when she first boards. Dr. Schumann observes her cornering and talking to a series of young men, weaving before each of them in a serpentine fashion: "Her eyes were like agates, and she swayed from side to side, stretching her neck, trying to force the boy to look her in the face" (p. 118). He is shocked to see her stroke her own breasts and thighs, and pat the face and heart of her listeners (p. 119). She is clearly a seducer, as Dr. Schumann himself will discover firsthand, a Lilith sent to punish and test the good intentions of Dr. Schumann's Adam and, not incidentally, a concrete threat to his weak heart.

A second familiar image is present in the traditional women—the wives and mothers on the ship. These women, like the temptresses, have also chosen to use their sexuality, and they prove to be no better off for having done so in a way sanctioned by society. In the first place, their names readily indicate that they have sacrificed long ago their personal identity for the sake of marriage, most graphically illustrated in the case of Frau Professor Hutten. But it is no less true of Frau Baumgartner, Frau Schmitt, Frau Lutz, or Senora Ortega.

Since Frau Hutten has so completely taken the traditional role to herself that her acquaintances call her "the ideal German wife," she may stand as a representative of the others. Her whole person is wrapped up in service and support of her husband and his ego. She has protected him from life's difficulties even to the point of becoming his beast of burden; he has never so much as carried a book to school in all his years of teaching. That once she was an independent personality which even now she has not totally repressed, is clear from the "traitorous" revery she falls into whenever her husband launches into one of his dull dinner table speeches. Musing about her husband's belief that they have never had a quarrel, she remembers bitter pills of submission she had to swallow for the health of her marriage:

> . . . the many lessons taught her then had gone into her blood and bones, and changed her almost beyond her own recognition. By now she remembered these hard lessons dimly and without that secret fury against her bridegroom which even at its hottest she had known for what it was—treachery to her marriage vow. She knew well that upon the woman depends the whole crushing weight of responsibility for happiness in marriage. At times this had seemed to be just one more unbearable burden which fell to the lot of wives. (pp. 284–285)

Seeing her resentment as baseness, she represses it in favor of her husband's patriarchal superiority, acquiescing in the delusion that she depends on him for everything. Indeed, her corpulence, symbol of the psychic burden she has taken on in making obeisance to him, means she cannot move off the floor without his help. Too often, however, as on the evening when she recognizes that he is seasick and gives him an excuse to leave the captain's table graciously, she must support him while appearing to need his assistance.

Surprisingly, she is not so very different from Amparo or Concha. Her man's career is built on her "slave labor," and if she doesn't sell her body for him, she has certainly had to sell her soul. Her reward is exactly the same as Amparo's, for her husband's fatherly instructions on her childlike responsibility to him always end with the two of them "in bed, always in bed, melting together in long loves so delicious and shameless it felt sinful, not like marriage at all" (p. 285). Porter women are not supposed to fall into that trap. If they have any sensibility at all, their psychic identity is at least as important to them as their sexual identity.

What they are supposed to do in the face of the necessity to marry is become mothers and sublimate sexual energy to an end that allows them an independent role. However, the women of the wasteland are noticeably infertile. Frau Hutten has desired children but not been granted them. In fact, her betrayal of her personhood is illustrated in the fact that she has become a devouring and hateful "mother" to her husband's recalcitrant students, the only children he has given her. Finally, she is reduced to surreptitiously nurturing her husband. Public mothering must be directed to Bébé, the bulldog, an abortion of the kind of matriarchy practiced by Granny Weatherall and Miranda's grandmother.

Frau Schmitt, with no children of her own, has also allowed her whole personality to be subsumed by her husband's. She has taught school because he was unable to hold a full professorship, and that, along with tending to her war-torn husband, has been her life:

> She was beginning to realize with astonishment that she had never really known any man but her husband; no women except wives of her husband's friends. . . . For years she had hardly seen anyone . . . except in the company of her husband: indeed, she had lived her married life almost literally in his presence. His state of health after the war had made it seem at times almost as if he were her child. . . . (p. 188)

She is identified by the heavy gold locket, containing his portrait, which she "cannot be without," and indeed it seems like a chain that ties her to him still. Having devoted herself totally to him, what she is left with is his corpse, which she longs to sit with in the hold of the ship. She is a small but unerring statement of what happens to women who depend too much on their relationship with a man.

Frau Baumgartner and Frau Lutz are each legitimate mother to one child, but the size of their families illustrates again that they cannot keep company with the pioneer mothers of Porter's canon. Each must cope with a husband for whom she has lost respect. Unable to expend their total energy as wives, they tend to overprotect their individual children in recompense. Consequently, Hans is a fearful child, and eighteen-year-old Elsa Lutz wears a foolishly small beret which suggests she is far more a child than the marriageable young woman she ought to be.

There remains only the young Mexican mother, Señora Ortega, "softened and dispirited by recent childbirth" (p. 29), whose maternity stands in sharp relief because she is unaccompanied by her husband and attended only by a primitive Indian nursemaid. Traveling with her first-born, she is hardly a matriarch, either, but has experienced enough of the pain of childbirth to show "a shade of terror in her face" (p. 54) at the thought of the other children she will bear. It is Frau Rittersdorf, happily childless, who romantically indulges her "womanly" feelings by mentally rhapsodizing over "the divine mystery of life" present in the new child, while his mother thinks painfully of the reality of motherhood: "how he woke and yelled in the night and pulled on her like a pig when she was tired to tears and wanted only to sleep" (p. 54).

Clearly, motherhood in a wasteland of infertility must be spent mostly on grown men, if it is to be spent at all. This in turn can only frustrate the women involved, causing them to lose respect for the husbands they must mother, thus further widening the rift between the sexes in this world where love is difficult if not impossible. The Mexican mother seems to suggest that even the happiest maternity, bringing forth a first-born son, is fraught with pain.

The androgynous women on the *Vera* don't confront this problem of utilizing maternal or even sexual energy. They are for the most part self-contained, sexually inactive, and dependent on no man. Frau Rittersdorf is the most obviously single of these women, returning unengaged from a trip to Mexico she felt sure would secure a wealthy Mexican husband for her mature years. Don Pedro has refused to take the bait, and Frau Rittersdorf is annoyed, but not devastated. She clearly can take care of the attentions a man is good for, as she demonstrates by sending bouquets of flowers—under the names of two deceased friends—to herself on board the *Vera*. By paying court to herself, Frau Rittersdorf does away with the necessity for confronting and coping with sexual feelings, a human flaw she has steadfastly resisted all these years. She has systematically repressed her sexual nature at the behest of her revered dead husband, Otto, who has instructed her in guarding against "impure" thoughts, even in the midst of intercourse.

Like Granny Weatherall, however, she has sexual potential, and when these emotions erupt, she cannot deal with them. This is clearly shown in the single dance she shares with Tito one evening, supposedly against her will. In phrasing that surely suggests masochistic rape, she thinks of how she "had felt herself taken without her consent and spirited away like a cloud, in the lightest, surest, gentlest embrace she had ever known, in such a dance as she had not even dreamed of since her innocent girlhood . . ." (p. 262). Like Granny Weatherall, she tries hard not to remember the incident, which makes her blush for shame, and she repeats over and over all the prayers she can remember "as an incantation against evil" (p. 262). "Though childless herself and never ceasing to be thankful for it" (p. 54), she too has spent her maternal instincts on her husband. She is finally contented with the memory of her husband's head cradled in her arms, she singing to him and rocking him to sleep "as if he were her little child" (p. 263).

Surely one of the most unfeminine women on the ship, despite her penchant for wearing lace and ounces of perfume, is Fraulein Lizzi Spockenkieker. Not a fraulein at all, as Herr Rieber muses, but a woman of the world, she is divorced, with the experience of several male "friends" behind her. Reminiscent of Rosaleen O'Toole in "The Cracked Looking-Glass," she nevertheless flirts and teases like a silly young girl. She readily provides a wasteland inversion of the notion of the innocent maiden. She is frequently described in animal imagery, most often referred to as a "peahen" or a "mare," and seems deliberately masculinized in several details: her hair is cropped short and she is flat-chested (Ric and Rac, surprising Lizzi and Rieber secreted on the ship's darkened deck, are disappointed to see that her unbuttoned blouse reveals no breasts); but it is her behavior more than anything else that marks her as androgynous.

She competes aggressively with Herr Rieber in the games they play, punishing him physically when she loses; nor is she a passive sexual playmate, biting him painfully during an amorous tussle one evening. The mothering the other fraus give their men is certainly missing here. But of course this is hardly surprising, for Lizzi is above all a businesswoman with a career; she is used to taking care of herself first, without the assistance of a man who might in the long run prove to be a bad investment. Her refusal to participate in sex is hardly from maidenly inhibition but rather because the right contract has not been struck. Again she is not unlike Amparo, for to Lizzi, sex is money, and she seems to lack any human passion of her own.

Androgynous but far more complex are the two most completely characterized women in the book: Jenny Brown and Mary Treadwell. Although basically different in personality, they are alike in small things: in their longing, for instance, for Paris, the City of Light; in the ties they feel (even while rejecting them) to their childhood homes; in their essential decision to be independent of any man for the sake of personal psychic survival. Interestingly, the man who becomes the scapegoat and therefore the outcast of the ship's "society," Wilhelm Freytag, is associated with them and with no other women on the voyage, suggesting that these two, more than any other women on the ship, are pariahs also. Nevertheless, they are distinct personalities and deserve individuated consideration.

Jenny Brown, the independent young American woman traveling with a man not her husband, is immediately defined as a dual creature. Although she has long hair modestly pulled back in an old-fashioned bun, she makes her first appearance among the other passengers in Vera Cruz wearing the shirt and trousers of a Mexican working man. The other passengers note her appearance with disdain, and the Mexican waiters in the piazza call her a mule.

More significant than physical appearance, however—which Jenny has sacrificed for the sake of free choice—is her opposition to David Scott, her lover. In the broadest terms of the novel, they represent yet another possible Adam and Eve, a couple who want to achieve a perfect, happy love—that is, unity and integration. Yet they are frustratingly separate. Although traveling "together," they cannot even agree on a common destination. Their physical separation and incessant quarreling on the ship suggests, on the simplest level, that their relationship is more grounded in sexual attraction than in a lasting love and, on a more complicated plane, that their division arises from the inherent opposition of warring personalities.

Porter readers have encountered this couple in "That Tree": the free artistic personality paired with the rigid, puritanical seeker of pristine, classical perfection. Here, however, although the struggle is similar and familiar, the terms are somewhat different. We are no longer dealing with two parts of one personality, waiting to see which will subsume and incorporate the other. Although Jenny has been influenced by David's taste and preference, even to the point of adopting his artistic technique and purity of color in dress, she recognizes her error and determines to reassert her own style. When a gypsy says a man is in her future, Jenny declares she doesn't need a man to survive. She is clearly a separate personality, sometimes irritatingly so, from David's point of view.

Jenny, with her easy gaiety, her light-heartedness, and her emotional readiness that allows her to picket for any political cause "for a lark," is promiscuously available as David sees it, inclined to tell strangers everything about herself and to creep off into corners with other men. She retains nothing, whereas he, like Mrs. Treadwell, reserves everything out of self-protection and lives "like a willful prisoner within himself, [who] would not let the door be unlocked" (p. 147). Whereas she gives it all away, David hungrily devours everything as if he can never get enough. Jenny thinks of him as a changeling child, belonging to no family, whose hunger is never really satiated. Having been a timekeeper in a Mexican mine, David further displays his rigidity in his fetish for cleanliness and his penchant for drawing only in black and white.

Such opposites ought to temper and ameliorate each other, but Jenny and David's relationship has been fated from the beginning. Only one month after she began to live with him, Jenny witnessed a tableau in a Mexican Indian village which becomes an emblem of their togetherness, first in her dreams and finally in her consciousness. What she has seen is a man and a woman locked in a death struggle amid the dust and heat of an Indian dwelling:

> They swayed and staggered together in a strange embrace, as if they supported each other; but in the man's raised hand was a long knife, and the woman's breast and stomach were pierced. The blood ran down her body and over her thighs, her skirts were sticking to her legs with her own blood. She was beating him on the head with a jagged stone, and his features were veiled in rivulets of blood. (p. 146)

This couple so bent on killing each other is "purified of rage and hatred." They cling together, "arms . . . wound about each other's bodies as if in love" (p. 146), finally resting their heads on each other's breast and shoulder while they gather strength to strike again.

The paradoxical necessity that men and women murder each other because they are joined together in love is but an extension of the inherent understanding of earlier Porter protagonists that love and sex place them in mortal danger. Only now men are perceived as victims as well.

Then too, Jenny has conflicts of her own apart from her relationship to David. In spite of her idealism, Jenny dares not allow herself to believe in love as she would like to do. When Freytag waxes poetic about the nature and possibility of love, Jenny listens hopefully, "as if hypnotized. The dreamy voice was soothing as a cradlesong, a song her own wishful deluded heart sang to itself" (p. 168). But she ends by asserting her "bitter mind" over her feelings and declaring these attitudes "sick, sentimental and false," declaring to Freytag with a vehemence which suggests how much it hurts her to say it: "I think it is a booby trap, . . . I hate it and I always did. It makes such filthy liars of everybody. But I keep falling into it just the same" (p. 168). Likewise, Jenny abhors the maternal feelings which well up in her easily, but they are what soften her to David time after time on the voyage. The inevitability of these emotions is evidenced when she determines to get away from David before they kill each other, but thinks to herself that she'll be "carrying David like a petrified fetus" for the rest of her life (p. 169).

Wilhelm Freytag, one of the more sensitively characterized men on board the *Vera*, functions as a perfect foil to both David and Jenny while simultaneously creating a romantic triangle with them. An emotional opposite to David, who, like Jenny, desires a good and true love, Freytag's presence makes it clear that Jenny has not chosen David idly. Ultimately, she prefers David, who "hates love worse" than she does. She supposedly resents this in him, but paradoxically it allows her to trust him. It is yet another convoluted statement of Jenny's rejection of her emotional nature and inner self, certainly a defense Porter women learn in order to protect themselves.

Jenny creates yet another triangle with Wilhelm Freytag and the wife whom he idealizes, Mary Champagne. Like Jenny, he has reached out for what seems pristine and perfect to him in a partner, and Mary Champagne's name indicates all that she is to him: virginal, pure, blond, beautiful, rich. Freytag constantly compares Jenny's ideas, attitudes, and behavior to Mary's perfection, thinking that "such follies as Jenny promised to be belonged to his other life . . . ; he knew what they were worth compared to the solid reality of his marriage" (p. 170). Yet Jenny, as an unmarried woman traveling with her lover, certainly represents sex, and Freytag's attraction to her, always clearly defined as a sexual one, is yet another reminder that perfect and pristine love does not exist—because we are sexual creatures.

Freytag tells Jenny that what she falls into isn't love, and she counters by insisting that one can't separate true love and sex. He says he agrees, but his private revery proves that, like the traditional male, he distinguishes sexual women from the ones worth marrying. Three months absent from his wife, he thinks of appeasing his sexual needs with Lola, the "basest-looking" of the Spanish dancers, with "something good and dirty and hot . . ." (p. 170). He continually talks to Jenny about his Mary, as if using an incantation against any sexual power Jenny might bring to bear over him.

But even Mary Champagne is a madonna with a flaw, for, contrary to all appearances and expectations, she is a Jew, a real enough stigma in pre–World War II Germany, but also a symbolic stigma: even a perfect woman is a sexual creature. Significantly, Freytag is chastised by his fellow Germans—not for anything he has done or for what he is, but for his connection with his wife. It is as if through his Jewish marriage he is punished both for his somewhat sentimental idealism and for the sexuality that is also cared for by the perfect woman he has set upon a pedestal.

Finally, Mary Treadwell is an androgynous woman so confirmed in her choice of independent singleness that it is horrifying even to David Scott, who is obviously nearly as bent on protecting himself emotionally as Mrs. Treadwell. From the beginning, Mary Treadwell is defined as retentive, and that quality is tied to her sexuality immediately. She has refused a beggarwoman alms and has been rewarded with a brutal pinch that has left her with a bad bruise on her arm. Dr. Schumann, watching her board the ship, easily decides that the bruise, "most likely the result of an amorous pinch, gave her a slightly ribald look . . ." (p. 29).

The significance of that assumption is not immediately apparent as we watch Mrs. Treadwell make her "escapes" from emotional entanglement, first with Frau Schmitt and then with Herr Freytag. She thinks prophetically that she will inevitably "sit down and have a good cry with somebody" (p. 40) before the voyage ends. That event does come about—but ironically because of her extreme reserve as well as her not completely repressed sexuality. She is not so uninterested in men that she has not noticed that Freytag is the only attractive man on the ship. Her mistake is to make his acquaintance, and because she gives no confidences herself, ever, she is totally unprepared to recognize one when Freytag tells her his wife is Jewish. Thus she repeats it casually to Lizzi, setting in motion Freytag's ouster from the company at the captain's table. Freytag's angry upbraiding brings on the tears she abhors. In a subtle way, her mild attraction to this good-looking man brings about the kind of trouble she has learned to expect from contact with the opposite sex.

Indeed, it is the intrusion of the opposite sex into her life that has ended the warmth and security of her long, luxurious childhood. She has lived in an emotional cocoon "that lay on the other side of that first love which had cut her life in two" (p. 207). Then, nightmare: "ten years of a kind of marriage, and ten years of divorce, shady, shabby, lonely, transient . . ." (p. 207). We meet her on the other side of a marriage defined primarily as a sexual experience in which she has tried hard to be "a slut" for her husband and has suffered his abuse. Mrs. Treadwell's experience proves the validity of the fear—shared by other Porter women—that sexual experience will change irrevocably the controlled maidenly life they know. She protects herself from the pain of this period by telling herself that "none of it had really happened" (p. 207), "not a word of it was true," and "I don't remember anything" (p. 208).

Recognizing that she has tried to obliterate the sexual period of her life and its painful aftereffects, we can better appreciate the subtle conflict in Mrs. Treadwell's psyche between her youth and the beginning of age, which she feels coming upon her with the advent of her forty-sixth birthday. Since she refuses to remember the middle of her life, her adult womanhood, there is no sense of continuity or progression for her. Under the mask of age she suddenly finds herself wearing, she hides carefully a "sixteen-year-old heart" (p. 397). No wonder that August, "the coarsened, sprawling, sunburnt afternoon of summer" (p. 247), seems most to resemble that age in life at which she has arrived. It is most antithetical to the person she feels herself to be.

She aptly illustrates the identity of this person in her behavior on board ship. During the day she practices detachment from the other passengers. When she parties in the evening she again illustrates not only her detachment but her foothold in her maidenhood. Her dancing, often with a handsome young officer, recalls the debutante balls of her youth, now a soft shimmer in her memory. But dancing for Mrs. Treadwell is also controlled sexual intimacy, an activity whereby she and her partner may be swept up and out of present time by the whirling motions of their bodies. As a young girl, she has learned, however, to control this intimacy by keeping her partner literally at arm's length. Control of her emotions, restraint, is the protective armor she wears against the kind of emotional ravages the wife in "Rope" suffers. Letting go can have fearsome consequences, as we will see on the climactic night of the voyage.

At night Mary Treadwell reverts completely to her maidenhood, putting on girlish nightgowns with full bishop sleeves that button to the neck and pulling her hair back "in the Alice in Wonderland style she had worn in bed since she was four or five" (p. 203). Her movements are all "very calm and orderly, like a convent-bred girl" (p. 206) as she sits playing game after game of solitaire on a small chessboard, which should be used by two. Significantly, she always loses at solitaire, but the game, along with the wine she drinks each night, is her distraction from remembering her painful disappointment in love.

The men of the *Vera* cannot be so easily classified as the women. For the most part they are individuated, but bound together by their clear disdain for women, which reflects the complete breakdown of rapport between the sexes. From the benign Dr. Schumann to the lewd William Denny, there is hardly a man on board who regards a woman as a person, much less an equal with whom he might share his self. Some pay lip service to that idea, but in their moments of anger, drunkenness, or anxiety, they all reveal the effects of drought on Eden: each has forgotten that woman is a part of himself.

In perhaps the mildest antiwoman revery, Dr. Schumann permits himself a "brief vengeful meditation on the crockery-smashing sex, . . . the sex that brought confusion into everything, religion, law, marriage; all its duplicities, its love of secret bypaths, its instinct for darkness and all mischiefs done in darkness" (p. 233). David Scott reveals his innate disdain for women when he feels a loss of self-respect because he has allowed Jenny to influence and to worry him, to affect his work and his life.

Herr Professor Hutten believes women are little more than children; on the other hand, Herr Baumgartner thinks *he* is the child: his wife is there to give him "freedom in all things while at the same time maintaining the restraints, appearances, and disciplines of daily life—what else was a wife for?" (p. 435). Arne Hansen, Johann, and Herr Rieber all regard women as sex objects; William Denny is the worst of all, having a whole slew of dirty epithets for women: "all women, the whole dirty mess of them. . . . one as much a bitch as the other . . ." (p. 304). The ship's captain feels that women must be kept in their place, and even so minor a character as the purser has an "utter contempt for the female sex" (p. 321).

In such an environment it is little wonder that the evil events of the voyage take place. The rising action, the events of the first half of the trip, are moved forward by the frenetic behavior of Ric and Rac, while the bride and groom stroll always on the periphery of the ship's activity. It is no mistake that the murderous twins, so sexual in nature, are linked to the sexual temptress La Condesa. From the beginning of the voyage all three are a threat to the doctor's weak heart. As a couple, he and La Condesa are the focus of the first half of the work and act as a paradigm for the other couplings taking place on board.

In their first attempted homicide, Ric and Rac have beguiled the ship's cat by petting him and so have managed to lay hands on him, intent on throwing him into the sea. Schumann, thoughtlessly putting himself in danger of a heart attack, rushes to the rescue and saves the cat, which has been "seduced within an inch of his life by a tickling of his nerve endings" (p. 117). That he is as vulnerable as the cat to seduction and death is clear: in the next moments he first sees La Condesa. He finds her beautiful and wishes for her attentions, feeling confused about her provocative behavior: does it reflect a nervous disorder or seductiveness? Actually, her poor health is but a metaphor for her sexual needs, and the doctor is the man who can cure both. She calls him to her cabin, and, despite his professional manner in examining her, she complains of her miserable fortune while openly stroking her breasts and telling the doctor she adores him. While he rebukes her sharply, he gives her a narcotic injection she does not need, symbolically giving in to his temptation to penetrate her.

Their next real encounter occurs again in the context of Ric and Rac's activities. This time the twins follow Herr Rieber and Lizzi to the darkened deck to watch their lovemaking. After Herr Rieber buys them off, they secrete themselves in a lifeboat and indulge in a little sex play themselves. Discovered and hauled before the doctor and La Condesa, they give her a chance to show her fellowship with them. She begins by dismissing their crime as amusement, then sarcastically suggests they be thrown overboard, an idea befitting the twins themselves. Finally, in a discussion of sin and innocence with the doctor, she tells lightly how she once gave her brother lye water to drink, saying she meant no harm, but was curious only "to see whether it would kill him" (p. 198).

Telling the doctor she loves him, she asks if he has never been unfaithful to his wife. Thus after warning him of his danger, she sets the snare and ends by begging him for an injection, saying, "Oh, quiet me—put me to sleep," the plea of a woman to be controlled or subdued in a sexual as well as a medical sense. And indeed, at the moment when he is about to plunge the needle into her upper arm, they smile "at each other lovingly" (p. 203). Furthermore, Dr. Schumann eventually uses his hypodermic in the way that more primitive man has always used sex against woman: to subdue her and assert his power over her. Feeling frustration over her confinement to her cabin by the captain, she expresses her contempt by smashing two bottles of *Schaumwein* in her basin. The doctor, even though he recognizes her motives and understands, still feels an uncontrollable urge to make her "feel his hand and will" (p. 233) and responds by roughly seizing her and plunging his needle into her arm.

Of course, despite his frantic rationalizations, there is never any doubt that he is much infatuated with her. Even unsuspicious observers like Frau Schmitt and members of the ship's crew can see it in his face. He behaves like a jealous lover, cutting off the visits of the Cuban students who are her only company. He then feels the need to confess and ask absolution for his mental capitulation to her charms. He correctly recognizes her as a demon lover who would drown him in the depths of the passion of which he fears himself capable, and so, like the Porter women who are always praying against remembering that they are sexual creatures, he repeatedly invokes the names of Jesus, Mary, and Joseph to ward off his demonic thoughts. When he finally does admit his love for her, he does so furtively, on the last night before she leaves the ship, when she is too drugged to respond.

As she is about to disembark, he admits his nocturnal declaration, but links this love to death. When they lovingly say good-bye to each other, he murmurs, "'Death, death,' . . . as if to some presence standing to one side of them casting a long shadow" (p. 355). It is what Mrs. Treadwell and Jenny fear, too; impending death, of one kind or another, is the threat of the voyage.

In counterpoint to the attempted couplings on the ship in the first half of the voyage is the essential separateness of the characters, one from the other. Amid the outbreak of fighting in the steerage, it is plain that the characters are divided—nationality from nationality, religion from religion, class from class—and they seem unwilling or unable to change. La Condesa tells Dr. Schumann that being German is "an incurable malady . . . as hopeless as being a Jew." To which he replies, "Or a woman" (p. 232). By implication, all humanity is imprisoned in the cage of its own kind, and attended there by prejudice and indifference, which are essentially refusals to love.

As the work moves toward the major events of the voyage, it begins to dramatize the old adage that for evil to triumph, it is necessary only for good men to do nothing. In four separate instances evil triumphs, aided and abetted by the passivity of those who witness it. In the first such instance, the social exclusion of the man wedded to a Jewish wife, Wilhelm Freytag, comes about because of the indifference of Mrs. Treadwell to her companion's secret, which in turn allows her to repeat it thoughtlessly to the prejudiced Lizzi. Freytag is right to be impassioned when Mrs. Treadwell says she gossiped only out of boredom: "Out of your boredom! What right have you to be bored? Indifference—what right have you to live in this world and care nothing for the human beings around you?" He further points out that her indifference is like a stone sending out ripples as it sinks in a pool: "It is not just this one thing—no no, it is a lifetime of it, it is a world full of it—it's not being able ever to hope for an end to it—" (p. 252).

Significantly, the petty evil present on the ship assumes a more sinister air directly following this exclusion. The members of the zarzuela company begin to plan their evil fiesta and to openly solicit money and heap insult and contempt on those around them. They are aided and abetted by the insensitive Cuban students. The heightening danger—as well as the echo of Eliot's clairvoyant's warning to "fear death by water"—is highlighted by the fact that Ric and Rac's evil becomes more overt. They threaten not only to throw Bébé, that "good innocent helpless dog," overboard, but Hans Baumgartner, too. Concha, meanwhile, is suggesting to Johann that he smother his uncle so that he will have money to spend on sex with her.

More than one kind of death occurs in *Ship of Fools*. When Ric and Rac finally succeed in laying hands on the stupefied Bébé and throwing him into the ocean without a second's thought, they represent the evil threatening to engulf and destroy the smug, self-satisfied, and complacent middle-class Germans (and by implication, the upper classes of other cultures), who are made defenseless by their self-centeredness.

Of course, it is not the death of the dog that results, but that of the innocent and helpless (weaponless) Etchegaray, who has acted to save life with a thoughtlessness equal to that of the evil children who have sought to destroy it. His lowly status at once recalls the senseless murder of the poor Indian boy in Vera Cruz and foreshadows the slaughter of the Jews. Naturally, it is aggravating that we know so little about him. Yet, in the terms of this moral fable, we know all we need to know about him: he is not indifferent. He doesn't wait to distinguish whether the living thing in the water is worth saving or not. He loves life, and he loves it enough to act to save it. Of the characters we know, the same can probably be said only of Dr. Schumann, who threatened his own life by rushing to save the ship's cat from the clutches of Ric and Rac at the beginning of the voyage.

Two important consequences result from this central incident. The first is sexual. The Huttens are suffering a serious breach in their marital relationship because Frau Hutten has dared to express an opinion different from her husband's—and in company, at that. His wife's distraction over Bébé's disappearance adds to his anger and irritation, but Frau Hutten's unintentional revolt is nipped in the bud when the water-logged Bébé is restored to her. Like the surrogate child that he is, Bébé represents the security of the Huttens' life together and the familiar solidity of their marriage, for which Frau Hutten has sacrificed everything. Bent over the half-drowned dog, she is reduced to weeping over their lost Eden in Mexico, their happiness in their youth. Feeling completely bereft, she throws herself on her husband's mercy, which triggers in him a sense of rightful power and therefore forgiveness and passion for his wife.

Emotionally restored to their familiar roles—she the child and he the almighty father—"grappled together like frogs" (p. 312), they make love passionately, in what is probably the most awkward sexual encounter in literature. Like others on the ship, their chance encounter with Ric and Rac has placed them in a sexual context. Their reunion has a longlasting and, at first glance, a good effect, since the status quo in their marriage is restored and their lovemaking renewed. But like Amparo and Pepe, they have a working sexual union based on inhuman premises. Frau Hutten has rediscovered power over her husband by learning again to be a sexual child. One can hardly applaud when she resolves near the end of the voyage to "save herself for love" (p. 375).

The second consequence has broader significance for the entire group. After Etchegaray's death, each person has a chance to demonstrate a capacity for commitment, that is, love; instead, each will demonstrate a capacity to do nothing. First, practically nobody understands what Etchegaray has done; practically nobody cares that he has done it, or that he has departed this life. Everyone's fear of death is highly personalized. Second, there is no one to speak against Ric and Rac for Etchegaray, and even the Huttens, most wounded by the twins after the poor carver, decline to accuse them. There is no law against drowning a dog, they say; they have no idea what the twins might have been thinking. Like the young woman in "Theft," they rationalize themselves out of the trouble of standing up and speaking out against a justifiable and obvious injustice done to their property and to the life of another human being.

The funeral the next morning is a mockery of the communal rite of passage it should be, with the first-class passengers acting like observers of a spectacle rather than participants and with violence breaking out among the fellows of the dead man. The portent of the failure of anyone to mourn properly the destruction in the wake of such evil is obvious. Ric and Rac ride high, enjoying themselves and the triumph of the "funeral of the man they had killed . . . [and] their fight on deck . . ." (p. 319). It is they who finally spot the course of three silver whales—a proper diversion that allows the spectators to consign the violence and death of the moments before to the past so that they can say, with the Huttens, "Well, it can't be helped, . . . it is done now, it is out of our hands" (p. 310).

That this malignity might be corralled is demonstrated by the final incident involving the malicious twins. Having stolen La Condesa's pearls, they race along the deck and nearly collide with the Lutzes, who are walking there. Frau Lutz instinctively grabs Ric and administers a maternal slap, causing him to drop the necklace, which Rac then throws into the sea. After arguing with his wife over the discretion and propriety of reporting what they have observed, Herr Lutz speaks to Dr. Schumann, the whole company is taken to task, and the children are punished and subdued (albeit for the wrong reasons). But, most important, the passengers are spared the children's mischief for the remainder of their stay on board.

Unfortunately, the passengers don't perceive that they have the power to oppose the encroaching malice of the dancing company. This is aptly demonstrated in what happens when they go ashore on Tenerife. A place of rough but incredibly lush beauty, it is the home of "beautiful and chaste" young girls who are water carriers. They are the very antithesis of the women of the wasteland, who not only can provide no water—that is, life—but who, if they are beautiful, are hardly chaste, and, if chaste, like Elsa Lutz, hardly beautiful.

Unlike the young girls "employed in making an honorable living," the Spanish company descends like a flock of crows on the island shops, shouting, insulting, thieving, stealing, scattering, creating chaos and fury wherever they turn, and leaving mayhem in their wake. Frau Rittersdorf records the details in her diary:

> "They are all over the shops, everywhere, like a pack of invading rats. I have watched them, and I know they are stealing right and left. . . . I feel they carry a kind of pestilence with them, they shed around them the true metaphysical odor of evil." (p. 367)

Of course, she feels no responsibility to do anything about this, and each of the others reacts in kind. The Americans gather with Freytag and follow the Spaniards about to see the show. The Huttens characteristically decide it is not their affair. Herr Glocken, probably the most timid member of the ship's company, is ironically the only one asked for assistance by a shopkeeper; he is completely routed by the Spaniards and must be assisted himself by Frau Lutz, who again steps in to discipline Ric and Rac as they chase Herr Glocken down the street. But neither do the Lutzes or the Baumgartners speak out against the thieves. Herr Glocken tries to focus on the enormity of what is going on:

"They were stealing everywhere today, they have been cheating on the ship all the time—that raffle—those children, those
little monsters, stole La Condesa's pearls and threw them overboard—" (p. 377)

Nevertheless, everyone goes on "gossiping all around the subject
and never once admitting guilt or complicity . . ." (p. 378).

After such knowledge, there can be no forgiveness. After the
thefts on Tenerife, the ship crosses into autumnal weather: a sunless
sky, gray water, and chill. The dancers announce their fiesta for that
evening, and it becomes plain that the capitulation of the "worthy"
members of this ship's society is complete. They gather out of curiosity to gawk at the stolen items displayed for raffle and wind up
buying chances on the prizes. If indifference has been their sin to
this point, the passengers now rationalize a direct participation in
the devil's dance to come. One by one they separate to rest, to shave,
to make a costume, to prepare for the party. The men think in terms
of seduction, whoring, and rape.

This *Walpurgisnacht* is the climax of *Ship of Fools* in more than
one sense. The two major themes of the work are brought together
in a nightmarish circle in which they chase each other's tails. The
ship's society is brought to complete chaos through its tacit acceptance of and connivance with evil. This destruction is spelled out in
sexual terms, and the myth of the perfect couple is all but destroyed
as one union after the other is frustrated or aborted.

By design of the dancing troupe, the whole evening becomes an
exercise in inversion. Ordinary place settings are disturbed, so that
there is confusion and commotion as people try to seat themselves
for dinner; and the stage is set for at least one violent argument, between Arne Hansen and Herr Rieber. Only the bridal couple conduct
themselves with a dignity that sets them apart from the rest. The
Spaniards, having established themselves at the head table, are purposely late, upsetting the captain and leading to his perfectly murderous reverie in which he fancies himself mowing down a riotous
mob with an "elegant portable machine gun" (p. 408). By the time
the Spaniards take possession of his table and run through a series of
inverted toasts, the captain is not sure whether he has been honored
or cursed. He flees the madhouse shouts of "To eternal confusion!
To dishonor! To shame!"—abandoning his ground to the invaders
who have turned his "correct" society into a hellish mockery. Already the passengers have begun to quarrel and to drink too much.
When the Spaniards begin the dancing by mimicking the dancing
styles of the other passengers, they bring to a fine point the insults

they have heaped upon the others in the previous several days. Herr Glocken, who wears a ridiculous tie inscribed "Girls, Follow Me," establishes the fact that sex is the business of the evening. And of course all this deviltry should end in orgy, but in the inverted terms of the evening, even orgy will be thwarted.

The image which ties together the chaotic violence inherent in the evening and the theme of aborted love is the raffle display of feminine finery, presided over by the Spanish women, who are available, like the frilly lace, for a price. The only real sexual union of the evening occurs when Johann finally succeeds in buying Concha.

For everyone else, there is frustration, violence, and despair. Elsa Lutz, finally confronted by the Cuban student whom she yearns for, cannot dance, and so loses the chance to fulfill her fantasy. Jenny and David quarrel and separate, and even Arne Hansen is forced to sit moodily nursing a beer because Amparo refuses to have anything to do with him. William Denny winds up literally chasing Pastora around the ship in an effort to get her into bed.

But even for those who might have greater expectations, things cannot work out. Jenny takes up with Freytag, who has designs on her, but she passes out before he can make love to her. Mrs. Treadwell gets drunk and allows her young officer to kiss her, but rejects him easily, out of habit, without a second thought. When Arne Hansen, drunk and already irritated by Herr Rieber, cracks a beer bottle over the bald man's skull, he recalls the similar incident in the steerage the day of Etchegaray's funeral. Hansen's act effectively ends not only Rieber's satyric reverie but also his prospects for seducing Lizzi that night or any other of the voyage.

It is, however, the violent and unlikely encounter between Mrs. Treadwell and William Denny that most effectively typifies and climaxes a whole voyage of misbegotten unions. We have already seen that Mrs. Treadwell is trying to gracefully negotiate a tightrope stretched between the fairy tale world of her youth—in which she was a princess—and the lonely mature years that stretch before her. What she ignores and cannot consciously deal with is the sexual period of her life, spent with her husband. Although she easily rejects the young officer's advances, he does stir in her a desire to try on that role again.

In a parody of Cinderella, who lost her slipper at the ball running from the prince, Mrs. Treadwell returns to her cabin half barefoot, having given a broken sandal to the steward for repair. There she sits down "to amuse herself" by painting on her own face a mask of "unsurpassed savagery and sensuality" (p. 442), not unlike Amparo's. She recognizes in it "a revelation of something sinister in her character" (p. 442), her sexuality and its attendant uncontrollable emotion, both of which she has so successfully repressed.

If Mrs. Treadwell is the princess who has once more successfully evaded marriage to the prince, William Denny, in a grotesque caricature of the prince come to claim his bride, forces her to confront reality. Seeing the mask of her repressed sexuality, he mistakes her for Pastora. In this he recognizes her as a sexual woman—in his parlance, then, a whore. He assaults her and she resists. Finding that he is too drunk to right himself when she pushes him to the floor, she does to him what Lacey Mahaffey does to her drunken husband in "A Day's Work." In what might be described as an inverted rape, *she* assaults *him*, punching him in the face and finally removing her remaining slipper to viciously pummel his head with its metalcapped heel, leaving her mark with every blow. Her anger with the man who has initiated her into the sexual world is thus spent by this passionate attack on another man who embodies carnality; after this she can wash her face of the terrible mask, restoring herself to princess-like maidenhood in a white satin bedgown, hair tied back like Alice in Wonderland. Restored to the equilibrium she understands, she sniffs the fresh sea air and remembers how, in the Maytime of her life, she saw the stars coming out one by one in the Paris sky.

Only the Baumgartners remain, and their riddled union is marked by the fact that their wedding anniversary occurs on this terrible night. Like all the others, they quarrel, primarily over Frau Baumgartner's refusal to play the angry mother to her husband's childish insistence that he will commit suicide by throwing himself into the ocean. The quarrel is not over before he has slapped her and they have made love in a kind of temporary reconciliation, but, significantly, their lovemaking is reported from the point of view of their young son, Hans, who sees in it violence and conflict:

> Something horrible was happening there in the dark, something frightful they were keeping from him—he strained his eyes staring, but there was only a wall of pure blackness mingled with the sounds of struggle. (p. 439).

And when Mrs. Treadwell passes them the next morning it is clear that, far from being renewed in each other, they are shamefaced, hiding "some sort of shabby little incident" (p. 460). She thinks to herself what the inhabitants of the wasteland really want from each other:

What they were saying to each other was only, *Love me, love me in spite of all! Whether or not I love you, whether I am fit to love, whether you are able to love, even if there is no such thing as love, love me!* (p. 460)

At Vigo, both the Spanish dancers and the Mexican bride and groom leave the ship, effectively stripping it of its sexual character. Like cockroaches, the dancers have survived the holocaust and seem none the worse for wear. The bride and groom leave without saying good-bye to anyone, and this is just, since they have never truly been part of this company. A kind of quiet settles on the ship after their departure, and denouement takes place.

However, the situation seems to have come almost full circle once again. As in Vera Cruz, the portents are bad. In every harbor, there are strikes, and cargo cannot be unloaded. The small boats that come out to meet the ship add confusion rather than gaiety, and there is no certainty that the captain will stop in any port but Bremerhaven.

Confusion abounds even for Jenny and David, on whom the action now focuses, even though they have finally decided to travel together to the same port. In spite of the fact that Jenny happily tells David she would like to "crawl back inside and be [his] rib again" (p. 467), this Adam and Eve have sinned against each other and will repeat their error. They find, first of all, that they cannot get visas for France, and then, determining finally to go to Bremerhaven, they find that David has mistakenly been issued a ticket for Southampton, which must be changed.

At Boulogne, where Mrs. Treadwell demonstrates how one gets to Paris—solitary and alone, her back turned against the ship she is leaving—Jenny weeps out of longing for the "blessed shores of France" (p. 469). At Southampton, an English-speaking newspaper boy, for some unexplained reason, won't—or can't—communicate with them, echoing an equally puzzling disagreement between the German captain and the British officers.

Finally, in Bremerhaven, a temporary commitment is made. Jenny asks, without rancor, why they are continuing when they are not going to spend their lives together. David replies that "maybe" they will never leave each other. The best thing they can think of is that they will sleep in the same bed that night. If unity can't be counted on, there is at least animal warmth for a time and the momentary staying of such loneliness as is imaged in the solitary, half-starved boy, a trumpet player in the ship's band, who stands on the deck of the *Vera* in Bremerhaven, whimpering, "Grüss Gott, Grüss Gott."

❖ Conclusion

We have already seen that Porter's work is an unfolding of a particular understanding of feminine experience. First of all, there exists within her women conflict between their natural desire for the warmth, security, and community of love, and their innate human desire to be autonomous and independent. Her traditional heroines begin by looking fervently for love, naïvely hoping for an Edenic, ordered world where they will live happily ever after. This is as evident in Isabel and Mrs. Whipple as it is in more complex characters like Granny Weatherall, Rosaleen O'Toole, and Miranda.

As they acquire, like Laura, a "developed sense of reality," they recognize that their sexuality complicates their choice of love or independence and precludes their having both. If a woman chooses love, with its attendant sexual relationship, she will surely lose her personal identity and possibly lose her life in childbirth. She may become a mother, thereby acquiring another new identity which lends autonomy and power. But it is inconceivable that she would use sex for its own sake, since she fears its unbridled power. Only the daring Amy toys with that prospect. However, if she eschews sex in favor of protecting her selfhood, she can become independent, although she must then suffer other frightening limitations which Porter women, like the protagonist of "Theft," discover only gradually and painfully.

The first evil inherent in independence is loneliness; these women must be entire to themselves. There is an even more insidious loss of sensitivity and repression of emotion which eventually withers the capacity to love at all and creates a vacuum of indifference where once there was personal desire and passion. Or, if one retains libidinal energy, it must be directed toward some other use: for Porter women, this is often art, religion, or political revolution.

By the time she comes to write *Ship of Fools*, Katherine Anne Porter is prepared to universalize her informing idea, and that is what her magnum opus is all about. Among the disparate company of passengers, someone has tried every tangled possibility in the web of human love. The book illustrates not only the personal pitfalls but the global implications for a society which finds it improbable, impractical, or impossible to love. In this concept, all the apparently separate issues of *Ship of Fools* are unified.

In the novel, Porter applies point for point what she knows about female conflict to the whole human gallery. Previously seen in terms of individual women and often internalized as a psychic struggle, the choice between secure love and independence is now the problem of men and women alike, and even of groups, classes, and nations of people. The same basic truth learned by Porter women as they come of age—that independence is lonely and that refusing to love breeds insensitivity—asserts itself in *Ship of Fools*. In addition, Porter suggests that collective loneliness and failure to love have sinister, staggering implications for human survival.

Once again, the desire for Eden is preeminent: in Mrs. Treadwell's wish to reach her utopian Paris; in the feeling of the Lutzes that they will be happy and Elsa will find a husband in Switzerland; in Frau Baumgartner's hope that her husband, removed from his old environment, will cease his drinking. But especially it is evident in the presence of so many potential Adams and Eves, couples who might succeed in creating a comfortable, secure nest together against the ravages of the outside world: Jenny and David, Freytag and his Mary, the Mexican bride and groom. They readily discover what all Porter women discover, that the first compromise necessary is some loss of identity. If the love relationship is to exist, concessions to the loved one are inevitable. Freytag is forced to admit, against all his inclinations, that prejudice is directed against his beautiful blonde Mary. If she cannot go out with him to public places, then he must elect to stay at home with her. In spite of the fact that he is still a prosperous German of good family, he must now accept her Jewishness as part of himself, even to being excluded from the dinner table society to which he has a perfect right. Jenny makes concessions to David's taste by drawing and dressing to please him; her gradual movement back toward her own preferences during the voyage signals the widening rift between them. Certainly the loss of the identity he knows—that of a God-fearing man—is what Dr. Schumann fears most in establishing a relationship with La Condesa. And their personal identity is something Frau Hutten and Frau Schmitt have long since forsaken in holding fast to marriage.

The second threat to selfhood, death, is also strongly evident in *Ship of Fools*. That one may lose one's life by loving is illustrated in Etchegaray's death. It is further illustrated in the precarious position of Dr. Schumann, whose heart is threatened by the passion he feels for La Condesa, and by the emblem of the Mexican Indian couple

engaged in mortal combat, who reflect most keenly the struggle between Jenny and David but also the conflicts of other couples on
board.

By the forties and fifties when *Ship of Fools* was being written,
the number of deaths in childbirth had been significantly reduced,
and birth control ensured that sexual activity need not cause pregnancy. Some women on board the *Vera* use sex as some men have
always done: as an isolated act separate from the context of any
larger emotional responsibility. That many of the characters equate
sex with love instead of seeing it as a part of a larger, more powerful
relationship between men and women suggests how wasted Eden
has become. Lola, Amparo, Concha, and Pastora are "something
good and dirty and hot," not women; Frau Hutten's marriage is restored by a renewal of sexual relations with her husband, suggesting
there is not much else to their partnership. Lizzi uses sex as a barter-
ing tool. Freytag worries that his sexual attraction to Jenny is dis-
loyalty to the pure wife he loves. And of course Dr. Schumann, in his
brush with the devil, mistakes his sexual attraction to La Condesa
for real commitment. This substitution of the part for the whole results in another kind of human death that Porter women have always innately feared. Those who use sex for its own sake or who fail
to control themselves in other ways—like Hansen, Denny, the Spaniards, and Lizzi—lose their humanity to animalism and are thus described in animal imagery.

Which brings us to the choice of independence, with the same
inherent problems Porter women have come to know, projected onto
larger numbers of people and, through them, all humanity. The first
of these problems is loneliness, imaged in Löwenthal the Jew. Frau
Rittersdorf and Frau Schmitt certainly reflect it, and David Scott
keeps loneliness for his real bedfellow. However, Mary Treadwell is
obviously the supreme example of it. She has so repeatedly and
forcefully repressed human feeling in herself that she exudes indifference and a terrifying complacency—ironically, a force which,
coupled with evil, can destroy the world.

Finally, what the floating wasteland of the *Vera* reflects is not
only a barren Eden weedy with failed lovers, but a confused and root-
less bunch of nomads, wandering in circles around the deck of the
ship, occasionally bumping into each other and experiencing momentary human contact, but never deriving the two things they need
most: a sense of belonging to each other and to something larger than
themselves, and a need to use their energy to foster the growth of that
larger reality, be it personal love, family, art, or principle.

In that poverty lies the horror of *Ship of Fools*. The *Vera* (ironically, "Truth") drives on toward Germany, at that point only a breeding ground for the deranged chauvinism and totalitarianism that will eventually kill six million Jews. In Porter's view, then, thwarted love, abused sexuality, and dishonored personal integrity are far more than women's problems, for the human hunger to belong and the need to use frustrated libidinal energy can then only be turned in upon oneself in an incestuous perversion of what is right and true affection. We see it in the Spanish twins and in the Spanish dancers, who, if nothing else can be said for them, are a tightly knit group, going everywhere in a knot, and content to be among themselves. The Germans are headed in the same evil direction, and the determined progress of the *Vera* indicates what the reader already ironically knows—that the Spaniards will end in a bloody civil war and the Germans in the holocaust of Nazism.

The indifference of the Mary Treadwells and the misdirected love of the Jenny Browns will conspire in a terrible union to allow evil to run rampant. Thwarted love may sound like the content of soap opera, but in Porter's hands, over several decades of writing, it becomes deadly nightshade with power to destroy the world.

The women in Katherine Anne Porter's fiction deserve to be studied first of all for the richness of characterization in them and for what they reveal about the psychic experience of womanhood. But they also deserve to be studied because in the largest sense they are feminine figures of the typical American hero: independent, isolated wanderers who choose rebellion (sometimes in the form of art) rather than love, marriage, or integration into civilization. They are also members of modern society, whatever their roots, and as much as the characters of Hemingway or Fitzgerald they chronicle what the advent of the twentieth century meant to the human race. Over and over, in the early stories as well as those focusing on Miranda, Porter's women must discover that love is usually attended by death and that independence is almost always lonely. They may have love or work, but not both. In that psychic reality, all these women—and their stories—come together. Whether the setting is Mexico, New York, a rural farm, or even the oceanbound *Vera* in *Ship of Fools*, Porter's women struggle with the tension between a desire to be feminine (in fairly traditional terms) and a desire—not to be alone—but to be free.

Appendix

Chronology of Katherine Anne Porter's Fiction

Date Written	Date Published	Title
1922?	December 1922	"María Concepción"
?	July 1923	"The Martyr"
1923	December 1924	"Virgin Violeta"
1924	December 1960	"Holiday"
?	October 1927	"He"
1927?	Summer 1928	"Magic"
?	1928	"Rope"
1927	February 1929	"The Jilting of Granny Weatherall"
1928	November 1929	"Theft"
1929	June 1960	"The Fig Tree"
1929	Spring 1930	"Flowering Judas"
1931	May 1932	"The Cracked Looking-Glass"
1931	1932, 1934	"Hacienda"
1931?	July 1934	"That Tree"
1933– 1934? {	January 1935	"The Witness"
	January 1935	"The Last Leaf"
	April 1935	"The Grave"
	July 1935	"The Circus"
1936	Spring 1936	"Noon Wine"
1936	Spring 1937	"Old Mortality"
1936	Winter 1938	"Pale Horse, Pale Rider"
?	Winter 1936	"The Old Order" (later "The Journey")
?	December 1939	"The Downward Path to Wisdom"
1937	February 1940	"A Day's Work"
?	Spring 1941	"The Source"
1940	Autumn 1944	"The Leaning Tower"
1942– 1962	1962	*Ship of Fools*

Note: Porter's statement in an interview clarifies the process by which the stories were ordered: "Surely we understand very little of what is happening to us at any given moment but by remembering, comparing, waiting to know the consequences, we can sometimes see what an event really meant, what it was trying to teach us. . . . In that sense it has sometimes taken me ten years to understand even a little of some important event that had happened to me . . ." (Barbara Thompson, "Katherine Anne Porter: An Interview," *Paris Review* 29 [1963]: 13). Dates of authorship in this chronology are based on a cursory reading of Joan Givner, *Katherine Anne Porter: A Life* (New York: Simon and Schuster, 1982), which was published just as this book went to press. Although it is difficult to date the "Old Order" stories, Givner states that many of them were "written during the Paris Years," probably in 1933 and 1934 (p. 339).

Notes

Introduction

1. Katherine Anne Porter, "Three Statements about Writing," in *The Collected Essays and Occasional Writings of Katherine Anne Porter* (1970; rpt. New York: Dell, 1973), p. 457. Hereafter cited as *CE*.
2. John W. Aldridge, "Art and Passion in Katherine Anne Porter," in *Time to Murder and Create: The Contemporary Novel in Crisis* (New York: David McKay, 1966), pp. 178–184; rpt. in *Katherine Anne Porter: A Critical Symposium*, ed. Lodwick Hartley and George Core (Athens: Univ. of Georgia Press, 1969), p. 97.
3. Edmund Wilson, review of *The Leaning Tower* by Katherine Anne Porter, *New Yorker*, September 30, 1944, pp. 72–74.
4. Cleanth Brooks, "The Southern Temper," in *A Shaping Joy: Studies in the Writer's Craft* (New York: Harcourt, Brace, 1971), pp. 205–208.
5. Robert Penn Warren, "Katherine Anne Porter (Irony With a Center)," *Kenyon Review* 4 (1942): 29–42; rpt. in *Katherine Anne Porter*, ed. Hartley and Core, pp. 51–66.
6. M. M. Liberman, "Lawrence, 'María Concepción,' and the Feminine," in *Katherine Anne Porter's Fiction* (Detroit: Wayne State Univ. Press, 1971), pp. 59–69.
7. Jane Flanders, "Katherine Anne Porter and the Ordeal of Southern Womanhood," *Southern Literary Journal* 9 (1976): 47–60.
8. Judith Fetterley, "The Struggle for Authenticity: Growing Up Female in *The Old Order*," *Kate Chopin Newsletter* no. 2 (1976):11–19.
9. Katherine Anne Porter, *The Collected Stories of Katherine Anne Porter* (1965; rpt. New York: New American Library, 1970), represents Porter's essential canon. Subsequent references to this work will occur in the text.
10. Thomas F. Walsh, "Deep Similarities in 'Noon Wine'," *Mosaic* 9 (Fall 1975): 83–91.
11. A complete and valuable study of the Great Mother archetype is Erich Neumann, *The Great Mother: An Analysis of the Archetype*, trans. Ralph Manheim, Bollingen Series, no. 47 (1955; rpt. Princeton: Princeton Univ. Press, 1972); also useful is C. G. Jung, "Psychological Aspects of the Mother Archetype," in *Four Archetypes: Mother, Rebirth, Spirit,*

Trickster, trans. R. F. C. Hull, Bollingen Series, no. 20 (1959; rpt. Princeton: Princeton Univ. Press, 1973) pp. 7–44.

12. A. E. Crawley, "Doubles," *Encyclopedia of Religion and Ethics* (New York: C. Scribner's Sons, 1911), vol. IV, p. 860.

13. Otto Rank, *The Double: A Psychoanalytic Study*, ed. and trans. Harry Tucker, Jr. (Chapel Hill: Univ. of North Carolina Press, 1971), p. xx. The double and its significance for literature is discussed at length in C. F. Keppler, *The Literature of the Second Self* (Tucson: Univ. of Arizona Press, 1972); and Robert Rogers, *A Psychoanalytic Study of the Double in Literature* (Detroit: Wayne State Univ. Press, 1970). Rogers' Chapter 7, "Fair Maid and Femme Fatale," is particularly relevant.

14. Sigmund Freud, "Taboo and the Ambivalence of Emotions," in *Totem and Taboo: Resemblances Between the Psychic Lives of Savages and Neurotics*, trans. A. A. Brill (1913; rpt. New York: Random House, 1918), pp. 26–97, is relevant here. Freud notes that "the projection creations of primitive man resemble the personifications through which the poet projects his warring impulses out of himself, as separated individuals" (p. 86, n. 54).

15. Anne Firor Scott, *The Southern Lady: From Pedestal to Politics 1830–1930* (Chicago: Univ. of Chicago Press, 1970), p. 4.

16. Ibid., p. 17.

17. Ibid., p. 43.

18. Ibid., pp. 14–16.

19. Helene Deutsch, *The Psychology of Women: A Psychoanalytic Interpretation*, 2 vols. (New York: Grune and Stratton, 1944, 1945).

20. Ibid., vol. I, p. 192.

21. Ibid., p. 283.

22. Juanita Williams, *Psychology of Women: Behavior in a Biosocial Context* (New York: Norton, 1977), p. 44.

23. Deutsch, *The Psychology of Women*, vol. I, p. 210.

24. Ibid., p. 287.

25. Ibid.

26. Williams, *Psychology of Women*, p. 44.

27. Deutsch, *The Psychology of Women*, vol. II, p. 93.

28. Ibid., p. 221.

29. "The Journey," *The Collected Stories of Katherine Anne Porter*, p. 334.

30. Scott, *The Southern Lady*, p. 39.

31. Quoted in Ibid.

32. Deutsch, *The Psychology of Women*, vol. II, p. 216.

33. Scott, *The Southern Lady*, p. 44.

34. "Ole Woman River," *CE*, p. 282.

35. "Three Statements About Writing," *CE*, p. 457.

36. In 1931, Porter left Mexico and sailed for Paris via Bremerhaven, the voyage which became the basis for *Ship of Fools*. Once in Paris, after publishing "Hacienda" and "That Tree," she wrote no more about Mexico. The objectification of character in "That Tree" suggests the emotional distancing that must have taken place after the writing of "Ha-

cienda." At this point, Porter took a new culture to her heart, married for the third time, and settled down to produce the Old Order series and to let other stories germinate from memories of her childhood. In these, she explores the inception of the psychological dichotomy she has chronicled so many times previously.

37. Barbara Thompson, "Katherine Anne Porter: An Interview," *Paris Review* 29 (1963): 87–114; rpt. in *Katherine Anne Porter*, ed. Hartley and Core, pp. 19–20.

1. *Reflections*

1. The following comment on Porter's use of Mexico in her stories: Drewey Wayne Gunn, "'Second Country': Katherine Anne Porter," *American and British Writers in Mexico, 1556–1973* (Austin: Univ. of Texas Press, 1969), pp. 102–122; William Nance, "Katherine Anne Porter and Mexico," *Southwest Review* 55 (1970): 143–153; Colin Partridge, "'My Familiar Country': An Image of Mexico in the Work of Katherine Anne Porter," *Studies in Short Fiction* 7 (1970): 597–614. See also *CE*, pp. 355–430.

2. James William Johnson, "Another Look at Katherine Anne Porter," *Virginia Quarterly Review* 36 (1960): 598–613; rpt. in *Katherine Anne Porter*, ed. Hartley and Core, pp. 83–96. Johnson, among others, has noted the opposition of the maternal and the love principle in "María Concepción."

3. When a rose is open, in full bloom, its petals create a pattern suggesting the mandala, a design in Oriental and Mexican mythology and art which is symbolic of the universe. The mandala image suggests in turn female genitalia. Thus, the rose is an effective symbol of María Rosa's role on several levels.

4. Neumann, *The Great Mother*, p. 190.

5. Ibid., pp. 196–197.

6. Ibid., p. 197.

7. Ibid.

8. Ibid., p. 207.

9. Possibly modeled on Diego Rivera.

10. George Hendrick, *Katherine Anne Porter*, United States Authors Series, no. 90 (New York: Twayne, 1965), p. 38.

11. It is interesting to note that Freud believed the cause of hysteria, so prevalent in Victorian women, to be a "traumatic seduction." Usually found in patients who claimed to have been seduced by a parent, hysteria resulted because sexual desire directed toward a person of such powerful authority was overwhelming.

12. Hendrick, *Katherine Anne Porter*, p. 83.

13. Ibid., p. 95.

14. Freud describes this homeopathic magic in *Totem and Taboo*, p. 106.

15. Porter's stories about unhappy marriages have often been cited as examples of her negativism. Her essays, however, suggest repeatedly that she

believes in the possibility and the importance of personal love between two people. For instance, she approves E. M. Forster for his "unalterable belief in the first importance of the individual relationship between human beings founded on the reality of love—not in the mass, not between nations, nonsense!—but between one person and another" (*CE*, p. 74). And in "Marriage Is Belonging," she states that "the blood bond, however painful, is the condition of human life in this world, the absolute point of all departure and return" (*CE*, p. 191).

What she eschews is not the possibility or the value of close interpersonal relationships, but the sentimental, mindless assumption that "romantic love is changeless, faithful, passionate, and its sole end is to render the two lovers happy. It has no obstacles save those provided by the hazards of fate . . . ; all real troubles come from without, [and the lovers] face them unitedly in perfect confidence" ("The Necessary Enemy," *CE*, p. 184).

Porter's stories suggest that she is an emotional and psychological realist who understands only too readily that all human beings, even those who love each other and marry in good faith, are subject to evil in themselves. Like the proverbial young wife in "The Necessary Enemy," all lovers will at times experience hatred of their spouses, Porter contends, along with an attendant guilt over what they feel is a betrayal of their promised love. Such an emotion helps to explain the irrational anger of the wife in "Rope," and subsequent guilt causes the emotional turn she takes at the end of the story. As an artist, Porter chooses to dramatize psychologically complex situations in which men and women, in spite of their intention to love each other, fail, and end in ironic difficulty.

16. Joseph Wiesenfarth has pointed out that the story's use of indirect discourse—with characters speaking but not being quoted directly—makes the narrative appear seamless and therefore ropelike. I am indebted to him for this insight.

2. A Closer Look

1. *The Complete Poems of Emily Dickinson*, ed. Thomas H. Johnson (Boston: Little, Brown and Co., 1960), pp. 702–703.
2. Daniel R. Barnes and Madeline T. Barnes, "The Secret Sin of Granny Weatherall," *Renascence* 21 (1969):162–165, argue that her constant reference to babies indicates Granny Weatherall had given her virginity to George and was pregnant when he jilted her. According to this interpretation, her maidenhood is what is "not given back."
3. *The Complete Poems of Emily Dickinson*, ed. Johnson, p. 160.
4. For a fascinating discussion of female doubling in "Snow White," particularly as it reflects fragmentation and division in literary women, see Sandra M. Gilbert and Susan Gubar, *The Madwoman in the Attic: The Woman Writer and the Nineteenth-Century Literary Imagination* (New Haven and London: Yale Univ. Press, 1979), pp. 3–92.
5. Karen Horney, "The Problem of Feminine Masochism," in *Psycho-*

analysis and Women, ed. Jean Baker Miller (New York: Penguin, 1973), p. 32, appears to be describing Rosaleen O'Toole when she writes about the way masochistic persons "find reassurance against deep fears": such a person needs to be loved but requires "constant signs of attention, and as he never believes in these signs except momentarily, he has an excessive need for attention and affection." He is easily attached to people, emotional in relationships, and easily disappointed because he can't get what he wants.

6. The best essay on the story is Joseph Wiesenfarth, "Illusion and Allusion: Reflections in 'The Cracked Looking-Glass,'" *Four Quarters* 12 (1962): 30–37. Wiesenfarth argues that in the conclusion, Rosaleen breaks with the pattern of her life and frees reality from her dreams and illusions, finally accepting her life with Dennis. In this view, then, the failure to replace the cracked glass is perhaps an acceptance of the imperfect that is most prevalent in life. Reprinted in *Katherine Anne Porter*, ed. Hartley and Core, pp. 139–148.

3. Shattering Illusions

1. William Nance, *Katherine Anne Porter and the Art of Rejection* (Chapel Hill: Univ. of North Carolina Press, 1964), p. 37.
2. The standard discussion of "Flowering Judas" is Ray B. West, Jr., "Symbol and Theme in 'Flowering Judas,'" *Accent* 7 (1947): 182–188; rpt. in *Katherine Anne Porter*, ed. Hartley and Core, pp. 120–128. West describes the intricate interrelationship of three "fields" of symbolism: Christian, mechanistic, and love symbols, which incorporate another triad—erotic, secular, and divine love. Leon Gottfried, "Death's Other Kingdom: Dantesque and Theological Symbolism in 'Flowering Judas,'" *PMLA* 84 (1969):112–124, illustrates that Porter has drawn on *The Inferno*, T. S. Eliot's poems, and both Cassian and Aquinas in creating the characters, action, and imagery of "Flowering Judas."
3. Thompson, "Katherine Anne Porter: An Interview," in *Katherine Anne Porter*, ed. Hartley and Core, pp. 15–16.
4. This aspect of Laura's psychology is discussed in Sam Bluefarb, "Loss of Innocence in 'Flowering Judas,'" *College Language Association Journal* 7 (1964):256–262. Bluefarb sees Laura as temporarily locked into the state of paralysis which automatically follows loss of innocence. But Sr. Mary Bride, O.P., "Laura and the Unlit Lamp," *Studies in Short Fiction* 1 (1963):61–63, sees Laura's inaction as a denial of and refusal to participate in life. Dorothy Redden, "'Flowering Judas': Two Voices," *Studies in Short Fiction* 6 (1969):194–204, comes closer to my view. She believes Laura survives only by maintaining equilibrium between dual forces in her life.

Porter herself elucidates and adds dimension to this issue in "Letters to a Nephew" (*CE*, p. 115). She appears to be describing Laura in discussing depression, which she equates with a general lethargy and unwillingness to act: "Psychologically, I believe it is supposed to have something to do with emotional and other frustrations due to inhibited libido due in turn to I forget what . . . firmly based on our hidden, long-denied wayward sexual impulses which keep us all feeling like criminals, or at least sinners. . . ." But what really interests her "is the theological view. It is called accidia or acedia, that is, Despair, and it is one of the deadliest of the seven deadly sins. All despair is, of course, in its deepest nature, despair of God's mercy, and you can hardly do worse. . . . my feeling is that the best thing you can do is say 'God be merciful to me, a sinner,' and try not to totter under your share of human perversity of thought and feeling." In other words, if one is to live, one must act.

5. One of Porter's most interesting pieces of nonfiction, "St. Augustine and the Bullfight" (*CE*, pp. 91–101), dwells on the psychological fascination that apparently repugnant forms of excitement provide to even a reluctant participant-spectator, a discussion that provides insight into the complex character of Laura. The "earmarks" of adventure as Porter describes them aptly characterize the environment from which Laura cannot run: she is surrounded by "violence of motive, events taking place at top speed, at sustained intensity, under powerful stimulus and a willful seeking for pure sensation . . ." (p. 101). Furthermore, Porter might be speaking of her protagonist's psychological recognition at the end of "Flowering Judas" when she writes: ". . . adventure is something you seek for pleasure . . . ; for the illusion of being more alive than ordinarily, . . . but experience is what really happens to you in the long run; the truth that finally overtakes you" (p. 92). Again, Porter might be speaking in Laura's voice when she says of the bullfight, "But this had death in it, and it was the death in it that I loved . . ." (p. 100).

4. *Recognition*

1. Lodwick Hartley, "The Lady and the Temple: The Critical Theories of Katherine Anne Porter," *College English* 14 (1953):386–391; rpt. in *Katherine Anne Porter*, ed. Hartley and Core, pp. 161–168.
2. Thomas F. Walsh, "Identifying a Sketch by Katherine Anne Porter," *Journal of Modern Literature* 7 (1979):555–561, uses a previously unpublished essay of Porter's to establish thematic meaning in "Hacienda." In a more recent essay, "Xochitl: Katherine Anne Porter's Changing Goddess," *American Literature* 52 (1980):183–193, he explains that the essay is the first expression of her yearning for perfect happiness. This "lost promise deepens her sense of terror" in "Hacienda," which becomes a paradigm for later stories "in which characters attempt to recover from their sense of betrayal when their dreams of Eden are shattered" (p. 192).
3. *CE*, p. 217.
4. The uroboros is an image of a circular snake biting its tail, a paradoxical symbol of the psychic origins of humanity in which all possible elements were present and undifferentiated. See Neumann, *The Great Mother*, pp. 18–21.

5. In similar language, in an essay entitled "The Mexican Trinity" (*CE*, pp. 399–403), Porter describes the collusion among Oil, Land, and Church which keeps Mexico from any meaningful revolution and its Indians from any real liberation.

5. *I Thought as a Child: The Old Order*

1. Written in 1929, but misplaced and not published until June 1960.
2. Edward G. Schwartz, "The Fictions of Memory," *Southwest Review* 15 (1960):204–215; rpt. in *Katherine Anne Porter*, ed. Hartley and Core, pp. 67–82, notes that all of Porter's fiction is related to Miranda. Flanders ("Katherine Anne Porter and the Ordeal of Southern Womanhood") agrees. She asserts that "the theme of woman's oppression, especially emotional and sexual inhibition, may be found in everything [Porter] wrote" (p. 48). She believes that the Old Order stories are "central to Porter's *oeuvre*, illuminating the fiction leading up to them and following them" (p. 50).
3. Ray B. West, Jr., *Katherine Anne Porter*, Univ. of Minnesota Pamphlets on American Writers, no. 28 (Minneapolis: Univ. of Minnesota Press, 1963), pp. 24–25. West notes that the stories of the Old Order are slight, and significant for the unity they have as a whole. It has been noted that this unity constitutes a *bildungsroman*. Fetterley ("The Struggle for Authenticity: Growing Up Female in *The Old Order*") believes these stories were "carefully ordered to reveal the drama of Miranda's growing up" (p. 11) and the primary concerns of that experience. Rosemary Hennessy, "Katherine Anne Porter's Model for Heroines," *Colorado Quarterly* 25 (1977):301–315, finds the Old Order sequence, "Old Mortality," and "Pale Horse, Pale Rider" a female *bildungsroman* which demonstrates that the price of self-knowledge is the sacrifice of romantic love.
4. According to West, *Katherine Anne Porter*, p. 27, "It is in the importance given these events by the authority of the teller that the story gains its significance. . . ."
5. Nance, *Katherine Anne Porter and the Art of Rejection*, p. 80. The autobiographical quality of much of Porter's work should be seen in the light of her comment on autobiography in her review of Eleanor Clark's *Rome and a Villa* (*CE*, p. 80): "This whole book is the distillation of a deep personal experience; it is autobiography in the truest sense, in terms of what outward impact set the inner life in motion toward its true relation to the world: the story of the search for what is truly one's own, and the ability to recognize it when found, and to be faithful in love of it." The same statement might be made of the Old Order stories and *Pale Horse, Pale Rider*.
6. Porter, "Reflections on Willa Cather," *CE*, p. 31. Of significance in relation to this comment is Hendrick's chronology of events in Porter's life (*Katherine Anne Porter*, p. 11). Her grandmother, Catherine Anne Porter, died in 1901 when Porter would have been entering her eleventh year.

7. Robert Seidenberg, "Is Anatomy Destiny?" in *Psychoanalysis and Women*, ed. Miller, p. 318.
8. Scott notes that many Southern women thought their situation comparable to that of slaves. She quotes Mary Chestnut: "There is no slave, after all, like a wife," and the saying that "the mistress of a plantation was the most complete slave on it" (*The Southern Lady*, pp. 50–51).
9. Sigmund Freud, *The Interpretation of Dreams*, ed. and trans. James Strachey (1900; rpt. New York: Avon, 1965), pp. 305–307.
10. Ibid., p. 430.
11. Bruno Bettelheim, *The Uses of Enchantment: The Meaning and Importance of Fairy Tales* (1976; rpt. New York: Random House, 1977), p. 210.
12. M. G. Krishnamurthi, *Katherine Anne Porter: A Study* (Mysore, India: Rao and Raghaven, 1971), p. 48, also concludes that Nannie's choice of a different life is "a quiet assertion of her separate identity."
13. Cleanth Brooks, "On 'The Grave,'" *Yale Review* 55 (1966):275–279; rpt. in *Katherine Anne Porter*, ed. Hartley and Core, pp. 115–119, is a seminal essay. Daniel Curley, "Treasure in 'The Grave,'" *Modern Fiction Studies* 9 (1963):377–384, also raises the story above the level of simple initiation. Seeing the "mind of the writer [as] the grave of the past," Curley believes writers resurrect their past in their art, and that this story is the paradigm of the "personal fable" which informs all of Porter's work.
14. Constance Rooke and Bruce Wallis have discussed the Adam and Eve myth in terms of the story in "Myth and Epiphany in Porter's 'The Grave,'" *Studies in Short Fiction* 15 (1978):267–275.
15. John Edward Hardy, *Katherine Anne Porter*, Modern Literature Monographs (New York: Frederick Ungar, 1973), p. 23, notes that the dove Paul claims is "a traditional Christian symbol of the soul's immortality." So the dove asserts resurrection as well as death. This ambiguity is appropriate as Miranda's last mental image at the end of the story. It is another manifestation of the duality which informs her vision of life.

6. *Face to Face*

1. Flanders, "Katherine Anne Porter and the Ordeal of Southern Womanhood," pp. 58–59.
2. For a very interesting discussion of the composition of "Old Mortality," see Liberman, *Katherine Anne Porter's Fiction*, pp. 37–57. Liberman clarifies the "conflict between the subjective person writing and the objective artist." It is further interesting to note that Porter saw her autobiographical use of family history as a complex derivation of legend and memory, a three-dimensional issue. She explained that her material consisted of "those things I have been told or that I read as a child; . . . and my own memory of events taking place around me at the same time. And there is a third facet: my present memory and explanation to myself of my then personal life, the life of a child, which is in itself a mystery, while being living and legendary to that same child grown up.

All this is working at once in my mind, in a confusion of dimensions. . . . So, I shall try to tell the truth, but the result will be fiction" ("My First Speech," *CE*, p. 433).

3. Hardy, *Katherine Anne Porter*, p. 32, makes the valid point that Gabriel, Amy, and Miranda's association with horses links them to the tradition of chivalry, a word which derives from the French *chevalier*, meaning horseman. Thus the family's interest in horses ought to equate them with the chivalric—or in its more contemporary connotation—the "gentlemanly" tradition. Nothing could be further from the truth about Gabriel, who in most unchivalric fashion "rides" or abuses both his horse, Miss Lucy, and his wife, Miss Honey, in an attempt to realize his dream of wealth.

4. Acanthus is a plant known for its thorns.

5. This is the same archetype Porter was drawn to in Aztec mythology. Sir James Frazer, *The Golden Bough: A Study in Magic and Religion*, abridged ed. (1922; rpt. New York: Macmillan, 1963), describes this sacrificial god as a lover of the mother goddess, who embodied "all the reproductive energies of nature." Her lover or consort was a "divine yet mortal [man] with whom she mated year by year, their commerce being deemed essential to the propagation of animals and plants, each in their several kind; and . . . ensuring the fruitfulness of the ground and the increase of man and beast" (p. 385). In ancient ritual, an effigy of the god was cut from his sacred tree and carried by lamenting women to the sea for burial. Sometimes the blood of priests or other human beings was shed to strengthen the god for his resurrection; in some places, the priest impersonating the god was hung or slain on a sacred tree to ensure the fruitfulness of the crops and continued life.

6. See ibid., chapters 29–40 for a full discussion of Adonis, Attis, and Osiris.

7. George Core, " 'Holiday': A Version of Pastoral," in *Katherine Anne Porter*, ed. Hartley and Core, p. 151, notes that the narrator reminds us of Miranda but discounts this similarity because he thinks "Holiday" is the Müllers' story, not the narrator's. I hope to show otherwise.

8. Liberman, *Katherine Anne Porter's Fiction*, pp. 80–87, discusses the relationship of Miranda to Ottilie.

PART 3. *Beyond the Looking-Glass*

1. A telling synthesis of Porter's understanding of the failure of love, so sharply dramatized in *Ship of Fools*, exists again in one of her essays: "It is hardly possible to exaggerate the lovelessness in which most people live, men or women: wanting love, unable to give it, or inspire it, unable to keep it if they get it, not knowing how to treat it, lacking the humility, or the very love itself that could teach them how to love: it is the painfullest thing in human life, and since love is purely a creation of the human imagination, it is merely perhaps the most important of all the examples of how the imagination continually outruns the creature

it inhabits. . . . Having imagined love, we are condemned to its perpetual disappointment; or so it seems" ("Orpheus in Purgatory," *CE*, p. 53).

7. Ship of Fools

1. Katherine Anne Porter, *Ship of Fools* (1962; rpt. New York: New American Library, 1963). Subsequent references to this edition of *Ship of Fools* will occur in the text. When Porter's much looked-for novel finally appeared, it was first greeted with overwhelming praise; within the year, however, a number of critics disagreed with that assessment, some of them rather violently and personally. For a discussion of the critical controversy surrounding the book, see Joan Givner, Jane DeMouy, and Ruth M. Alvarez, "Katherine Anne Porter," in *American Women Writers: Bibliographical Essays* (Westport, Conn.: Greenwood Press, forthcoming).

Bibliography

Primary Sources

Kiernan, Robert F. *Katherine Anne Porter and Carson McCullers: A Reference Guide*. Boston: G. K. Hall, 1976.
Porter, Katherine Anne. *The Collected Essays and Occasional Writings of Katherine Anne Porter*. 1970; rpt. New York: Dell, 1973.
Porter, Katherine Anne. *The Collected Stories of Katherine Anne Porter*. 1965; rpt. New York: New American Library, 1970.
Porter, Katherine Anne. *Ship of Fools*. 1962; rpt. New York: New American Library, 1963.
Waldrip, Louise, and Bauer, Shirley Ann. *A Bibliography of the Works of Katherine Anne Porter and A Bibliography of the Criticism of the Works of Katherine Anne Porter*. Metuchen, New Jersey: Scarecrow Press, 1969.

Secondary Sources

Barnes, Daniel R., and Barnes, Madeline T. "The Secret Sin of Granny Weatherall." *Renascence* 21 (1969):162–165.
Bettelheim, Bruno. *The Uses of Enchantment: The Meaning and Importance of Fairy Tales*. 1976; rpt. New York: Random House, 1977.
Bluefarb, Sam. "Loss of Innocence in 'Flowering Judas.'" *College Language Association Journal* 7 (1964):256–262.
Bride, Sr. Mary, O.P. "Laura and the Unlit Lamp." *Studies in Short Fiction* 1 (1963):61–63.
Brooks, Cleanth. "The Southern Temper." In *A Shaping Joy: Studies in the Writer's Craft*. New York: Harcourt, Brace, 1971.
Crawley, A. E. "Doubles." *Encyclopedia of Religion and Ethics*. New York: C. Scribner's Sons, 1911.
Deutsch, Helene. *The Psychology of Women: A Psychoanalytic Interpretation*. 2 vols. New York: Grune and Stratton, 1944, 1945.
Fetterley, Judith. "The Struggle for Authenticity: Growing Up Female in *The Old Order*." *Kate Chopin Newsletter* 2, no. 2 (1976):11–19.
Flanders, Jane. "Katherine Anne Porter and the Ordeal of Southern Womanhood." *Southern Literary Journal* 9 (1976):47–60.

Frazer, Sir James George. *The Golden Bough: A Study in Magic and Religion*. Abridged ed. 1922; rpt. New York: Macmillan, 1963.

Freud, Sigmund. *The Interpretation of Dreams*. Ed. and trans. James Strachey. 1900; rpt. New York: Avon, 1965.

———. *Totem and Taboo: Resemblances between the Psychic Lives of Savages and Neurotics*. Trans. A. A. Brill. 1913; rpt. New York: Random House, 1918.

Gilbert, Sandra M., and Gubar, Susan. *The Madwoman in the Attic: The Woman Writer and the Nineteenth-Century Literary Imagination*. New Haven and London: Yale University Press, 1979.

Givner, Joan. "The Genesis of *Ship of Fools*." *Southern Literary Journal* 10 (1977):14–30.

Gunn, Drewey Wayne. "'Second Country': Katherine Anne Porter." *American and British Writers in Mexico, 1556–1973*. Austin: Univ. of Texas Press, 1969.

Hardy, John Edward. *Katherine Anne Porter*. Modern Literature Monographs. New York: Frederick Ungar, 1973.

Hartley, Lodwick, and Core, George, eds. *Katherine Anne Porter: A Critical Symposium*. Athens: Univ. of Georgia Press, 1969.

Hendrick, George. *Katherine Anne Porter*. United States Authors Series, no. 90. New York: Twayne, 1965.

Hennessy, Rosemary. "Katherine Anne Porter's Model for Heroines." *Colorado Quarterly* 25 (1977):301–315.

Johnson, James William. "The Adolescent Hero: A Trend in Modern Fiction." *Twentieth Century Literature* 5 (1959):3–11.

Johnson, Shirley E. "Love Attitudes in the Fiction of Katherine Anne Porter." *West Virginia University Philological Papers*, 13 (1961):82–93.

Johnson, Thomas H., ed. *The Complete Poems of Emily Dickinson*. Boston: Little, Brown and Co., 1960.

Jung, C. G. *Four Archetypes: Mother, Rebirth, Spirit, Trickster*. Trans. R. F. C. Hull. Bollingen Series, no. 20. 1959; rpt. Princeton: Princeton Univ. Press, 1973.

Keppler, C. F. *The Literature of the Second Self*. Tucson: Univ. of Arizona Press, 1972.

Krishnamurthi, M. G. *Katherine Anne Porter: A Study*. Mysore, India: Rao and Raghaven, 1971.

Liberman, M. M. *Katherine Anne Porter's Fiction*. Detroit: Wayne State Univ. Press, 1971.

Miller, Jean Baker, ed. *Psychoanalysis and Women*. New York: Penguin Books, 1973.

Mooney, Harry John, Jr. *The Fiction and Criticism of Katherine Anne Porter*. Pittsburgh: Univ. of Pittsburgh Press, 1957.

Nance, William L. *Katherine Anne Porter and the Art of Rejection*. Chapel Hill: Univ. of North Carolina Press, 1964.

Neumann, Erich. *The Great Mother: An Analysis of the Archetype*. Trans. Ralph Manheim. Bollingen Series, no. 47. 1955; rpt. Princeton: Princeton Univ. Press, 1972.

Partridge, Colin. "'My Familiar Country': An Image of Mexico in the Work of Katherine Anne Porter." *Studies in Short Fiction* 7 (1970):597–614.

Rank, Otto. *The Double: A Psychoanalytic Study.* Ed. and trans. Harry Tucker, Jr. Chapel Hill: Univ. of North Carolina Press, 1971.

Rogers, Robert. *A Psychoanalytic Study of the Double in Literature.* Detroit: Wayne State Univ. Press, 1970.

Scott, Anne Firor. *The Southern Lady: From Pedestal to Politics 1830–1930.* Chicago: Univ. of Chicago Press, 1970.

Walsh, Thomas F. "Deep Similarities in 'Noon Wine'." *Mosaic* 9 (Fall 1975): 83–91.

———. "Identifying a Sketch by Katherine Anne Porter." *Journal of Modern Literature* 7 (1979):555–561.

———. "Xochitl: Katherine Anne Porter's Changing Goddess." *American Literature* 52 (1980):183–193.

West, Ray B., Jr. *Katherine Anne Porter.* Univ. of Minnesota Pamphlets on American Writers, no. 28. Minneapolis: Univ. of Minnesota Press, 1963.

Williams, Juanita A. *Psychology of Women: Behavior in a Biosocial Context.* New York: Norton, 1977.

Wilson, Edmund. Review of *The Leaning Tower* by Katherine Anne Porter. *New Yorker*, September 30, 1944.

Index

115–120, 128, 138, 146–147, 158, 167, 215nn.2,3,5; "Pale Horse, Pale Rider," 6, 13, 17, 94, 113, 117, 128, 131, 157–166, 167, 215n.5; "Rope," 13, 40–44, 192, 211–212n.15, 212n.16; *Ship of Fools*, 3, 6, 7, 17, 18, 95, 113, 118, 177–178, 179–202, 203–206, 218n; "The Source," 11, 13, 113, 115, 116, 117, 120–122, 127; "That Tree," 11, 16, 73–78, 188; "Theft," 11, 12, 14, 15, 16, 40, 55–61, 73, 79, 80, 92, 99, 117, 197, 203; "Virgin Violeta," 16, 30–36, 40; "The Witness," 115, 117, 127–129
Pregnancy, 12–13; in "Flowering Judas," 88; in "The Grave," 143; in "Holiday," 167–168, 170; in "The Jilting of Granny Weatherall," 50; in "María Concepción," 21–23; in "Old Mortality," 153–154. *See also* Great Mother; Motherhood
Prince Charming, 33, 66–67, 201
Psychic conflict in women. *See* Female conflict

Quetzalcoatl, 25

Rape, 86, 92, 178, 199
Revolution. *See* Mexico
Ric and Rac, 181–182, 187, 193–194, 196–198, 206
Rites of passage, 86–87, 61, 197. *See also* Initiation

Snow White, 62, 71, 212n.4
Southern belle, 9–10, 12, 14. *See also* Belle; Woman as angel; Woman as virgin

Tammuz, 163
Tantalus, 166
Terrible Mother, 8, 23–25, 29, 75–76, 185. *See also* Great Mother
Tree as symbol of motherhood, 75

Vegetation myths, 24–25, 105–106, 110–111, 217n.5. *See also* Eden;

Gods; Wasteland
Virginity, 12–14, 29; in "Flowering Judas," 78–92; in "The Grave," 142–143; in "The Journey," 124–126; in "Old Mortality," 146–154; in "Virgin Violeta," 30–36; in white Southern women, 9–10. *See also* Female sexuality; Frigidity; Woman as virgin

Wasteland: central to *Ship of Fools*, 178; reflective of human barreness, 73, 158, 160–161, 167, 201, 205; women in, 185, 186, 187, 193, 198
Woman and anger: Isabel, 29; Miriam, 75, 77; Mrs. Treadwell, 201; wife in "Rope," 41–43; woman in "Theft," 60
Woman and autonomy. *See also* Matriarchs; Woman and freedom
—through art, 6, 7; Jenny Brown, 188–190; writer in "Hacienda," 97–101, 107
—through emotional restraint: Laura, 79; Mrs. Treadwell, 191; writer in "Theft," 56–61
—through self-assertion: Mother Müller, 169; Nannie, 133–135
—through sexual restraint: Amy, 148, 150; Laura, 79
Woman and freedom
—absence of, 19; Amy, 150, 153; the Grandmother, 116, 123; Isabel, 29; Laura, 81, 86–87; Miranda and María, 154; Ninette, 39–40; Rosaleen, 66, 72; Violeta, 31, 33, 35; wife in "Rope," 41–42, 44; women in *Ship of Fools*, 184–185
—desire for: Laura, 79; Miranda, 144; Violeta, 32, 36
—and loneliness, 6, 15, 17–18, 58, 93, 99–100, 165–166
Woman and identity: asserted, 133–135; asserted through art, 93; female need for, 14–16, 36, 66; gained through marriage and motherhood, 48–50, 169–170; lost through marriage and motherhood, 154, 183, 184–185, 203, 204. *See also* Female conflict